28TH LIFE: MY COMPLETELY ORDINARY LIFE I

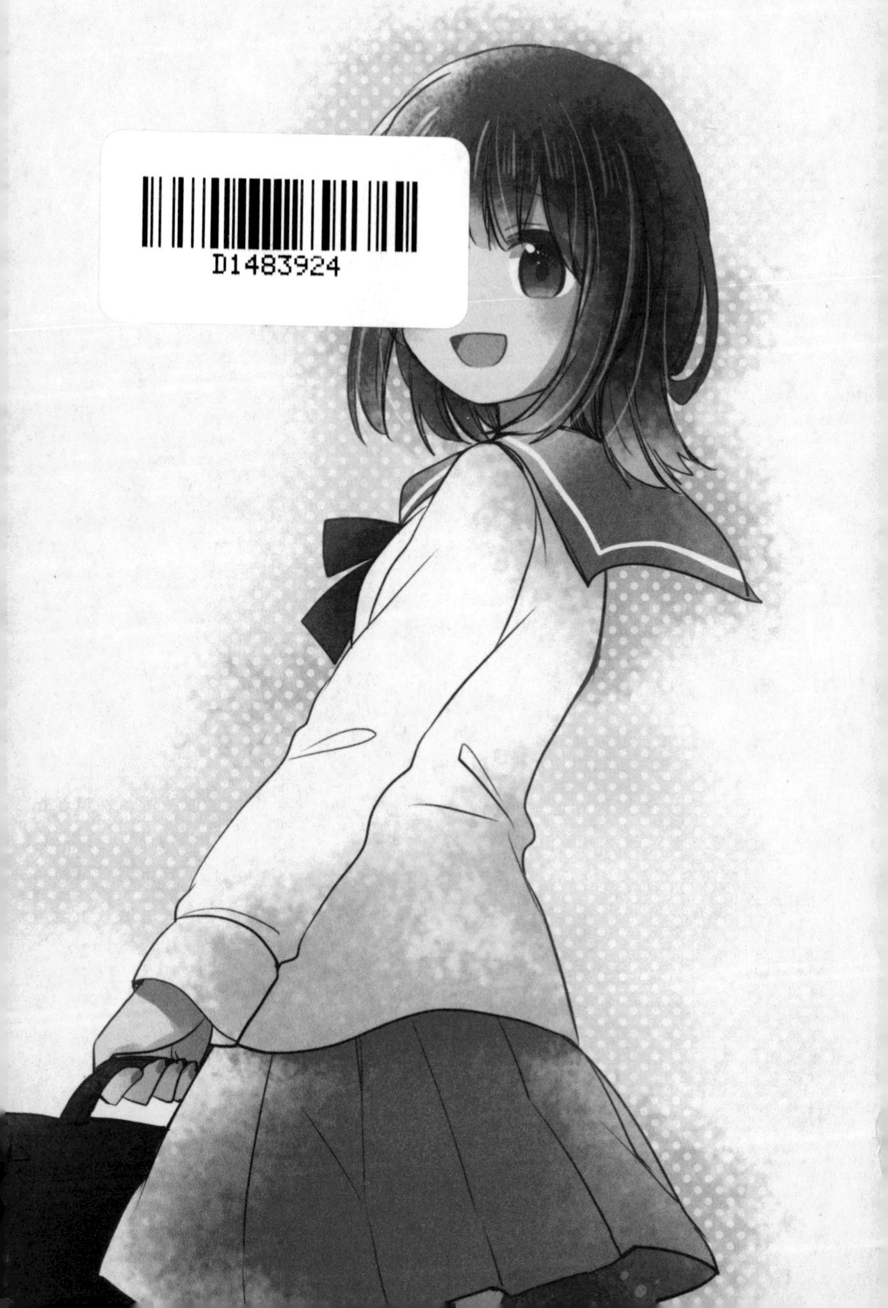

Happy
Sugar
Life

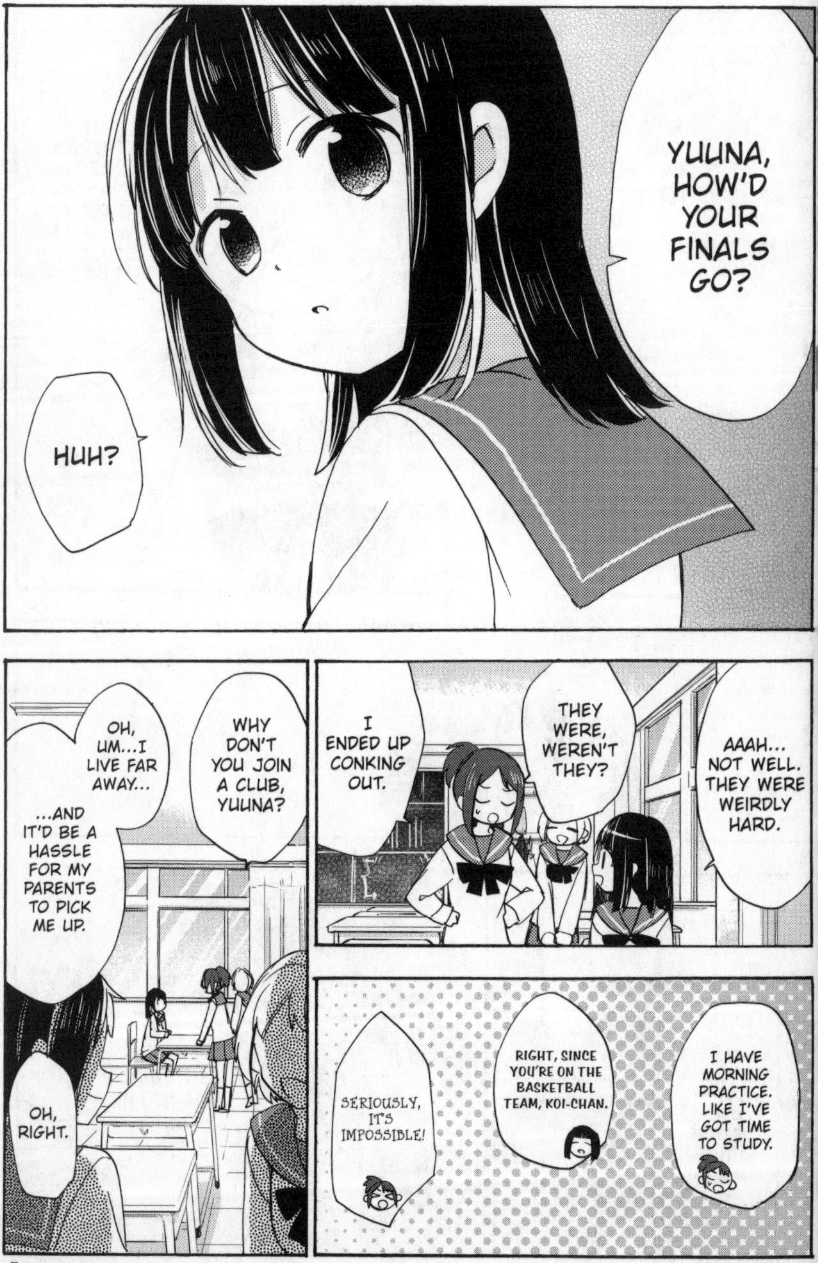
YUUNA, HOW'D YOUR FINALS GO?
HUH?
AAAH... NOT WELL. THEY WERE WEIRDLY HARD.
THEY WERE, WEREN'T THEY?
I ENDED UP CONKING OUT.
I HAVE MORNING PRACTICE. LIKE I'VE GOT TIME TO STUDY.
RIGHT, SINCE YOU'RE ON THE BASKETBALL TEAM, KOI-CHAN.
SERIOUSLY, IT'S IMPOSSIBLE!
WHY DON'T YOU JOIN A CLUB, YUUNA?
OH, UM...I LIVE FAR AWAY...
...AND IT'D BE A HASSLE FOR MY PARENTS TO PICK ME UP.
OH, RIGHT.

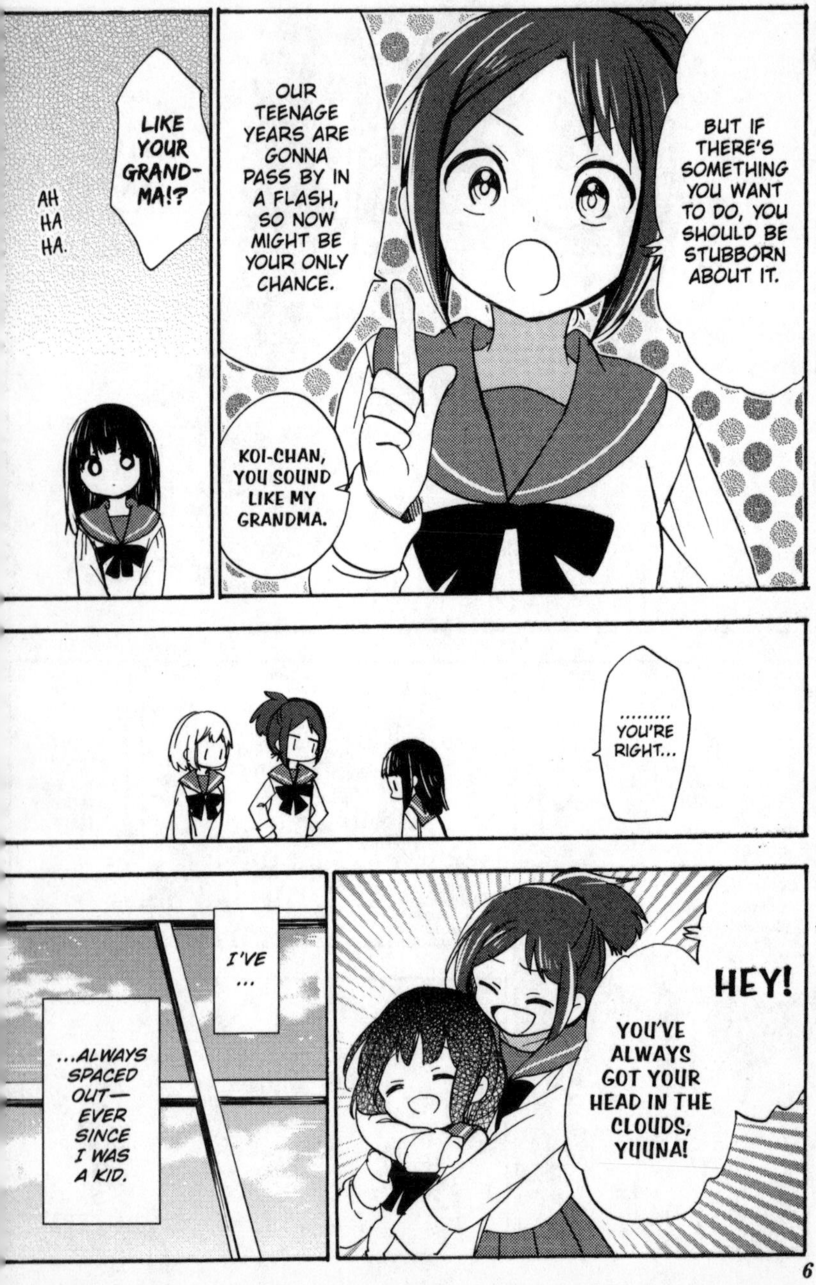
BUT IF THERE'S SOMETHING YOU WANT TO DO, YOU SHOULD BE STUBBORN ABOUT IT.
OUR TEENAGE YEARS ARE GONNA PASS BY IN A FLASH, SO NOW MIGHT BE YOUR ONLY CHANCE.
KOI-CHAN, YOU SOUND LIKE MY GRANDMA.
LIKE YOUR GRANDMA!?
AH HA HA.
.... YOU'RE RIGHT...
HEY!
YOU'VE ALWAYS GOT YOUR HEAD IN THE CLOUDS, YUUNA!
I'VE ...
...ALWAYS SPACED OUT— EVER SINCE I WAS A KID.

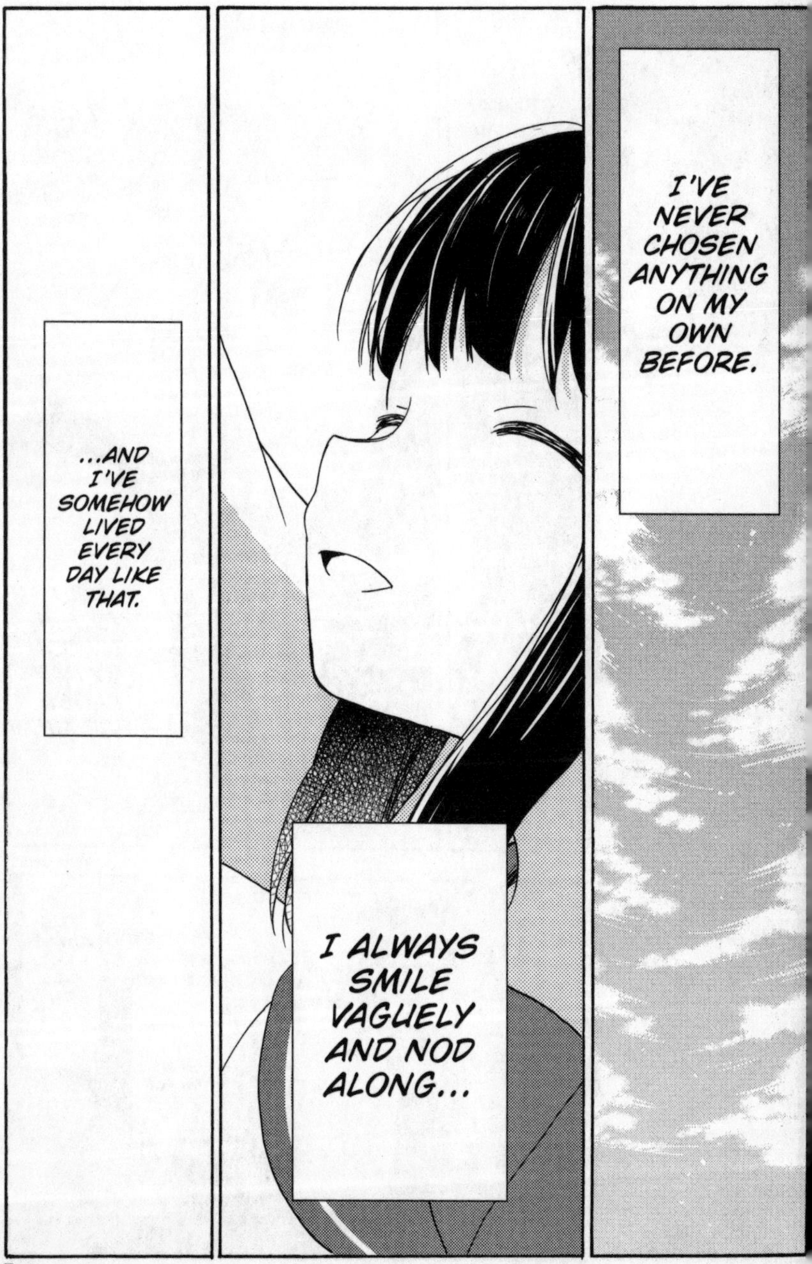
I'VE NEVER CHOSEN ANYTHING ON MY OWN BEFORE.
I ALWAYS SMILE VAGUELY AND NOD ALONG...
...AND I'VE SOMEHOW LIVED EVERY DAY LIKE THAT.

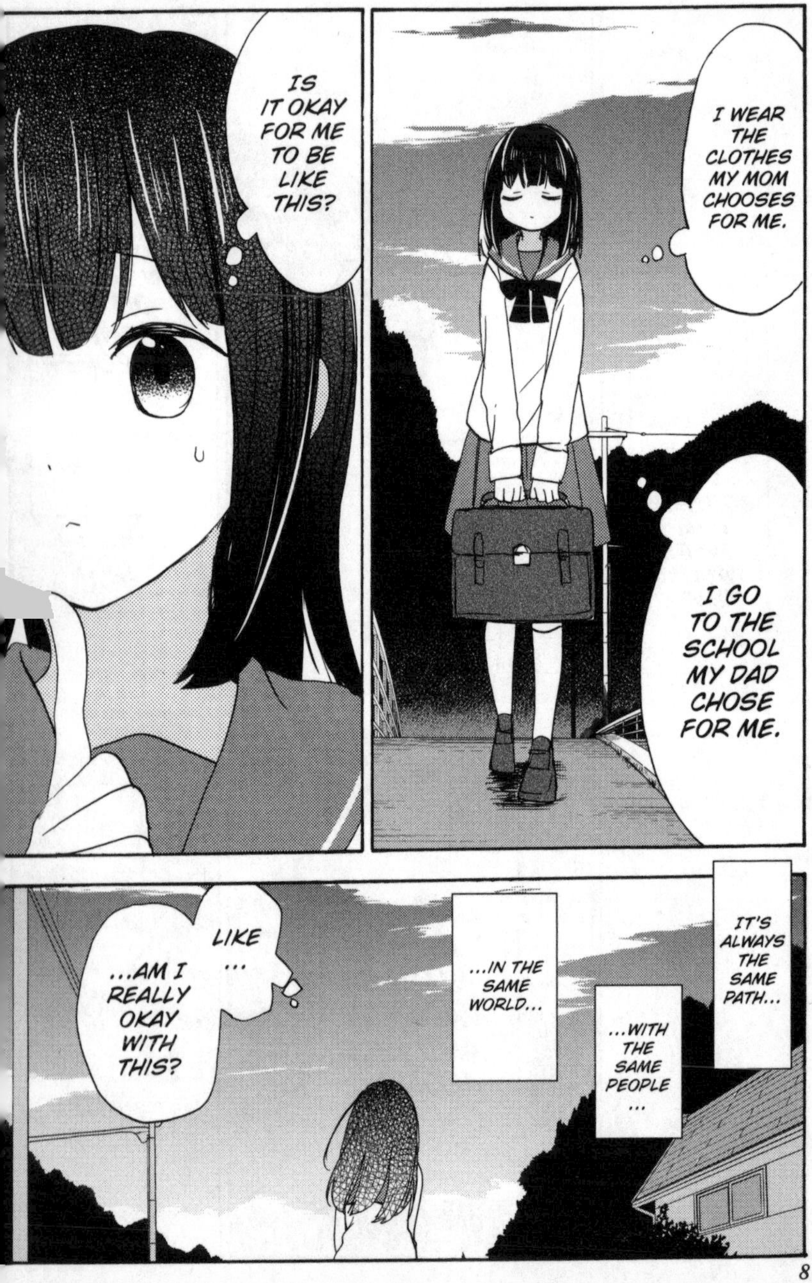
I WEAR THE CLOTHES MY MOM CHOOSES FOR ME.
I GO TO THE SCHOOL MY DAD CHOSE FOR ME.
IS IT OKAY FOR ME TO BE LIKE THIS?
IT'S ALWAYS THE SAME PATH...
...IN THE SAME WORLD...
...WITH THE SAME PEOPLE...
LIKE...
...AM I REALLY OKAY WITH THIS?

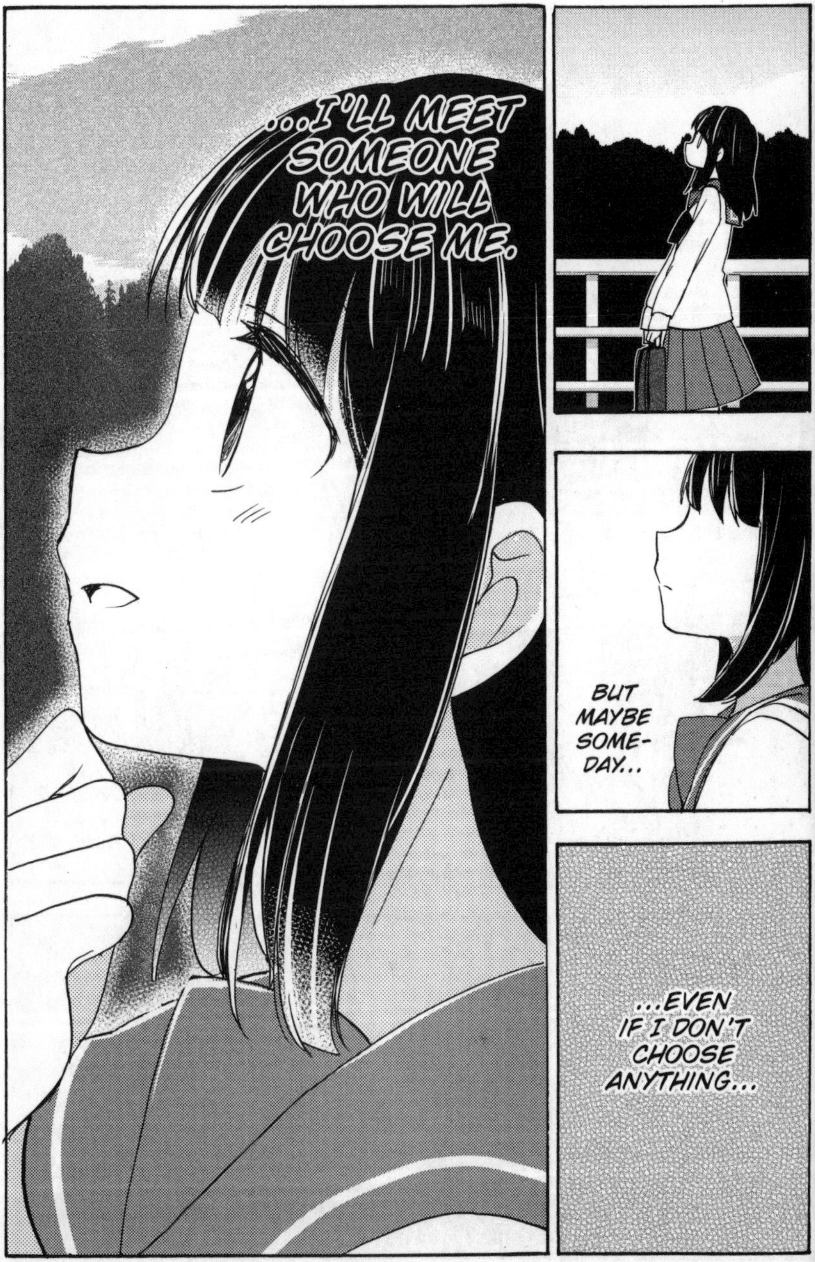
BUT MAYBE SOME-DAY...
...EVEN IF I DON'T CHOOSE ANYTHING...
...I'LL MEET SOMEONE WHO WILL CHOOSE ME.

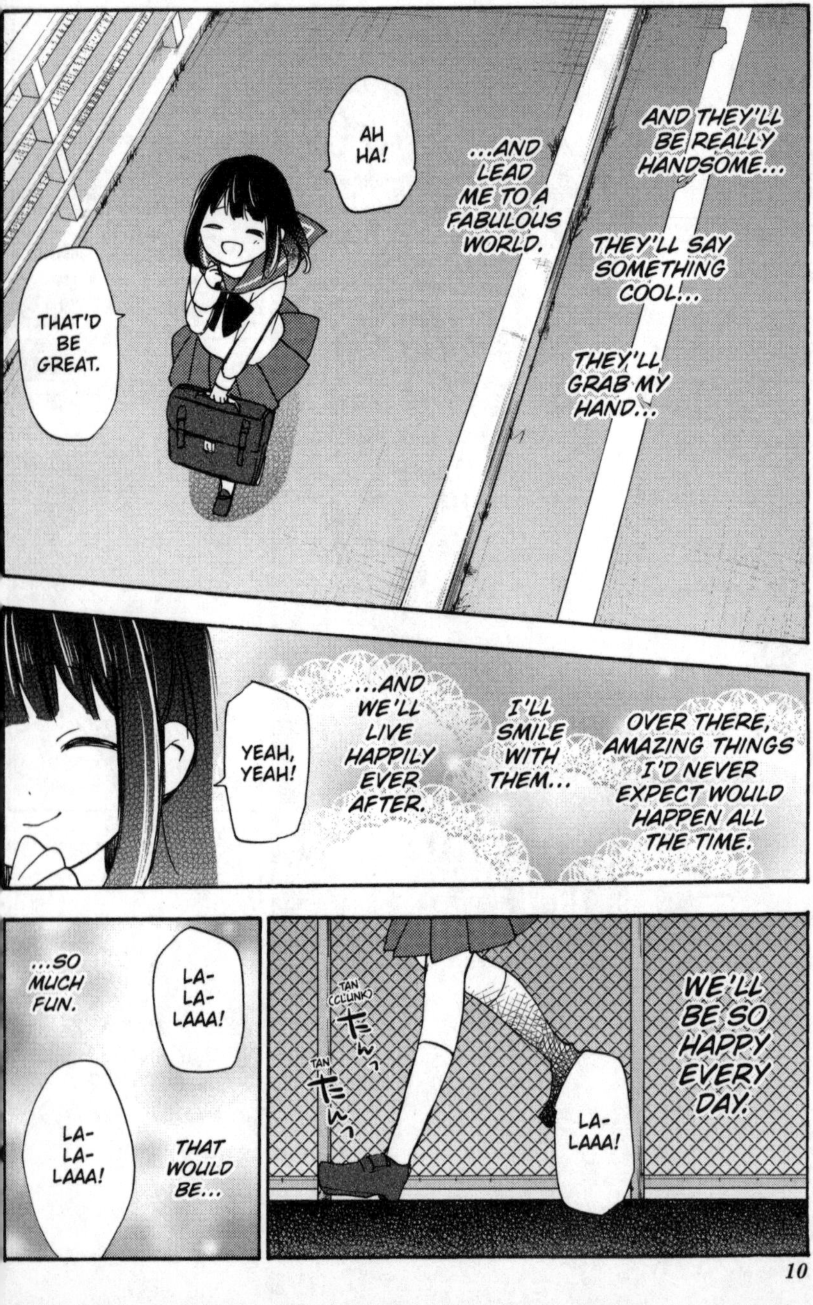
AND THEY'LL BE REALLY HANDSOME...
THEY'LL SAY SOMETHING COOL...
THEY'LL GRAB MY HAND...
...AND LEAD ME TO A FABULOUS WORLD.
AH HA!
THAT'D BE GREAT.
OVER THERE, AMAZING THINGS I'D NEVER EXPECT WOULD HAPPEN ALL THE TIME.
I'LL SMILE WITH THEM...
...AND WE'LL LIVE HAPPILY EVER AFTER.
YEAH, YEAH!
WE'LL BE SO HAPPY EVERY DAY.
LA-LAAA!
TAN (CLUNK) だんっ
TAN だんっ
LA-LA-LAAA!
...SO MUCH FUN.
THAT WOULD BE...
LA-LA-LAAA!

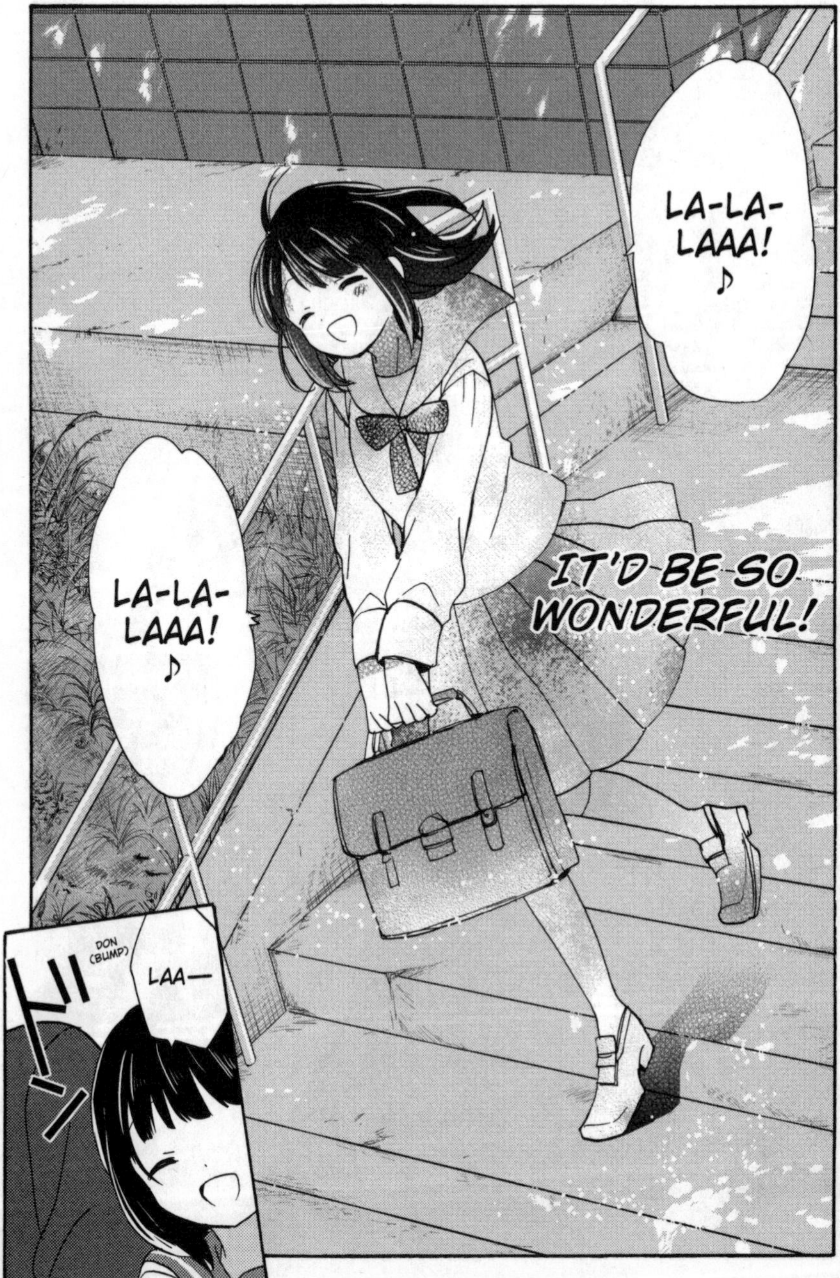
LA-LA-LAAA! ♪
IT'D BE SO WONDERFUL!
LA-LA-LAAA! ♪
LAA—
DON (BUMP)

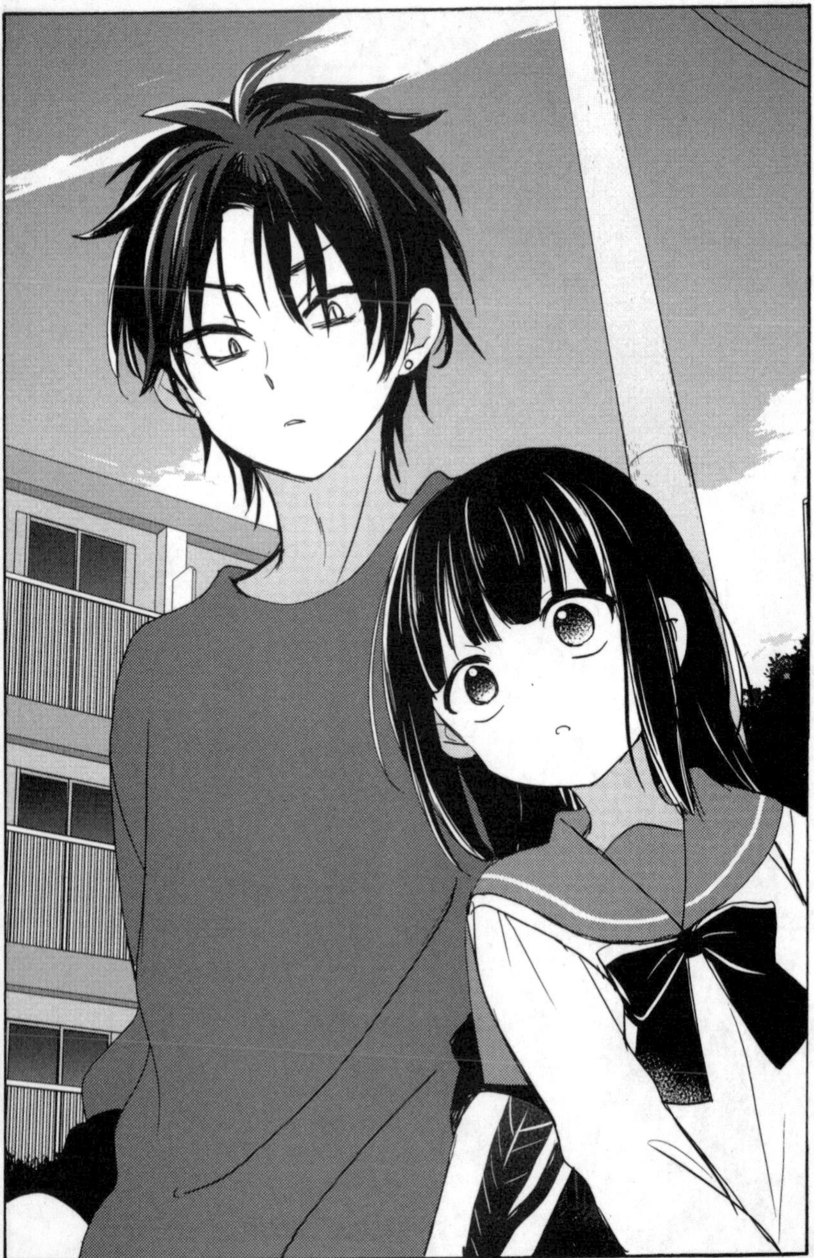

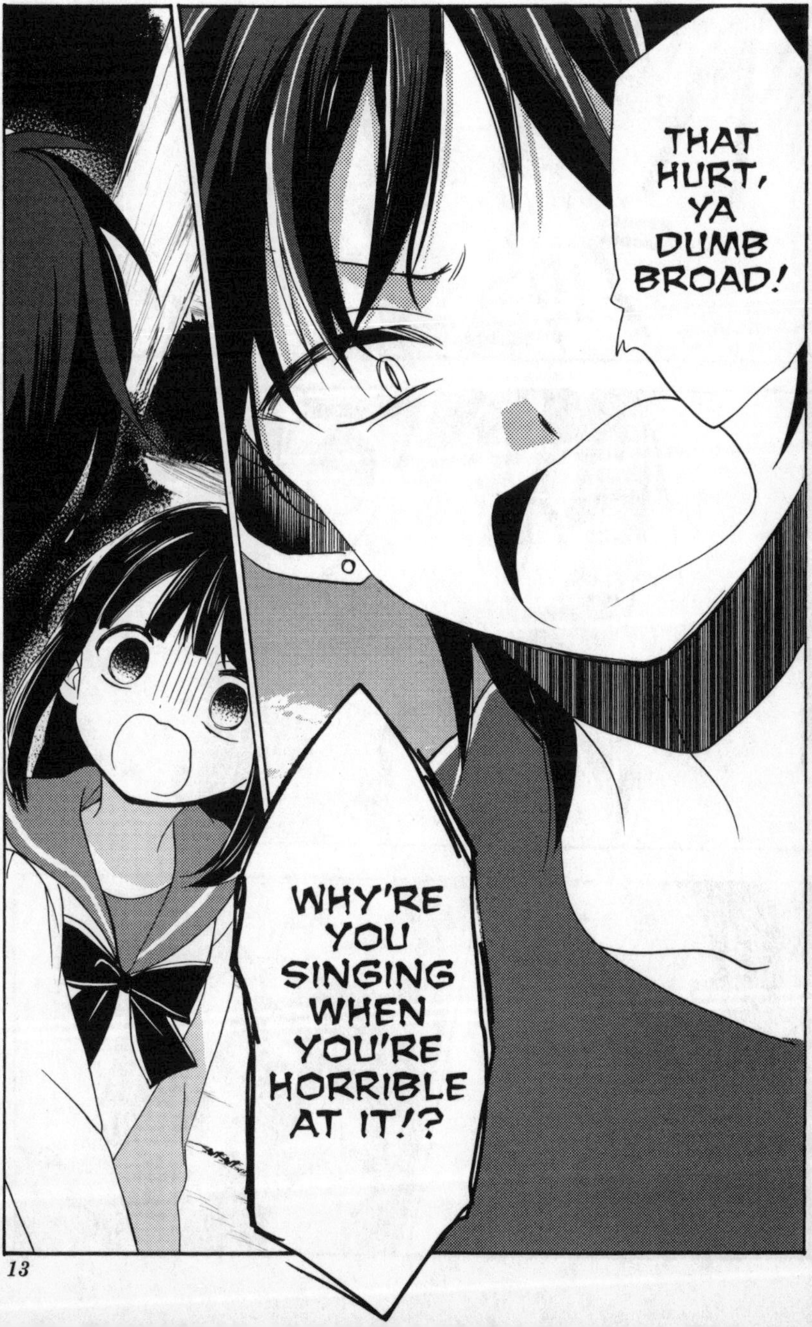
THAT HURT, YA DUMB BROAD!
WHY'RE YOU SINGING WHEN YOU'RE HORRIBLE AT IT!?

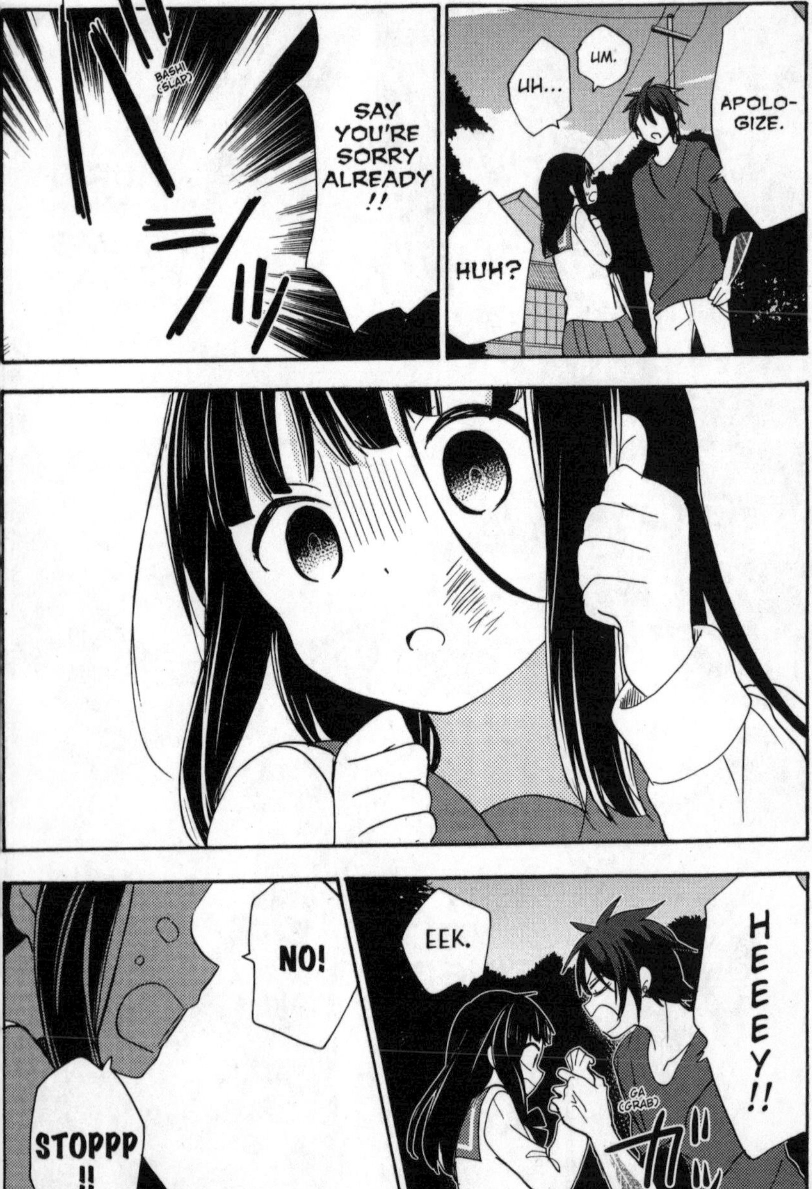
APOLO-GIZE.
UM.
UH...
HUH?
BASHI (SLAP)
SAY YOU'RE SORRY ALREADY!!
HEEEEY!!
EEK.
GA (GRAB)
NO!
STOPPP!!

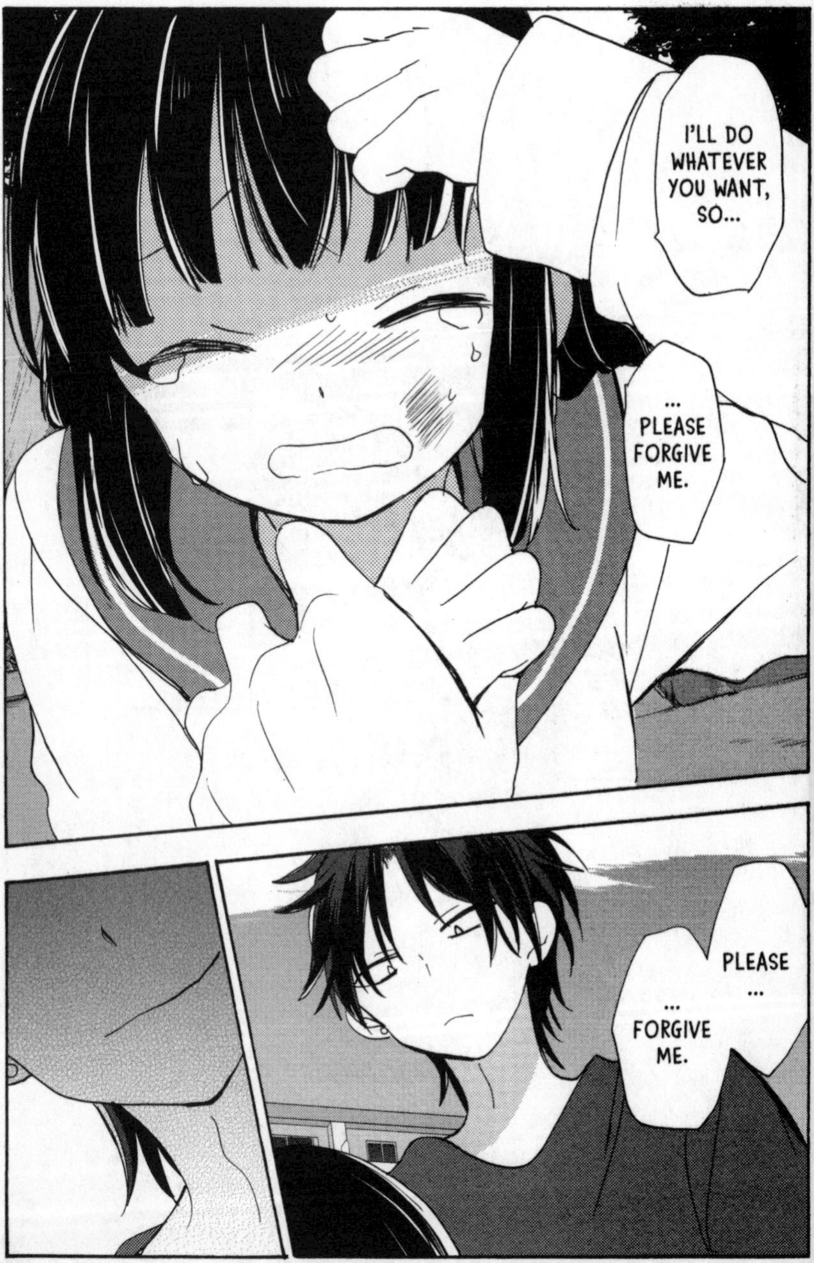
I'LL DO WHATEVER YOU WANT, SO...
... PLEASE FORGIVE ME.
PLEASE ...
... FORGIVE ME.

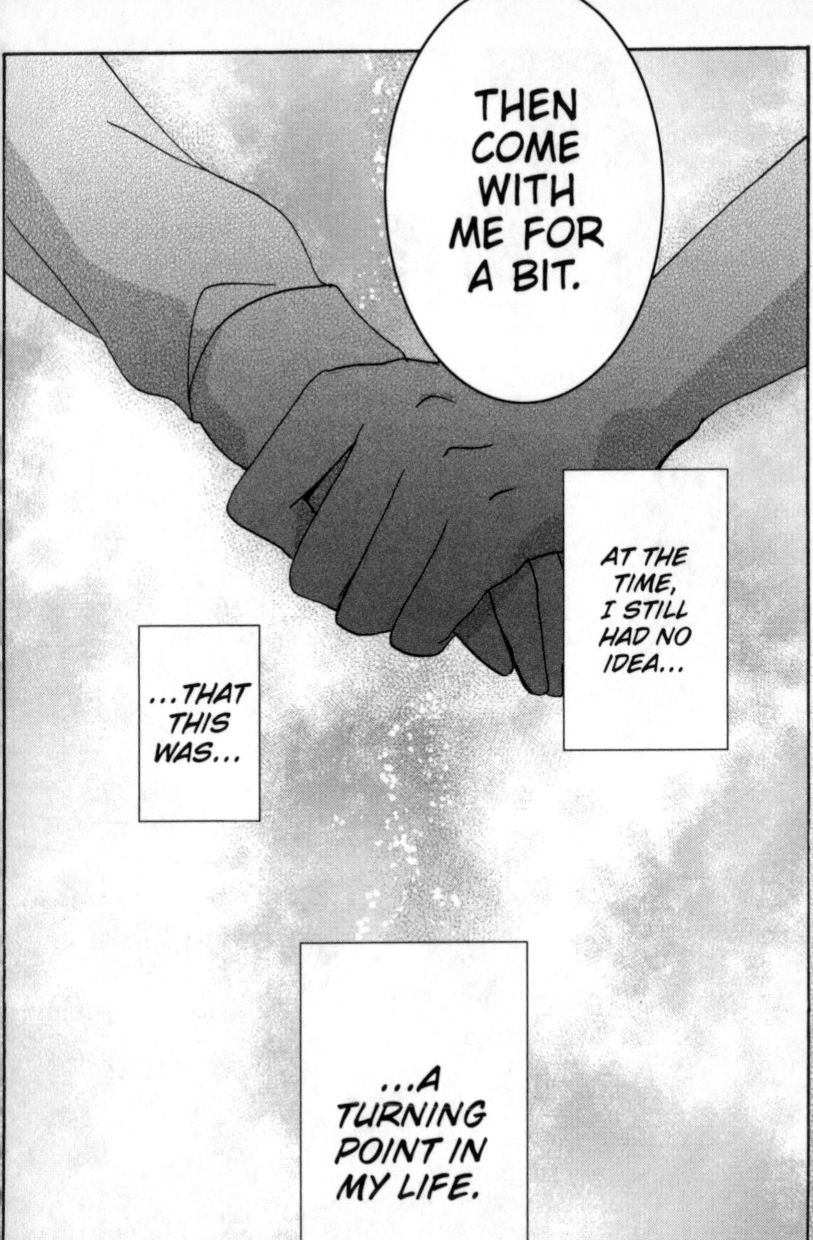
THEN COME WITH ME FOR A BIT.
AT THE TIME, I STILL HAD NO IDEA...
...THAT THIS WAS...
...A TURNING POINT IN MY LIFE.

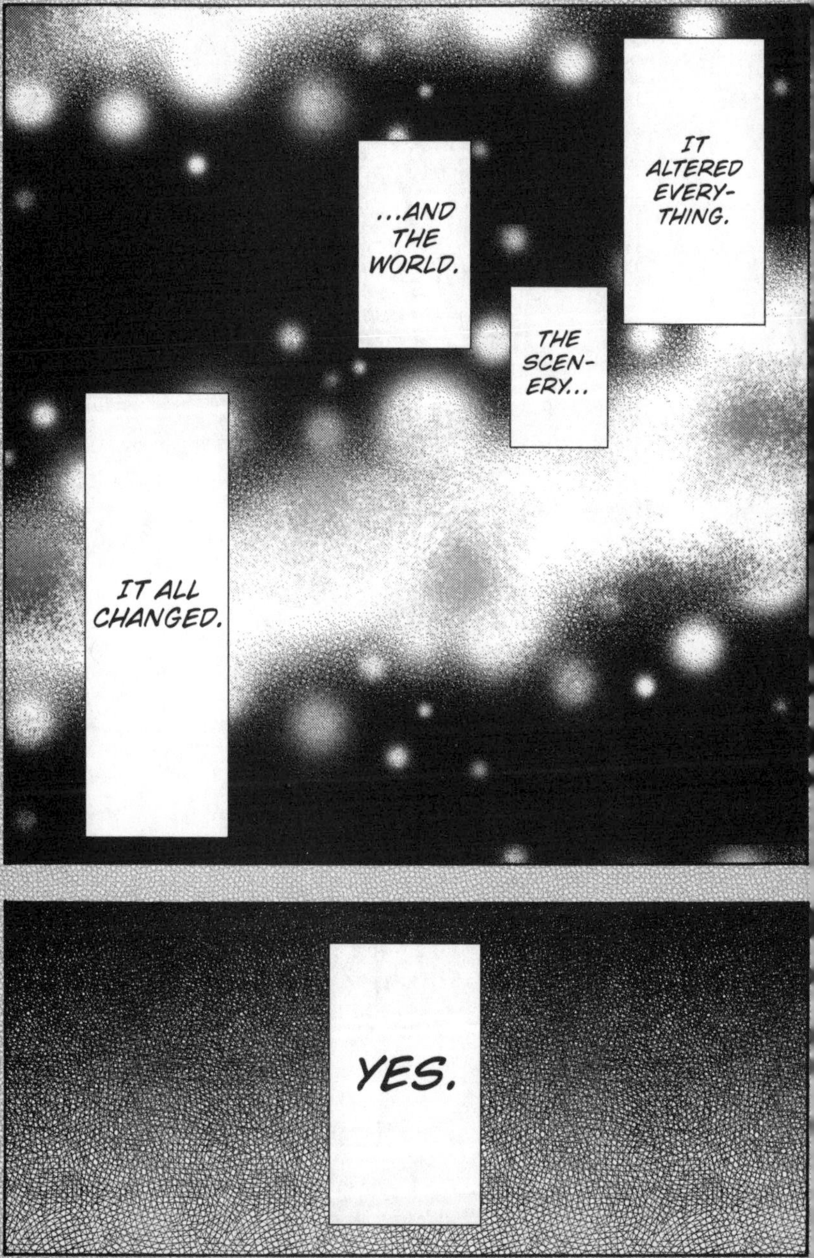
IT ALTERED EVERYTHING.
THE SCENERY...
...AND THE WORLD.
IT ALL CHANGED.
YES.

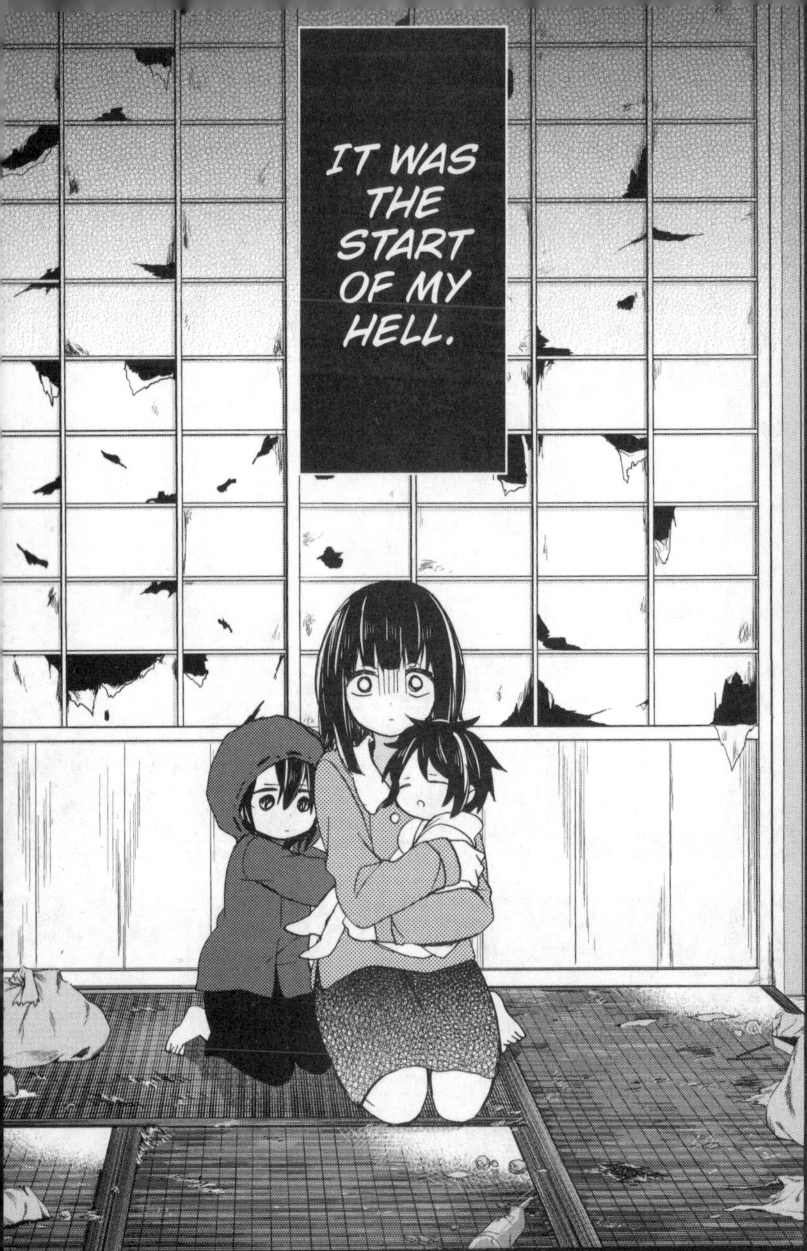
IT WAS THE START OF MY HELL.

Happy
Sugar
Life

Happy
Sugar
Life

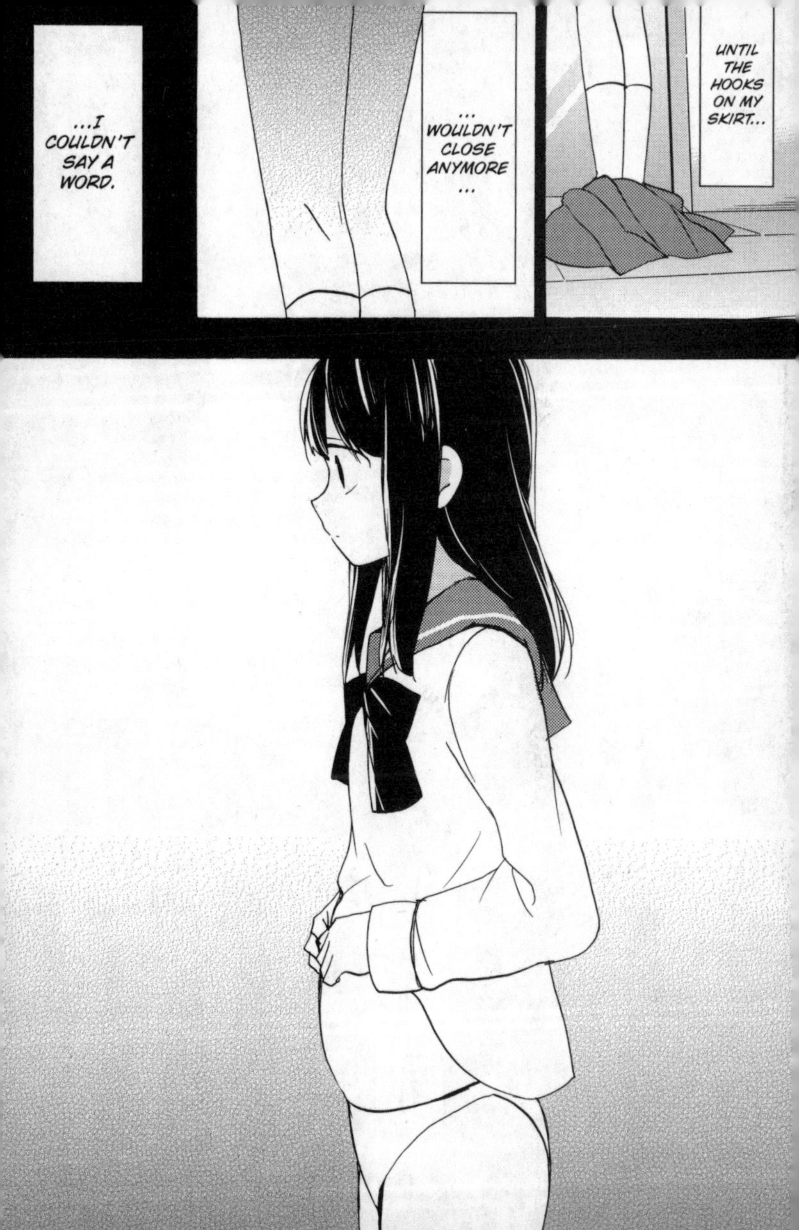
UNTIL THE HOOKS ON MY SKIRT...
...WOULDN'T CLOSE ANYMORE...
...I COULDN'T SAY A WORD.

29TH LIFE: MY COMPLETELY ORDINARY LIFE II

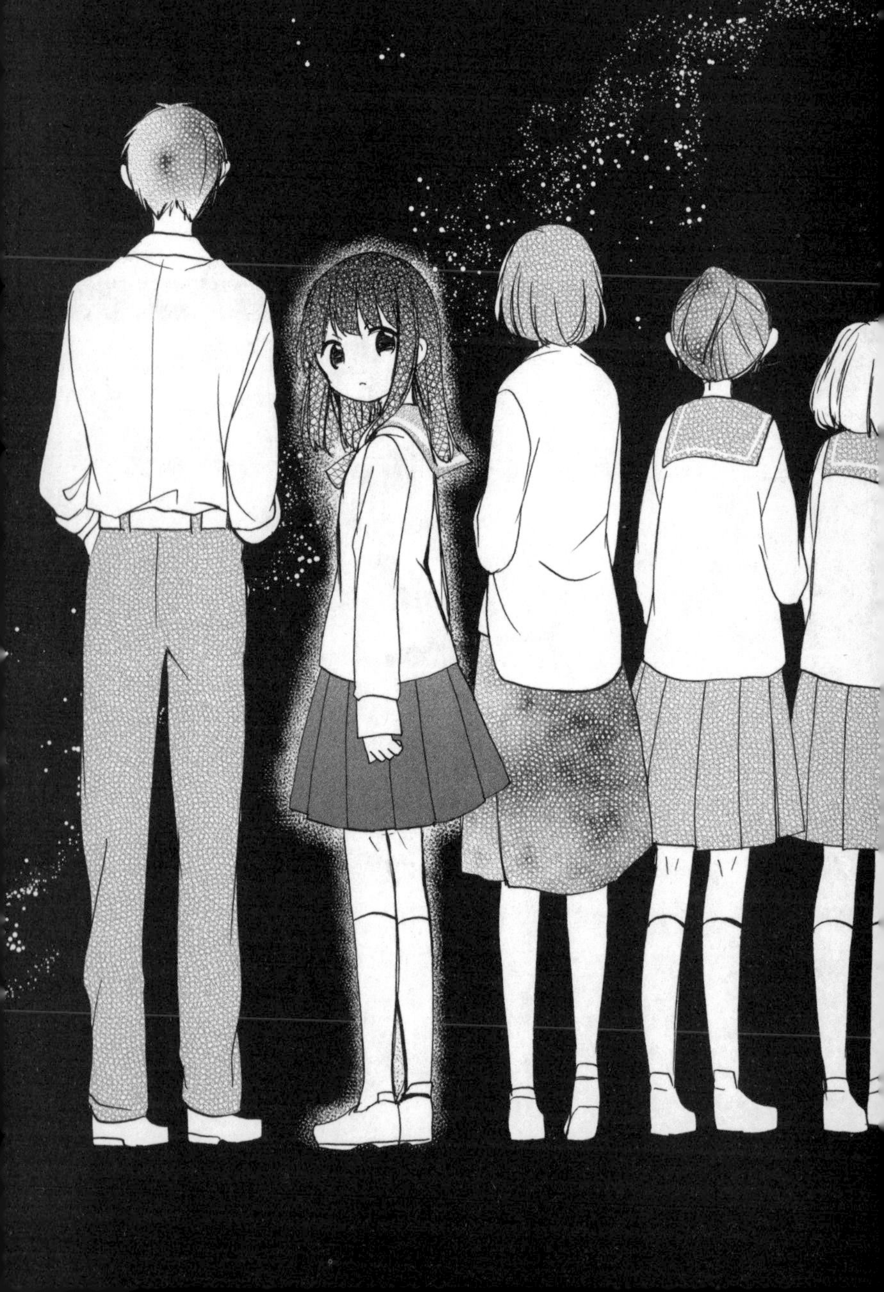

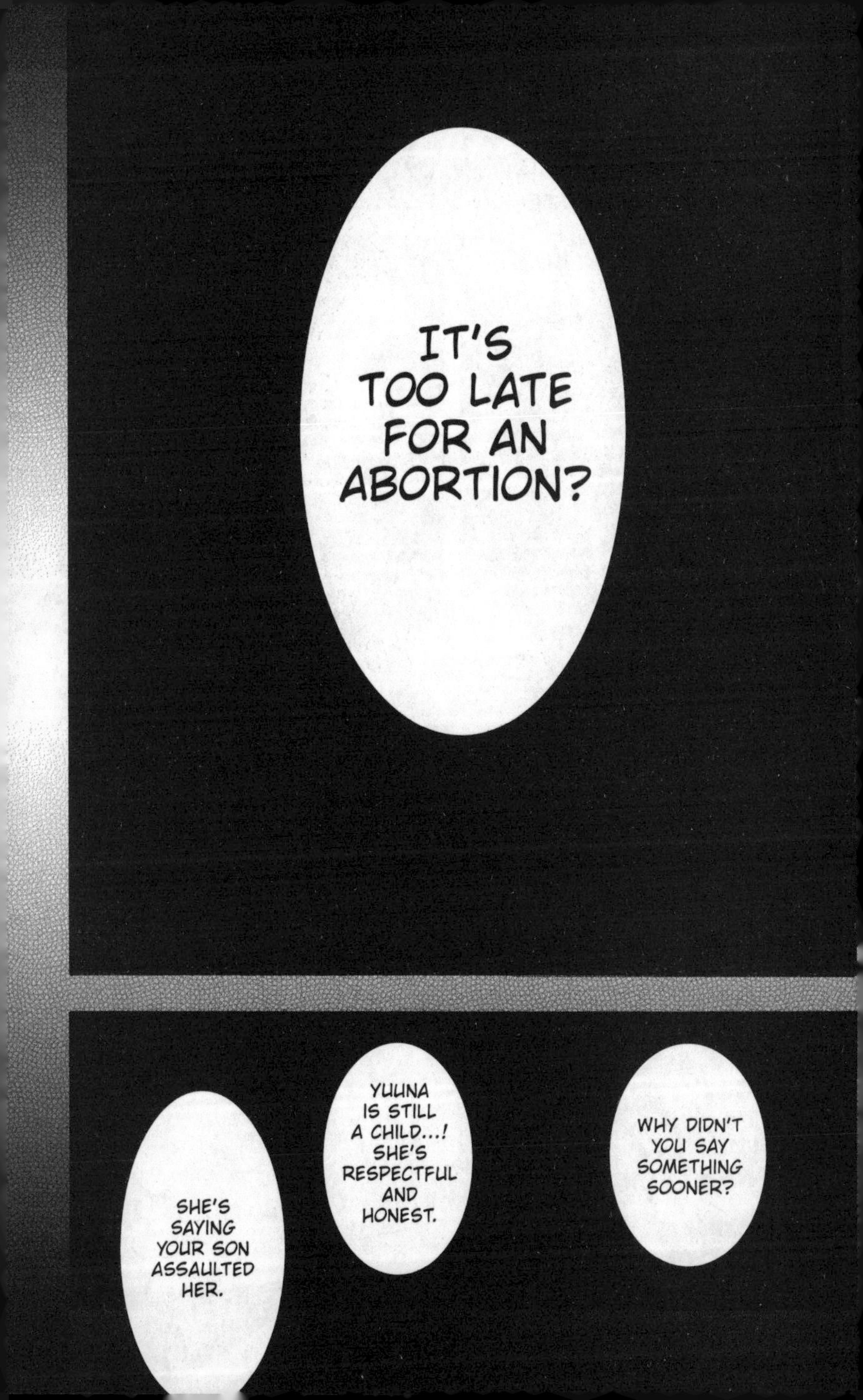
IT'S TOO LATE FOR AN ABORTION?
WHY DIDN'T YOU SAY SOMETHING SOONER?
YUUNA IS STILL A CHILD...! SHE'S RESPECTFUL AND HONEST.
SHE'S SAYING YOUR SON ASSAULTED HER.

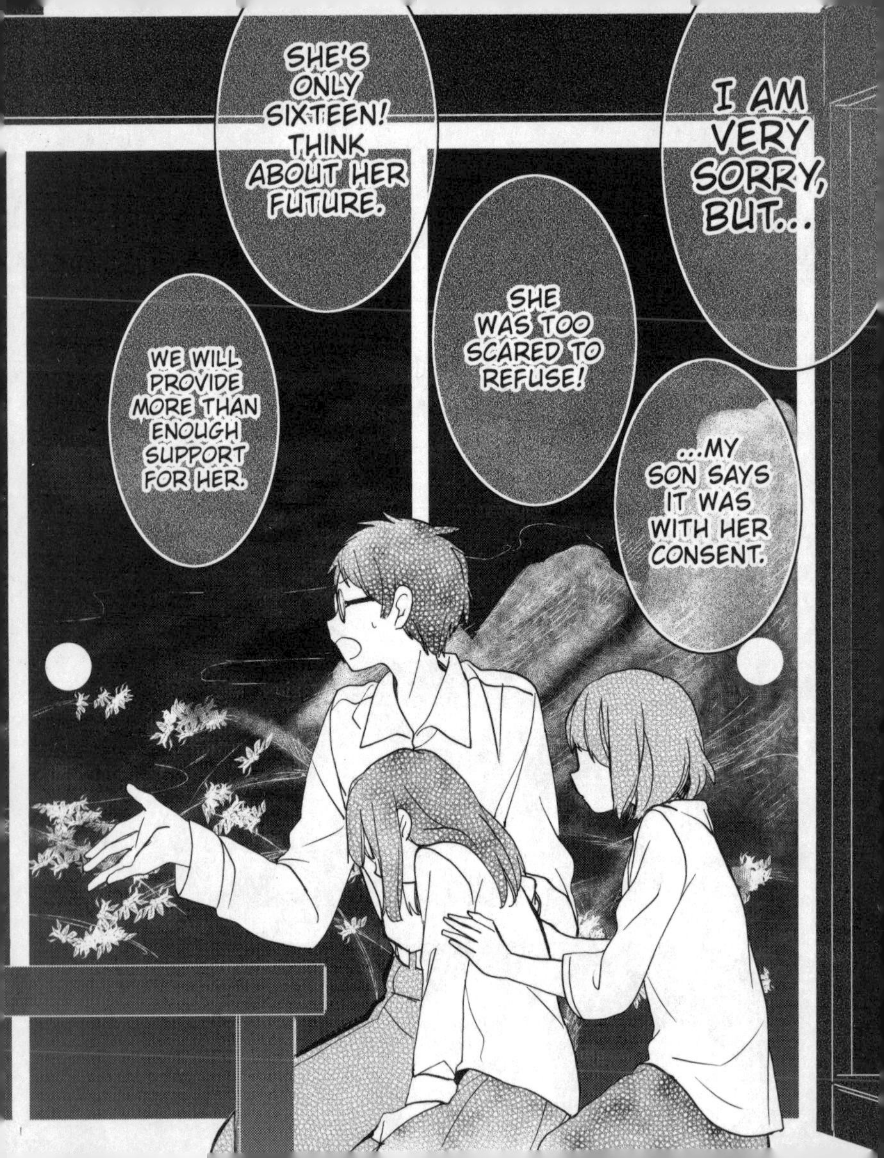
I AM VERY SORRY, BUT...
...MY SON SAYS IT WAS WITH HER CONSENT.
SHE'S ONLY SIXTEEN! THINK ABOUT HER FUTURE.
SHE WAS TOO SCARED TO REFUSE!
WE WILL PROVIDE MORE THAN ENOUGH SUPPORT FOR HER.

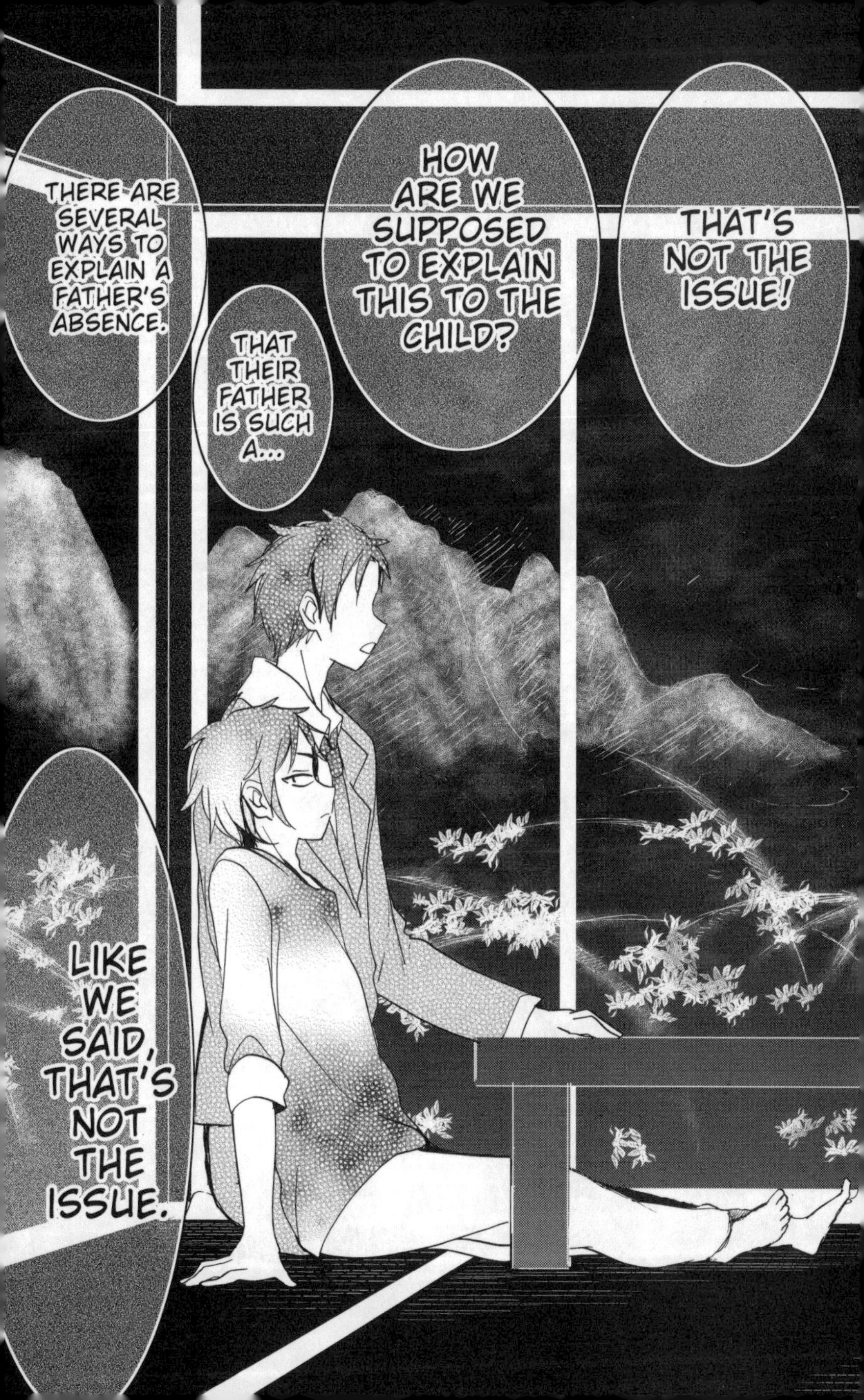

THAT'S NOT THE ISSUE!
HOW ARE WE SUPPOSED TO EXPLAIN THIS TO THE CHILD?
THAT THEIR FATHER IS SUCH A...
THERE ARE SEVERAL WAYS TO EXPLAIN A FATHER'S ABSENCE.
LIKE WE SAID, THAT'S NOT THE ISSUE.

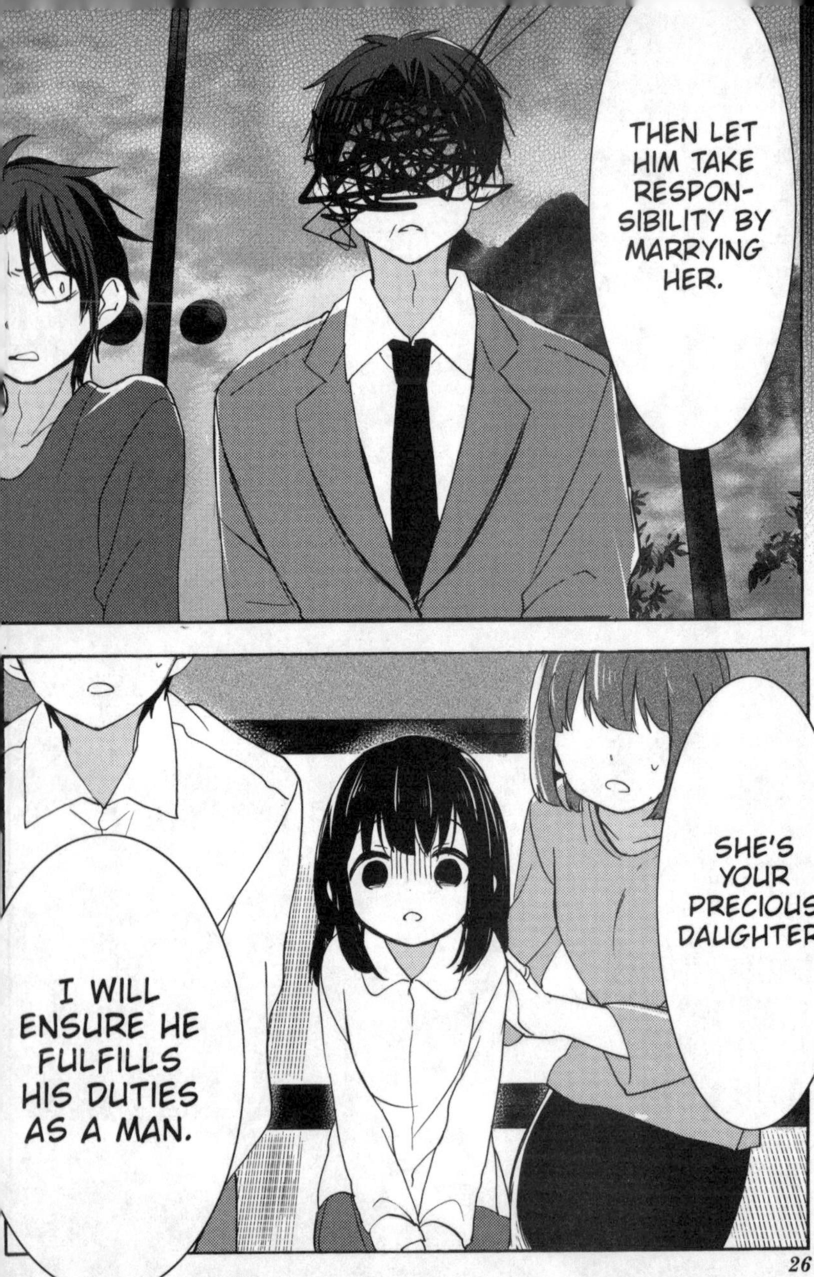
THEN LET HIM TAKE RESPON-SIBILITY BY MARRYING HER.
SHE'S YOUR PRECIOUS DAUGHTER.
I WILL ENSURE HE FULFILLS HIS DUTIES AS A MAN.

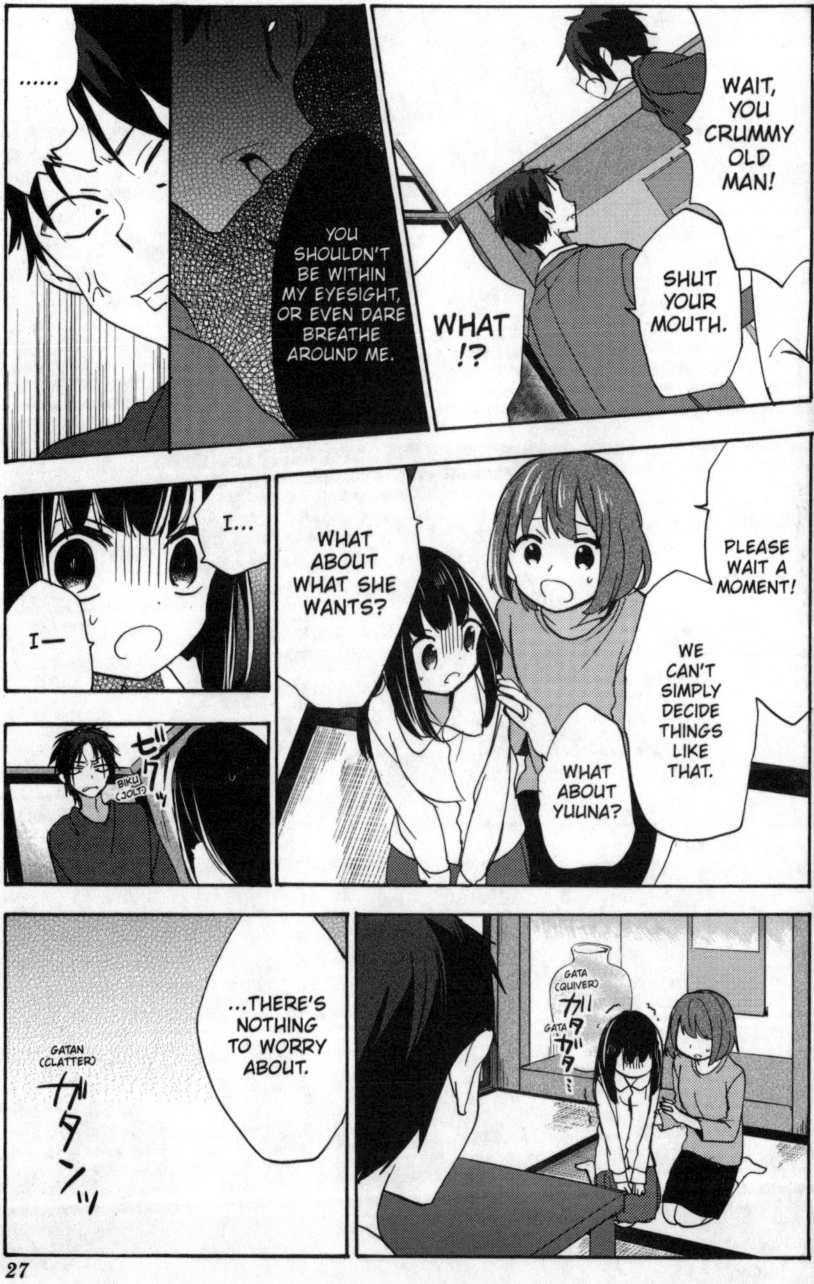
WAIT, YOU CRUMMY OLD MAN!
SHUT YOUR MOUTH.
WHAT !?
YOU SHOULDN'T BE WITHIN MY EYESIGHT, OR EVEN DARE BREATHE AROUND ME.
......
PLEASE WAIT A MOMENT!
WE CAN'T SIMPLY DECIDE THINGS LIKE THAT.
WHAT ABOUT YUUNA?
WHAT ABOUT WHAT SHE WANTS?
I...
I—
ビクッ
BIKU (JOLT)
GATA (QUIVER)
ガタ
GATA
ガタ...
...THERE'S NOTHING TO WORRY ABOUT.
GATAN (CLATTER)
ガタンッ

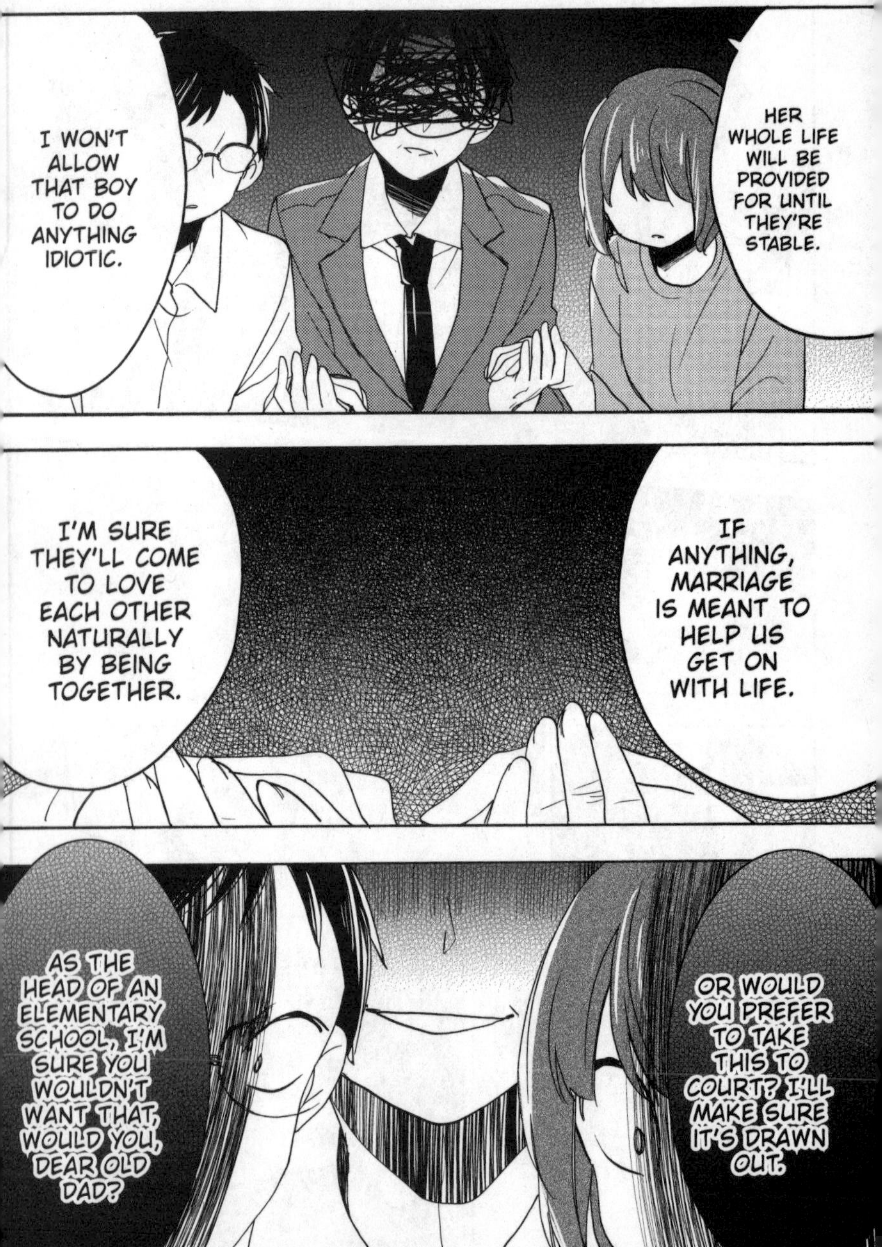
HER WHOLE LIFE WILL BE PROVIDED FOR UNTIL THEY'RE STABLE.
I WON'T ALLOW THAT BOY TO DO ANYTHING IDIOTIC.
IF ANYTHING, MARRIAGE IS MEANT TO HELP US GET ON WITH LIFE.
I'M SURE THEY'LL COME TO LOVE EACH OTHER NATURALLY BY BEING TOGETHER.
OR WOULD YOU PREFER TO TAKE THIS TO COURT? I'LL MAKE SURE IT'S DRAWN OUT.
AS THE HEAD OF AN ELEMENTARY SCHOOL, I'M SURE YOU WOULDN'T WANT THAT, WOULD YOU, DEAR OLD DAD?

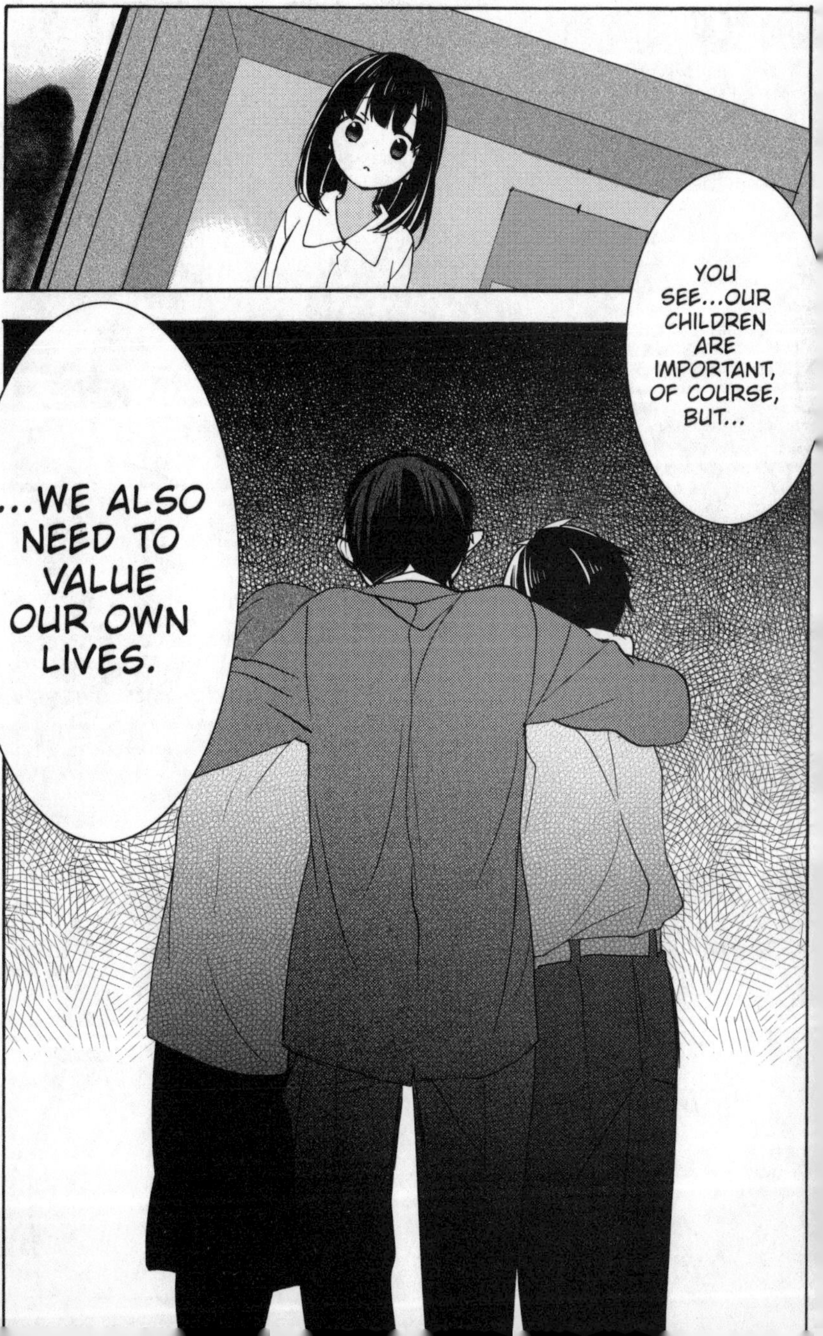
YOU SEE...OUR CHILDREN ARE IMPORTANT, OF COURSE, BUT...
...WE ALSO NEED TO VALUE OUR OWN LIVES.

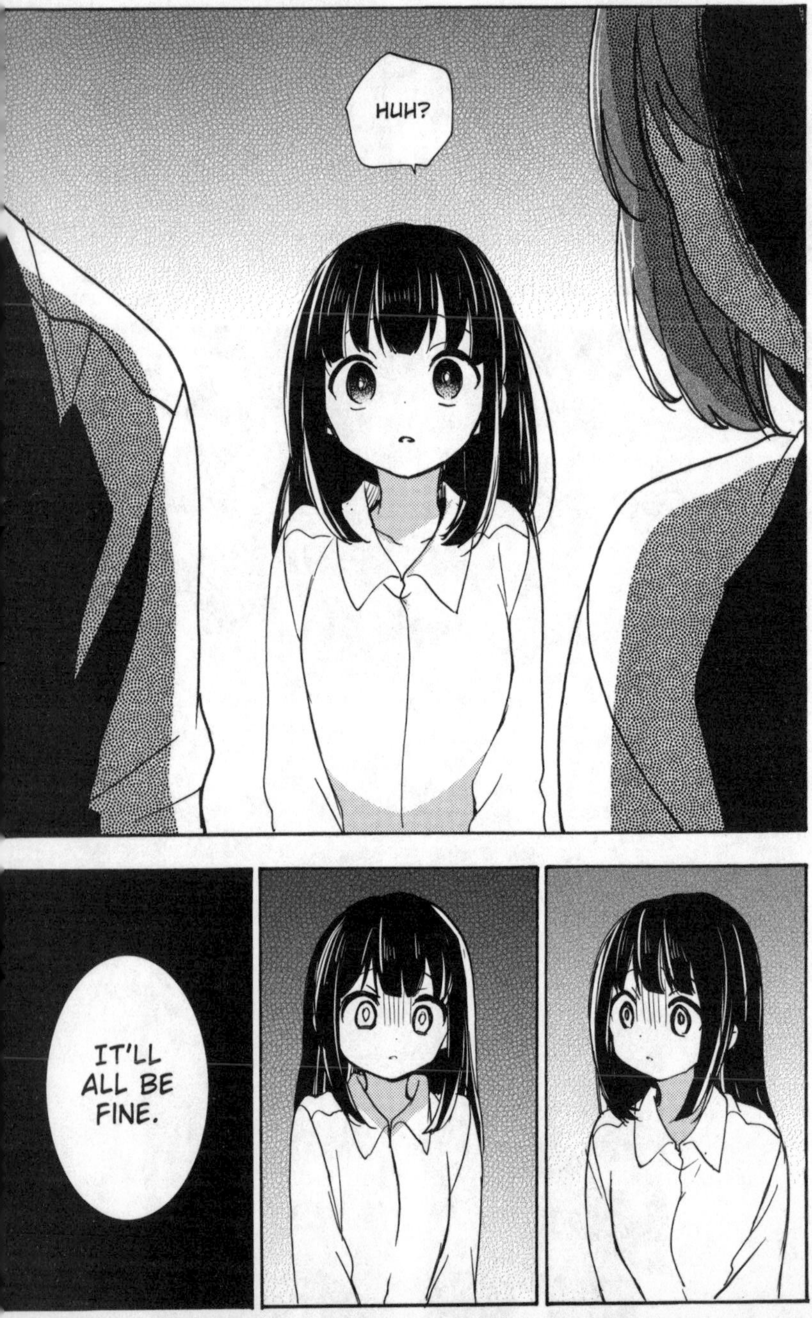
HUH?
IT'LL ALL BE FINE.

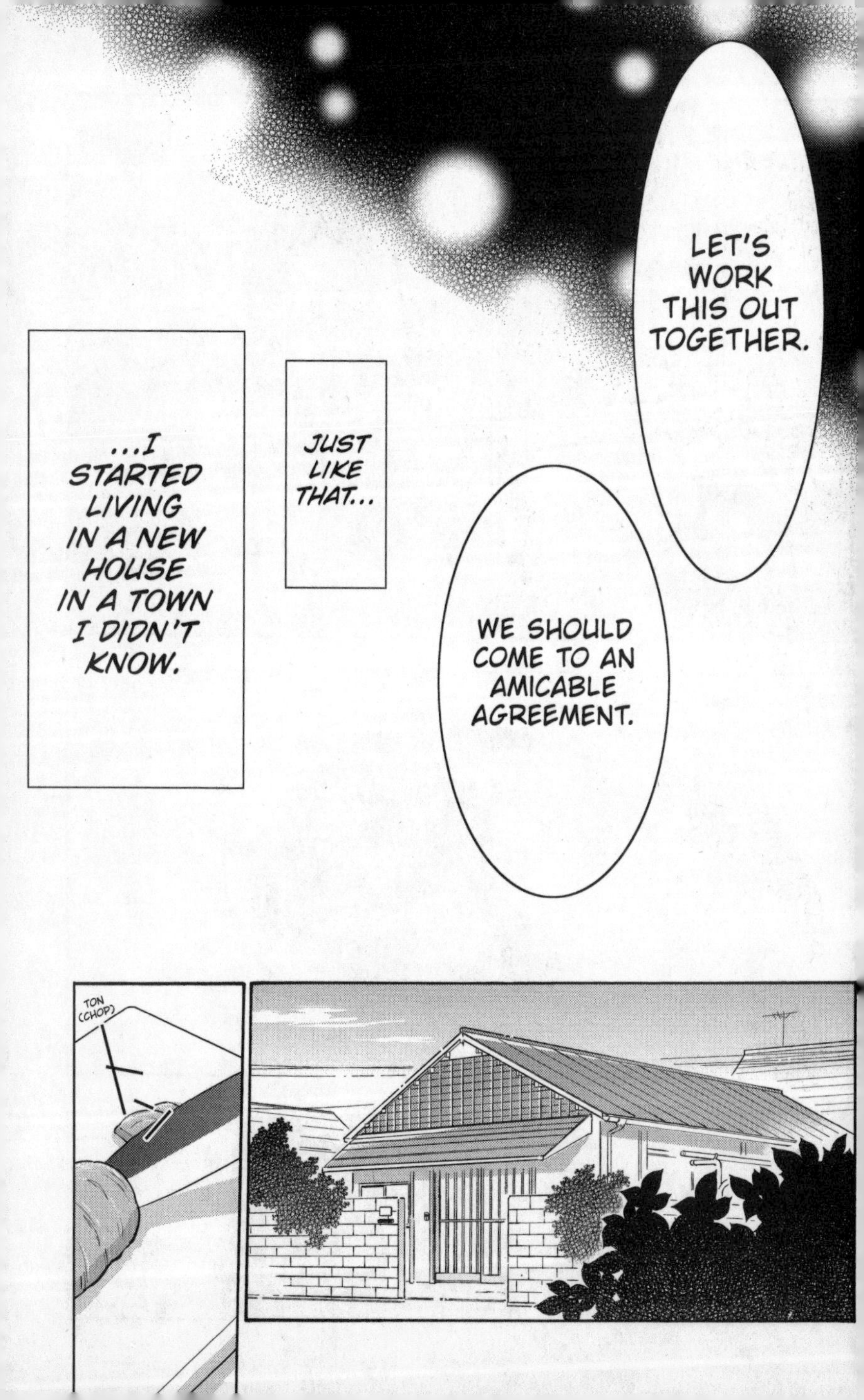
LET'S WORK THIS OUT TOGETHER.
WE SHOULD COME TO AN AMICABLE AGREEMENT.
JUST LIKE THAT...
...I STARTED LIVING IN A NEW HOUSE IN A TOWN I DIDN'T KNOW.
TON (CHOP)

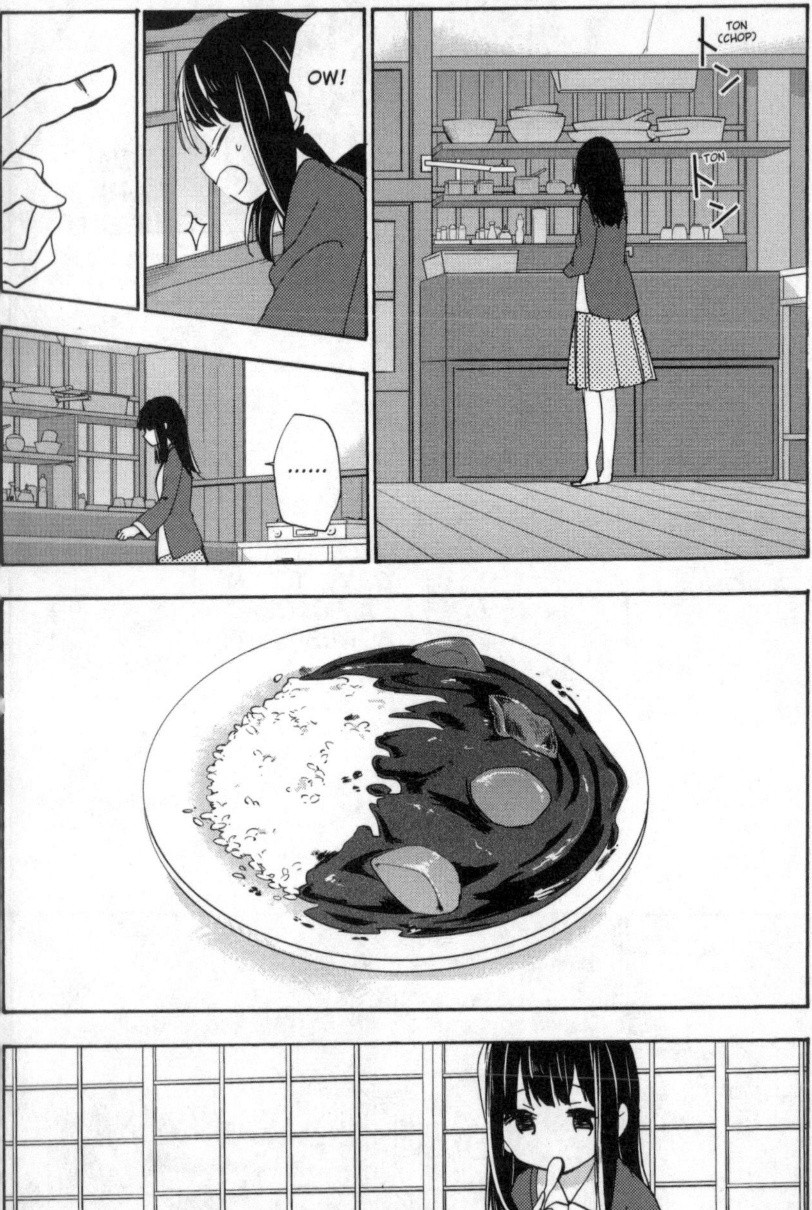
TON (CHOP)
TON
OW!
....

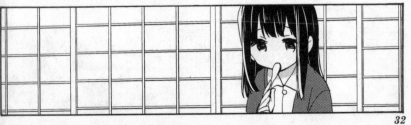

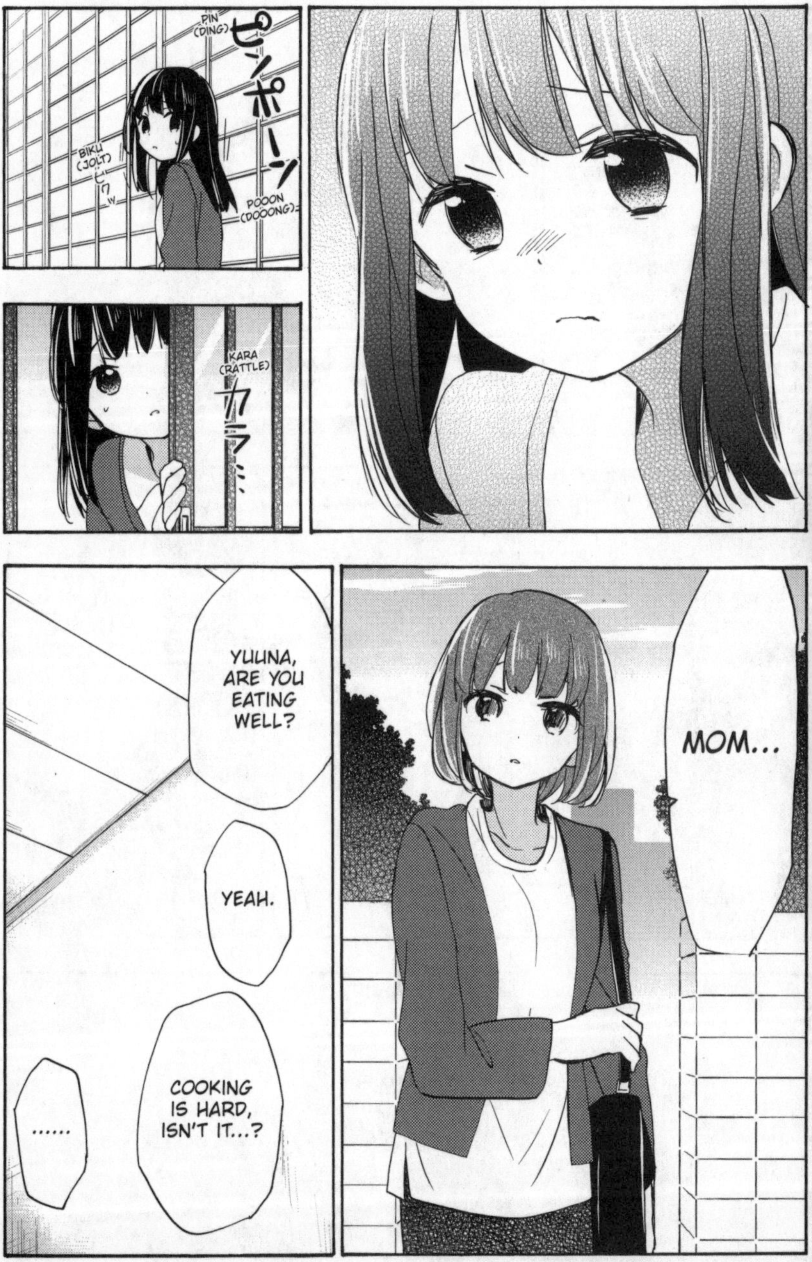
PIN (DING)
ピンポーン
POOON (DOOONG)
BIKU (JOLT)
ビクッ
KARA (RATTLE)
カラ…
MOM...
YUUNA, ARE YOU EATING WELL?
YEAH.
COOKING IS HARD, ISN'T IT...?
......

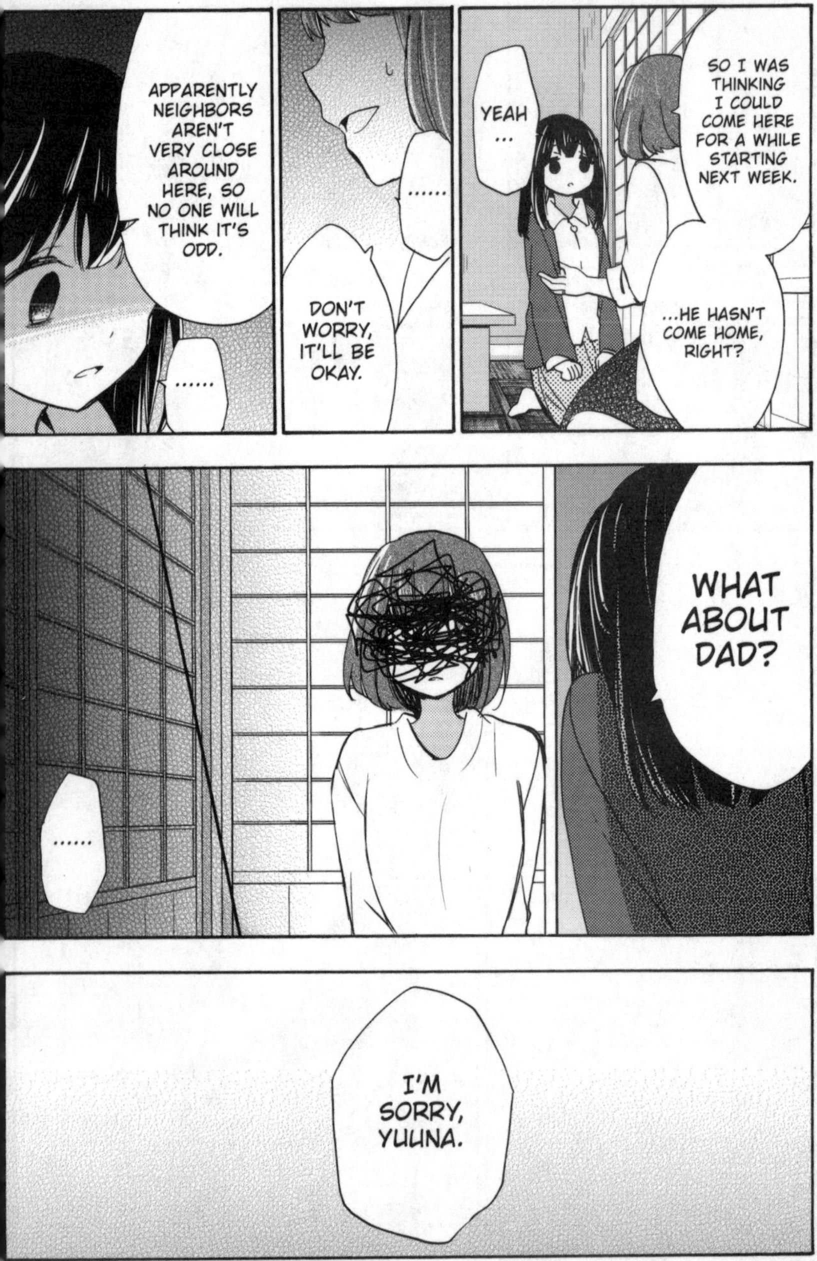
SO I WAS THINKING I COULD COME HERE FOR A WHILE STARTING NEXT WEEK.
YEAH ...
...HE HASN'T COME HOME, RIGHT?
......
DON'T WORRY, IT'LL BE OKAY.
APPARENTLY NEIGHBORS AREN'T VERY CLOSE AROUND HERE, SO NO ONE WILL THINK IT'S ODD.
......
WHAT ABOUT DAD?
......
I'M SORRY, YUUNA.

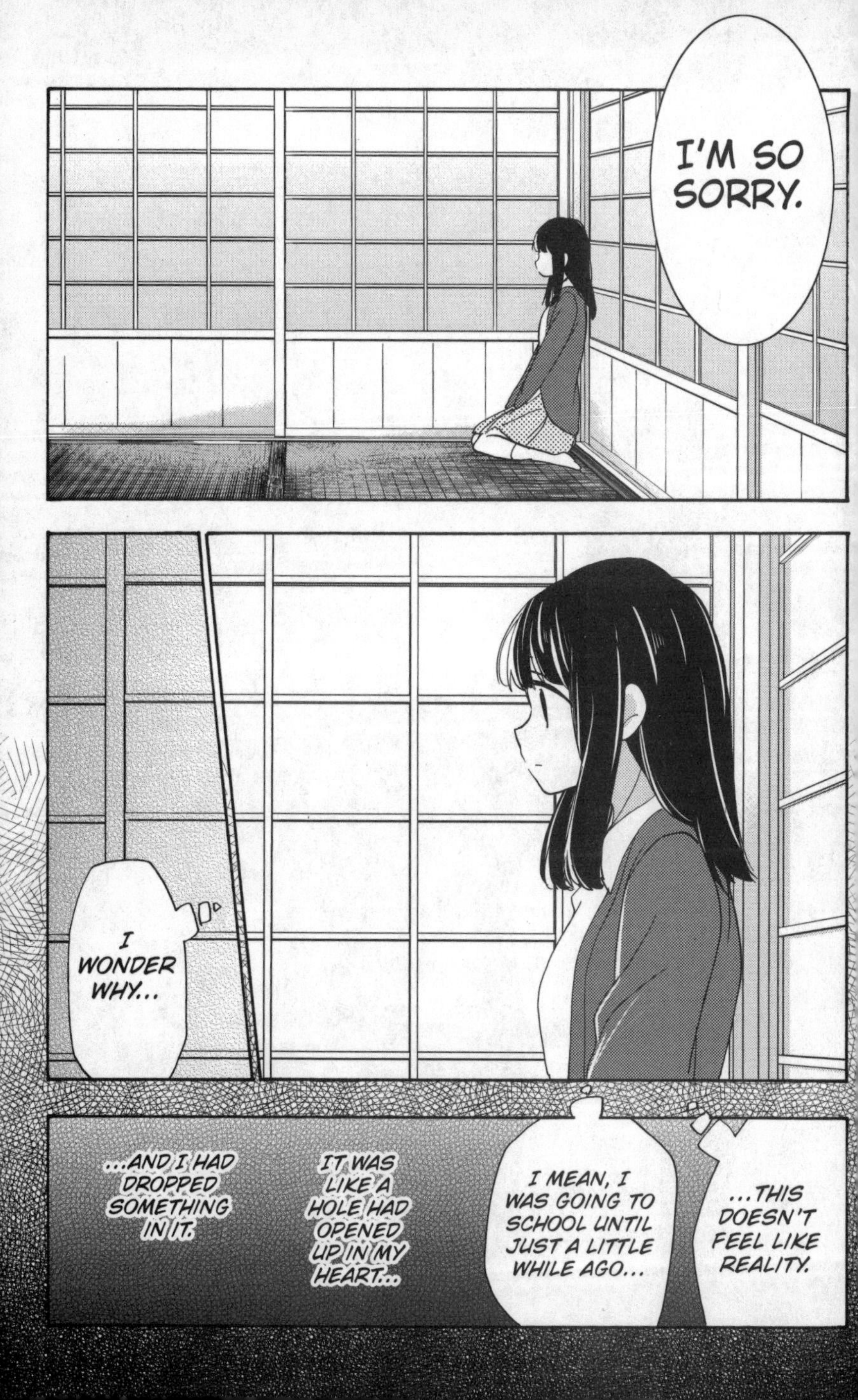
I'M SO SORRY.
I WONDER WHY...
...THIS DOESN'T FEEL LIKE REALITY.
I MEAN, I WAS GOING TO SCHOOL UNTIL JUST A LITTLE WHILE AGO...
IT WAS LIKE A HOLE HAD OPENED UP IN MY HEART...
...AND I HAD DROPPED SOMETHING IN IT.

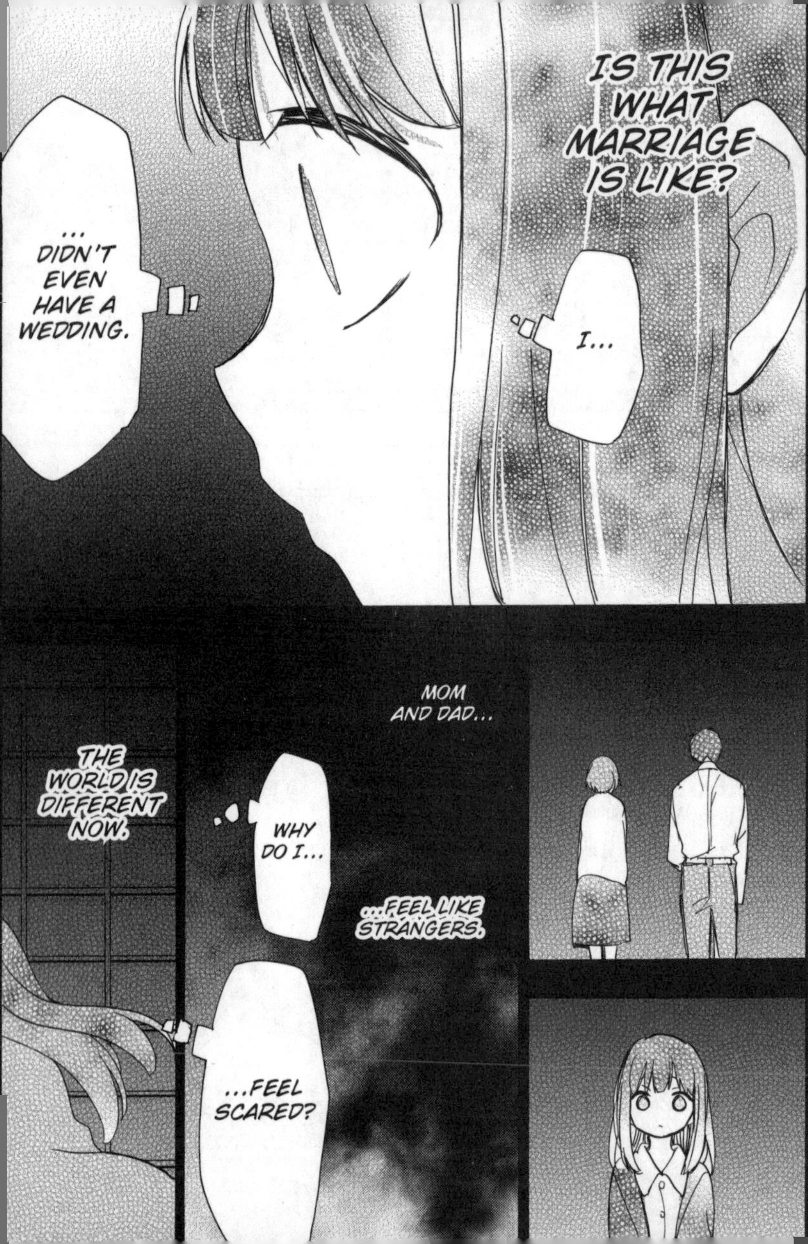
IS THIS WHAT MARRIAGE IS LIKE?
I...
...DIDN'T EVEN HAVE A WEDDING.
MOM AND DAD...
...FEEL LIKE STRANGERS.
WHY DO I...
...FEEL SCARED?
THE WORLD IS DIFFERENT NOW.

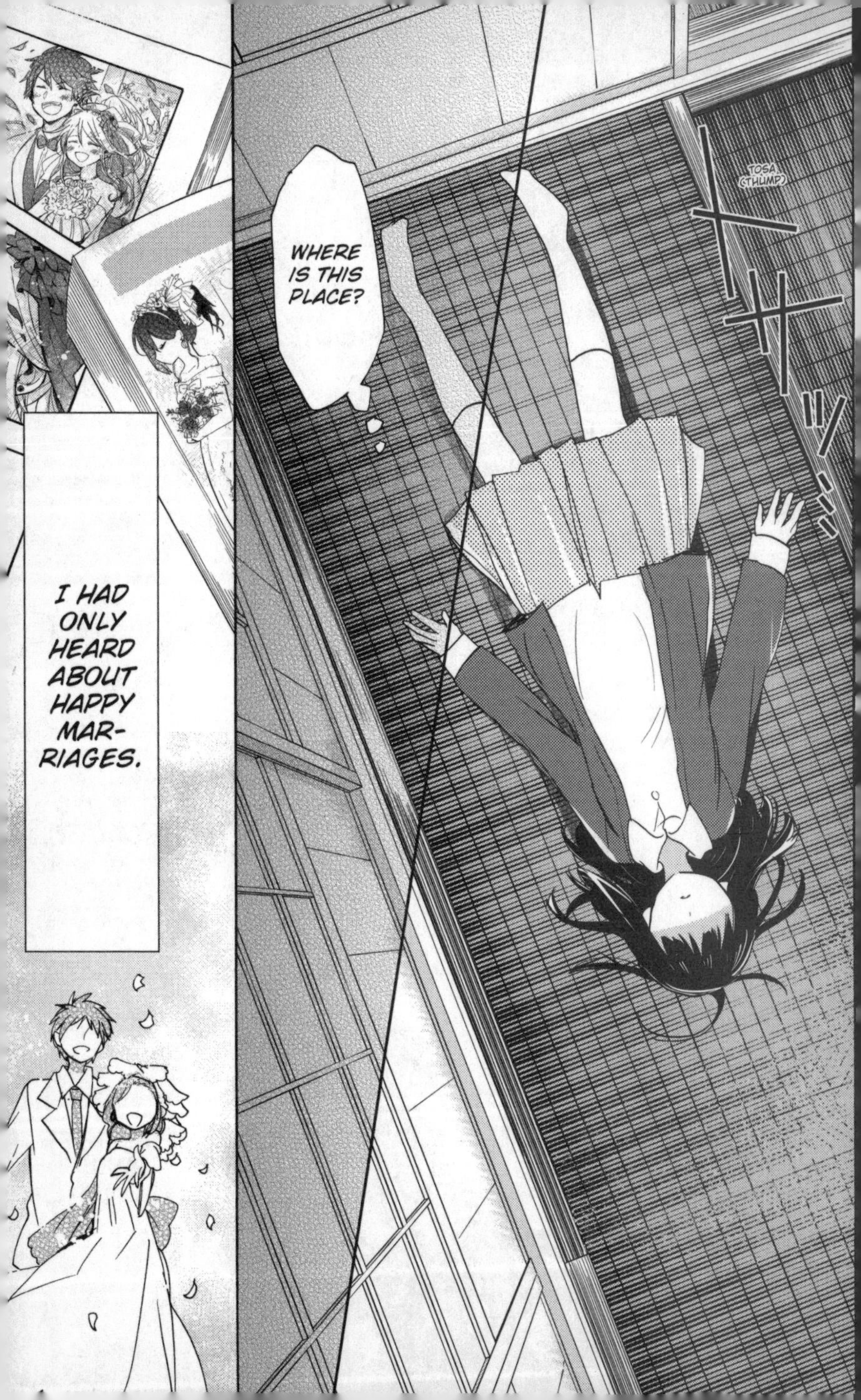
TOSA (THUMP)
WHERE IS THIS PLACE?
I HAD ONLY HEARD ABOUT HAPPY MAR-RIAGES.

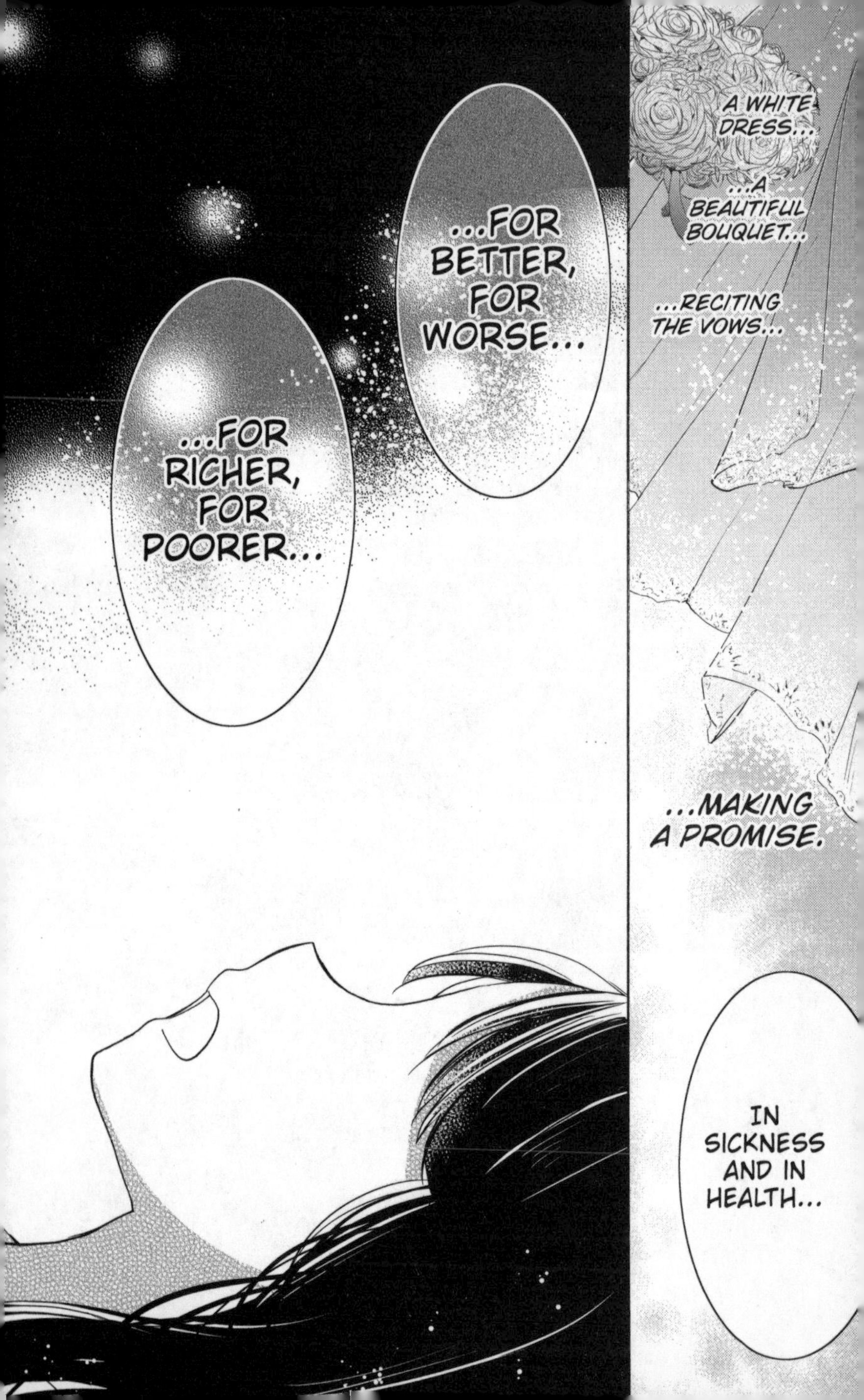
A WHITE DRESS...
...A BEAUTIFUL BOUQUET...
...RECITING THE VOWS...
...MAKING A PROMISE.
IN SICKNESS AND IN HEALTH...
...FOR BETTER, FOR WORSE...
...FOR RICHER, FOR POORER...

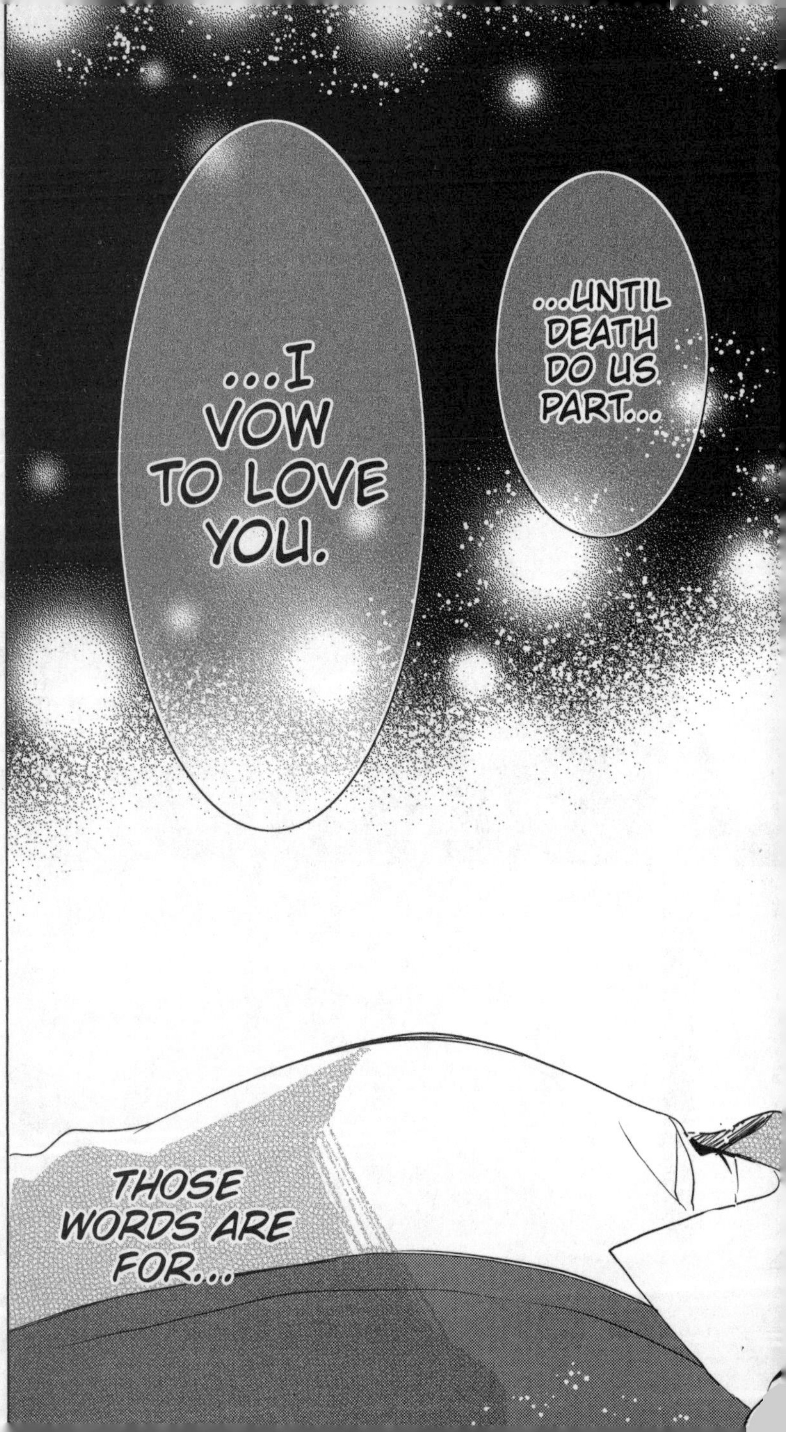

...THE ONE YOU LOVE.

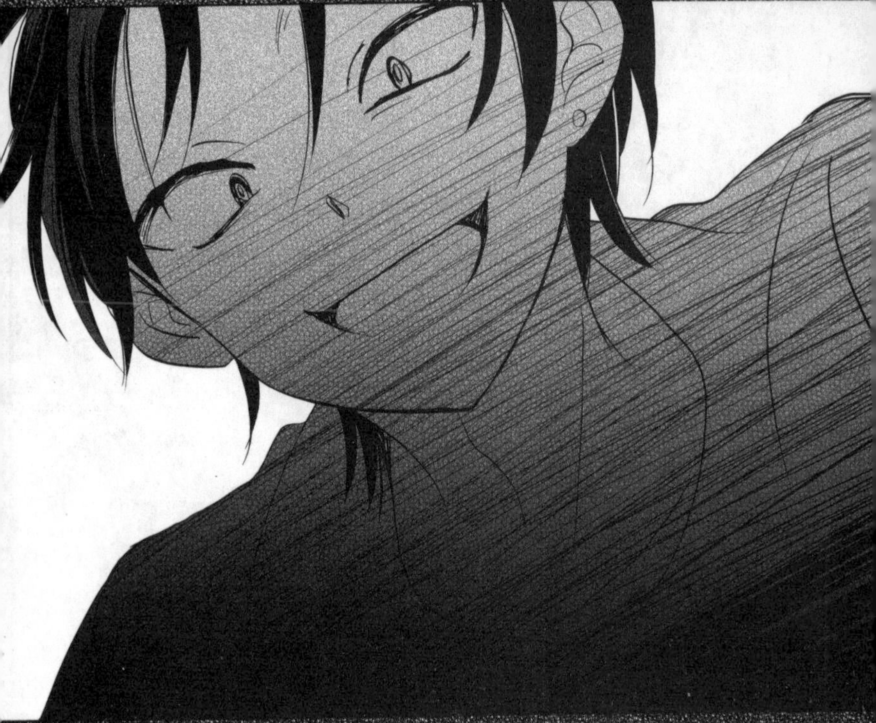
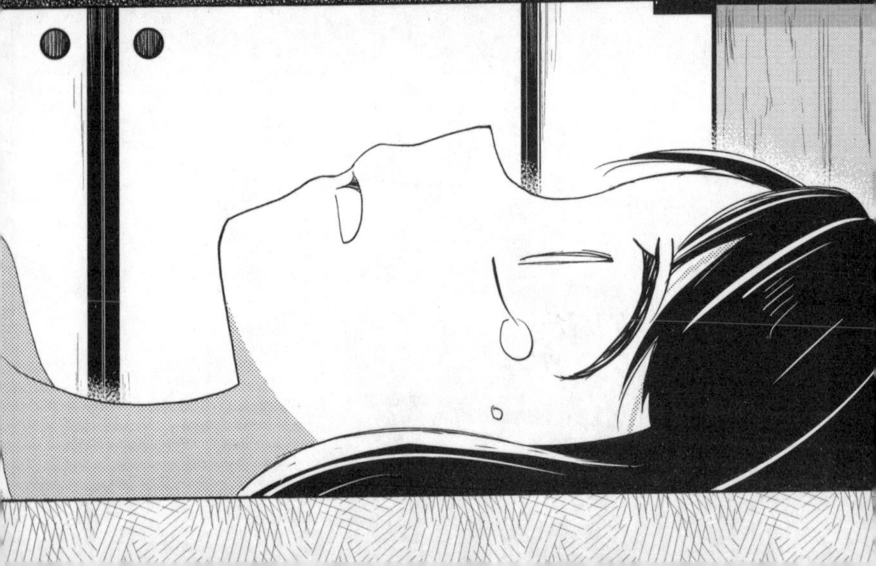

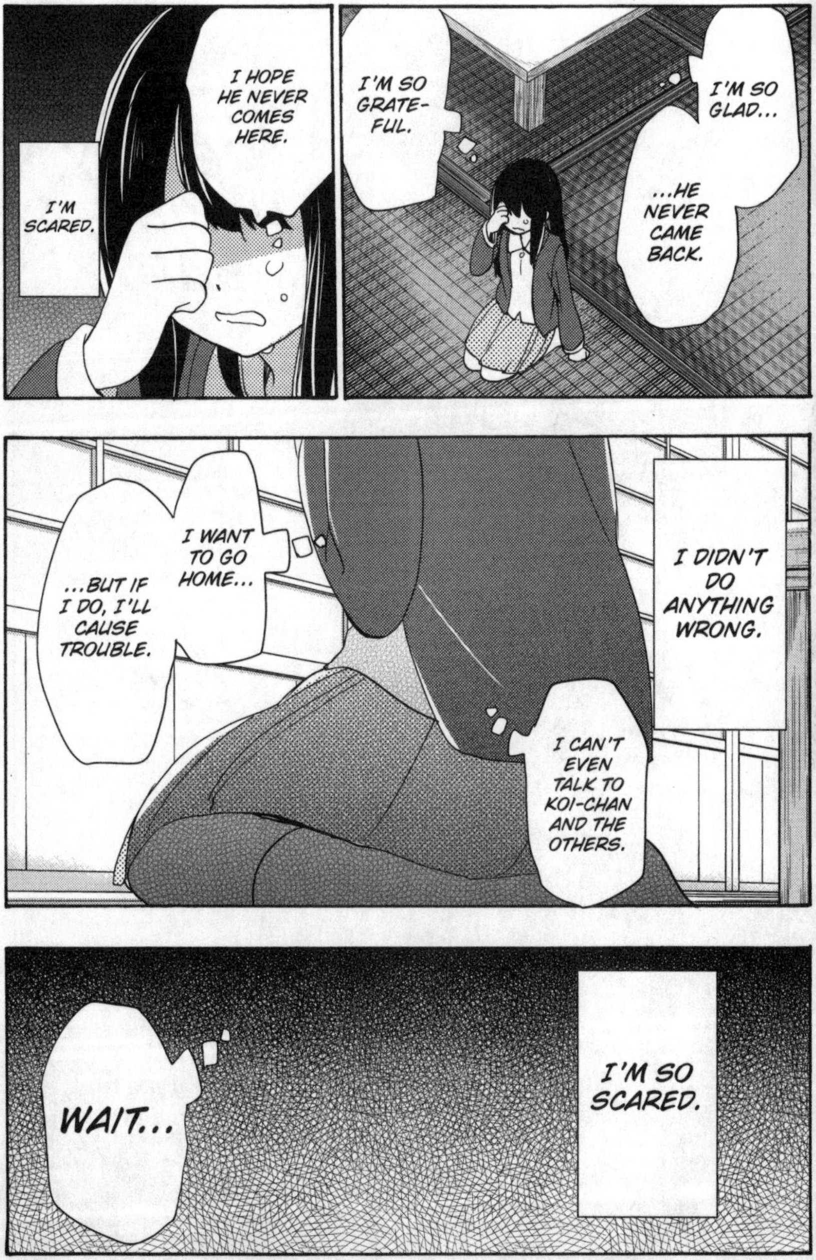
I'M SO GLAD...
...HE NEVER CAME BACK.
I'M SO GRATE-FUL.
I HOPE HE NEVER COMES HERE.
I'M SCARED.
I DIDN'T DO ANYTHING WRONG.
I WANT TO GO HOME...
...BUT IF I DO, I'LL CAUSE TROUBLE.
I CAN'T EVEN TALK TO KOI-CHAN AND THE OTHERS.
I'M SO SCARED.
WAIT...

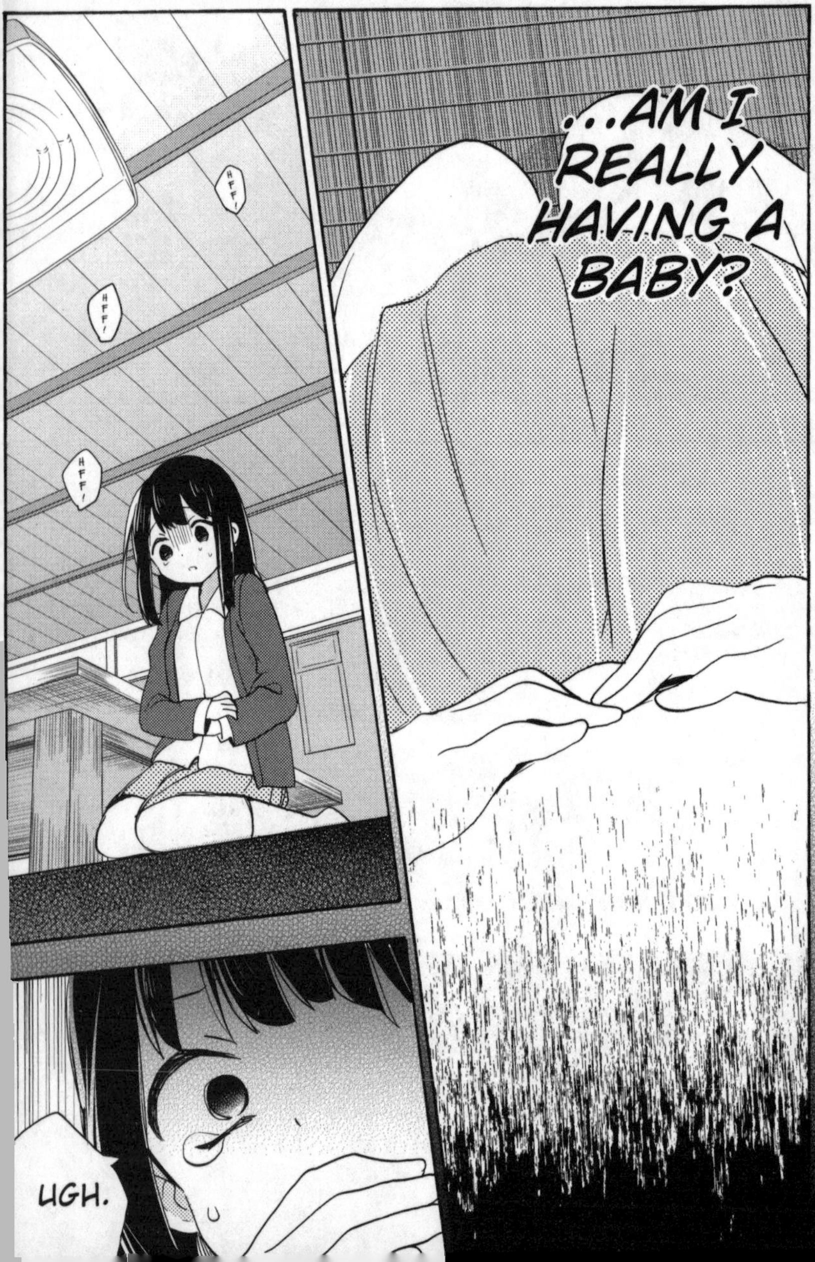
...AM I REALLY HAVING A BABY?
HFF!
HFF!
HFF!
UGH.

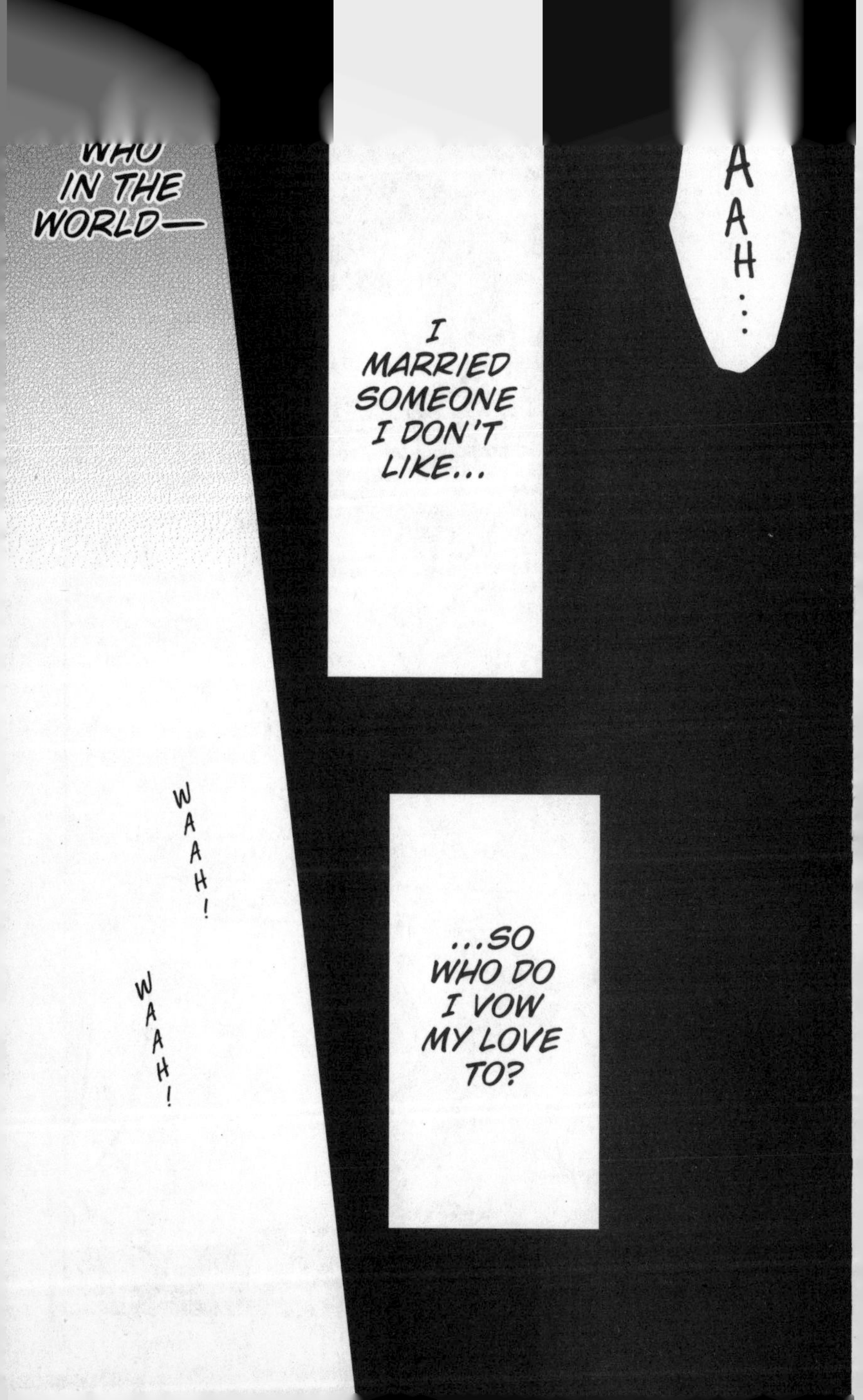
AAH...
I MARRIED SOMEONE I DON'T LIKE...
...SO WHO DO I VOW MY LOVE TO?
WHO IN THE WORLD—
WAAH!
WAAH!

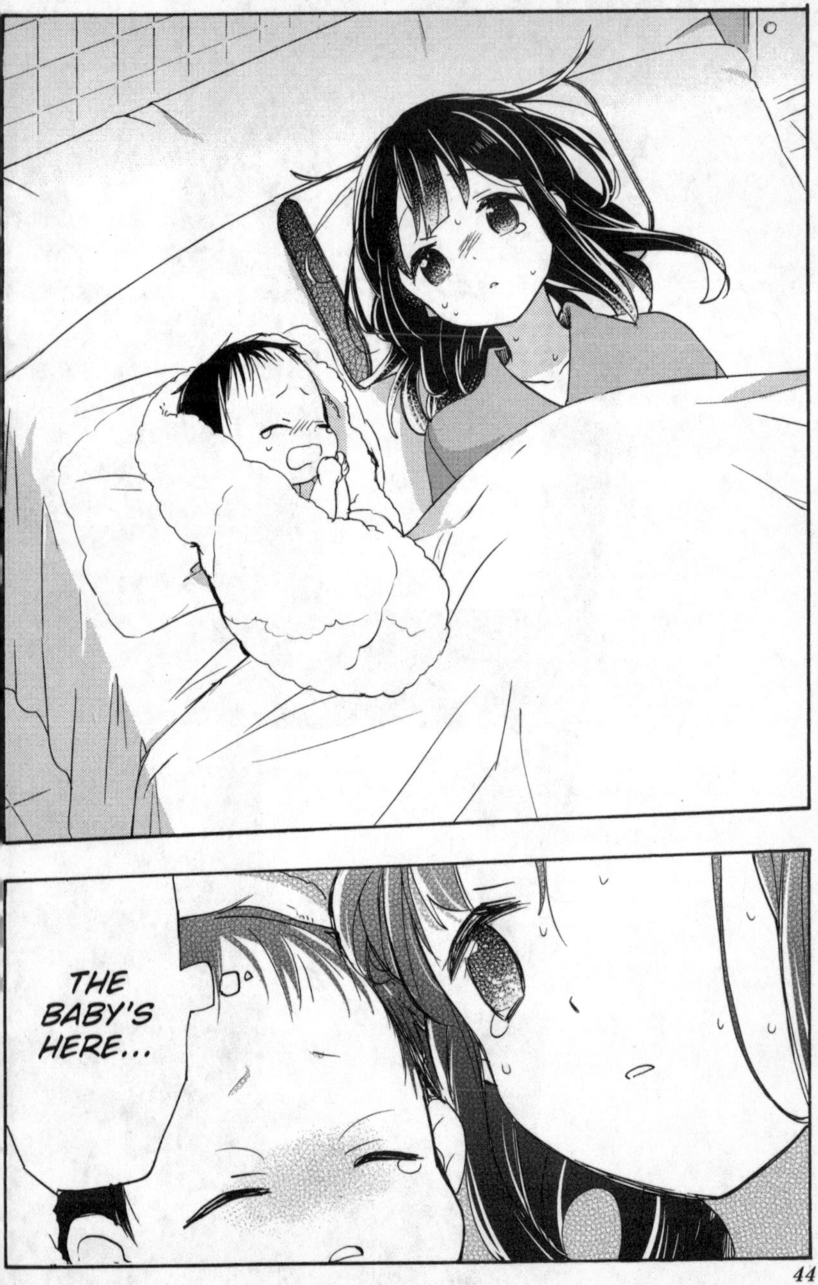
THE BABY'S HERE...

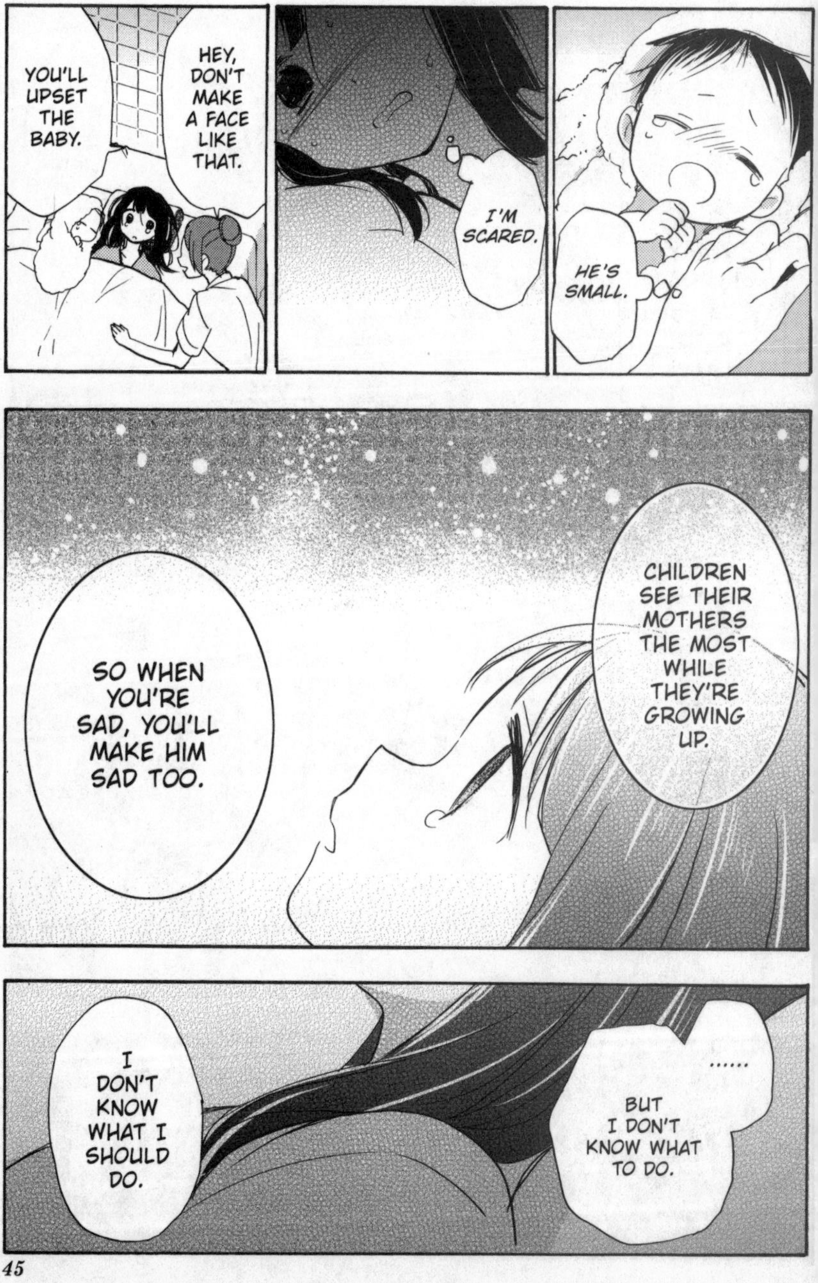
HE'S SMALL.
I'M SCARED.
HEY, DON'T MAKE A FACE LIKE THAT.
YOU'LL UPSET THE BABY.
CHILDREN SEE THEIR MOTHERS THE MOST WHILE THEY'RE GROWING UP.
SO WHEN YOU'RE SAD, YOU'LL MAKE HIM SAD TOO.
......
BUT I DON'T KNOW WHAT TO DO.
I DON'T KNOW WHAT I SHOULD DO.

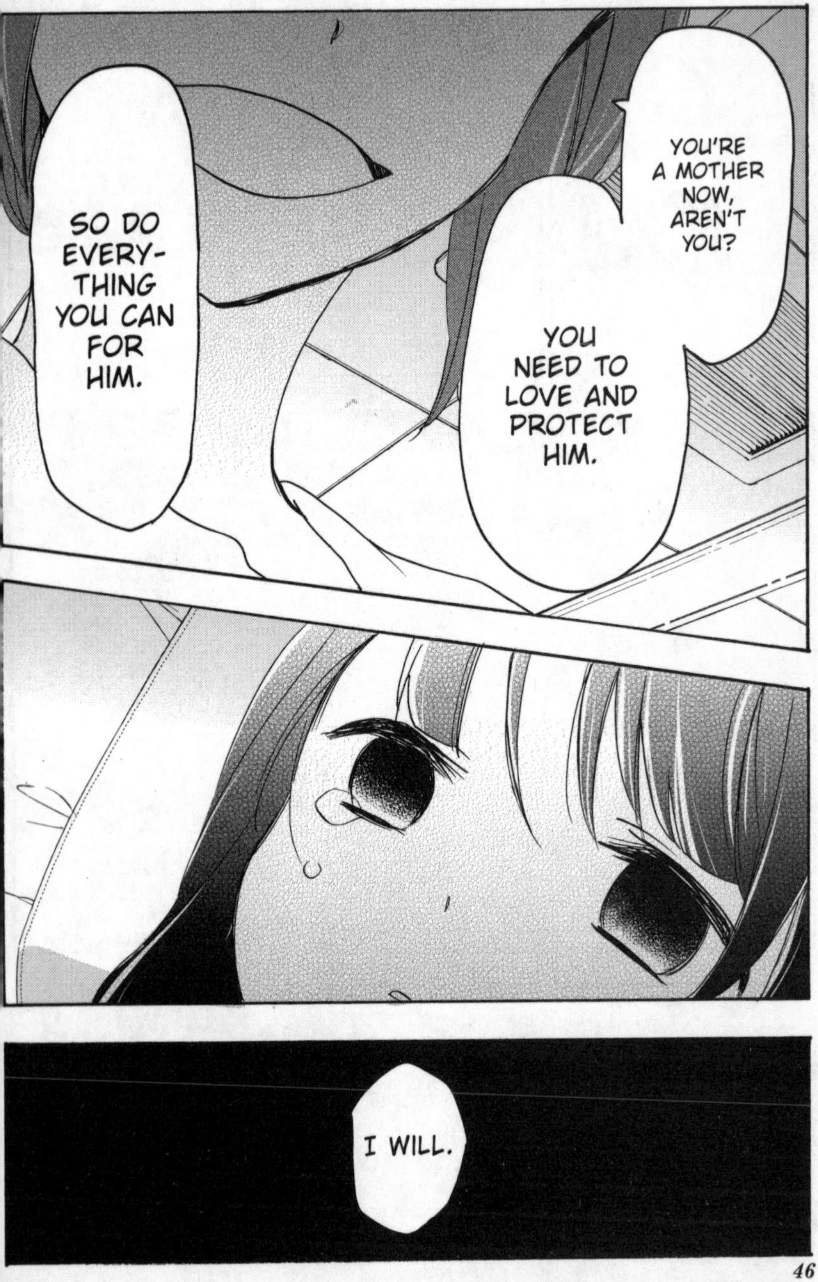
YOU'RE A MOTHER NOW, AREN'T YOU?
YOU NEED TO LOVE AND PROTECT HIM.
SO DO EVERY-THING YOU CAN FOR HIM.
I WILL.

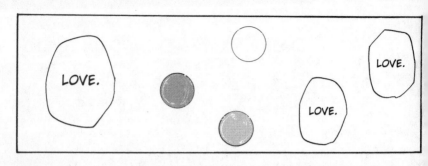

PARALLEL LIFE: THE SWEET, THE TWISTED, THE PAINED

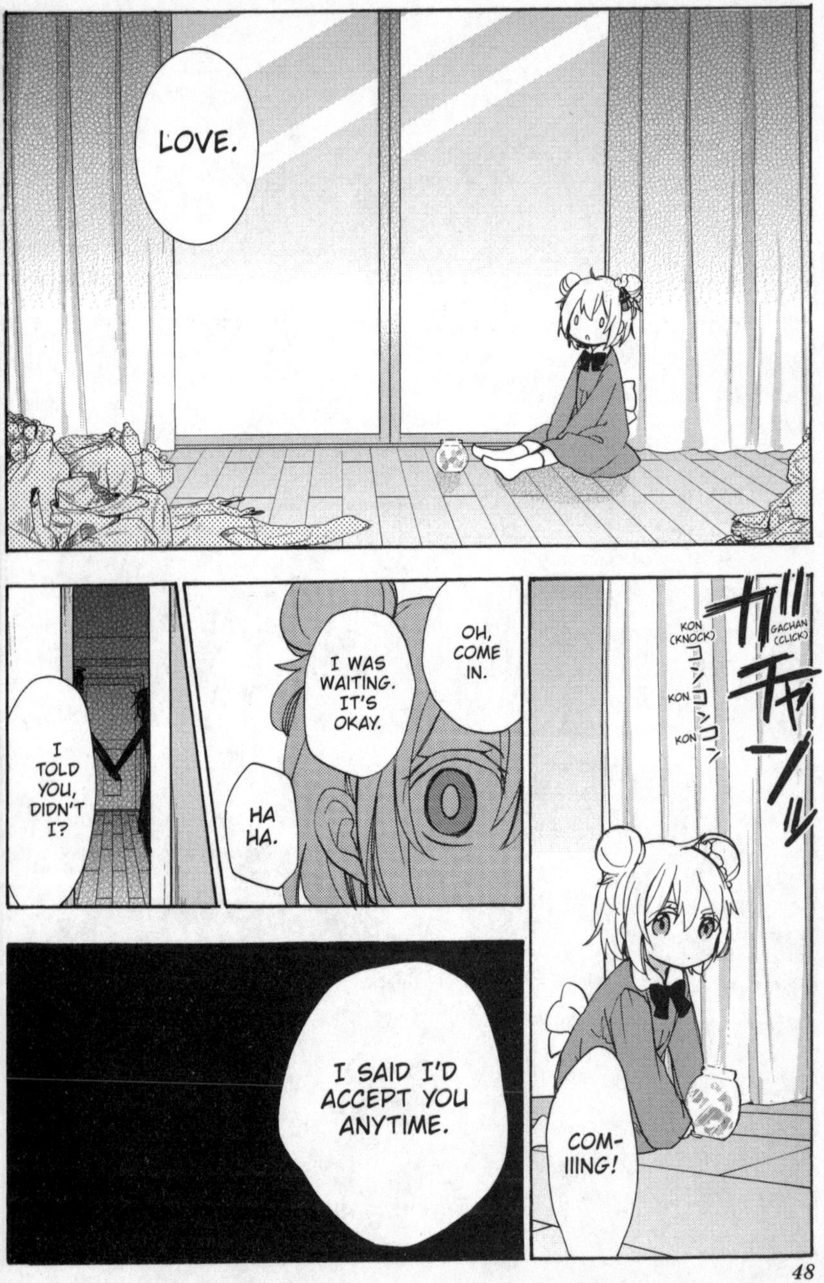
LOVE.
ガチャン
GACHAN (CLICK)
コンコンコン
KON (KNOCK)
KON
KON
COM-IIING!
OH, COME IN.
I WAS WAITING. IT'S OKAY.
HA HA.
I TOLD YOU, DIDN'T I?
I SAID I'D ACCEPT YOU ANYTIME.

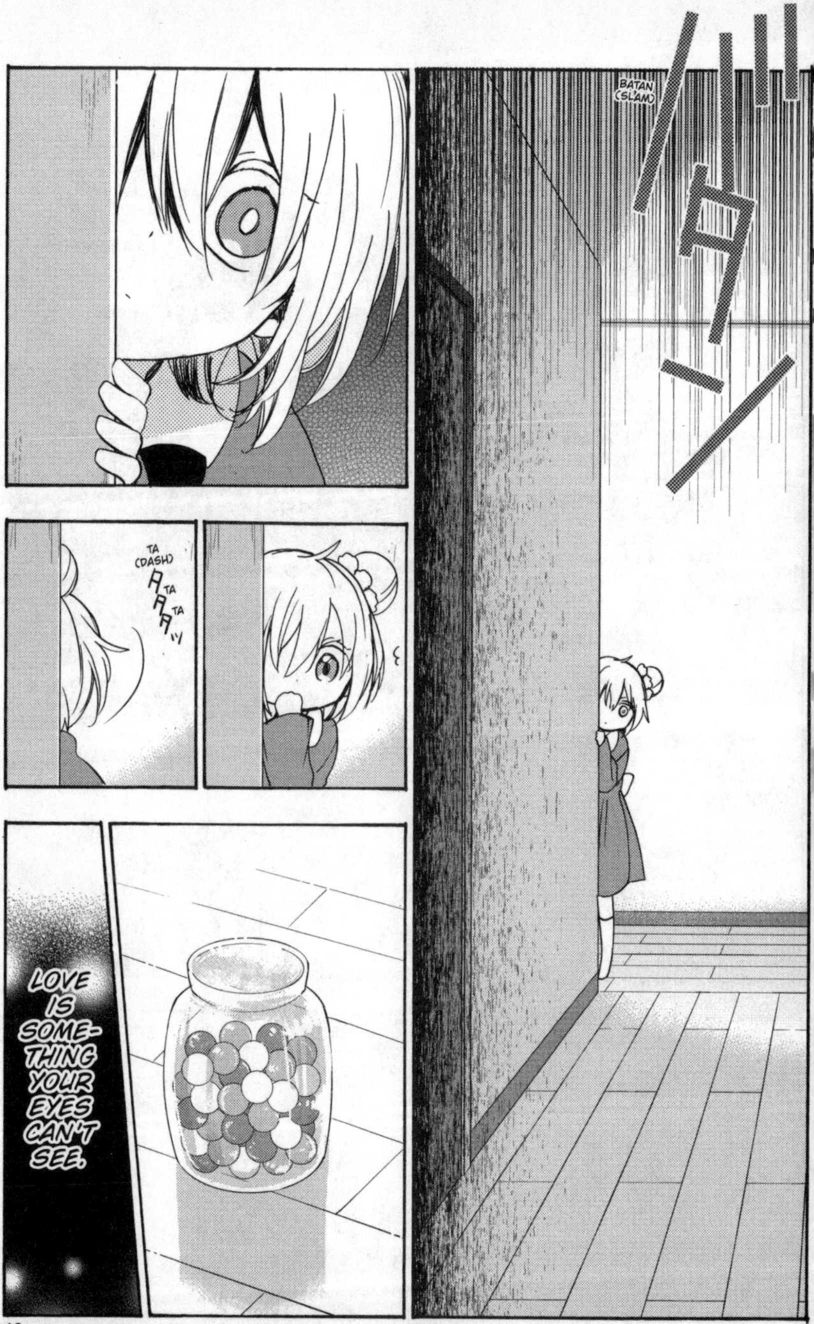
BATAN (SLAM)
TA (DASH) TA TA TA
LOVE IS SOME-THING YOUR EYES CAN'T SEE.

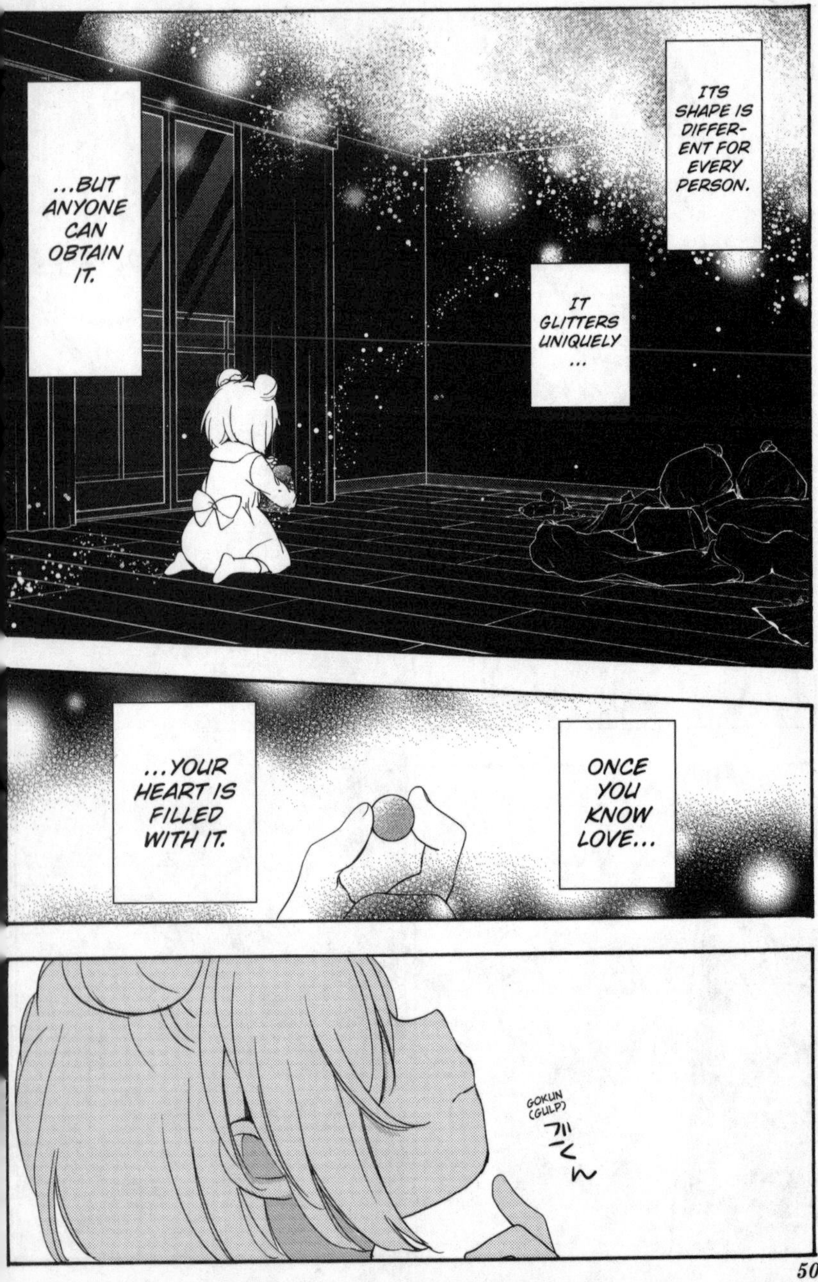
ITS SHAPE IS DIFFER-ENT FOR EVERY PERSON.
IT GLITTERS UNIQUELY ...
...BUT ANYONE CAN OBTAIN IT.
ONCE YOU KNOW LOVE...
...YOUR HEART IS FILLED WITH IT.
GOKUN (GULP)
ゴくん

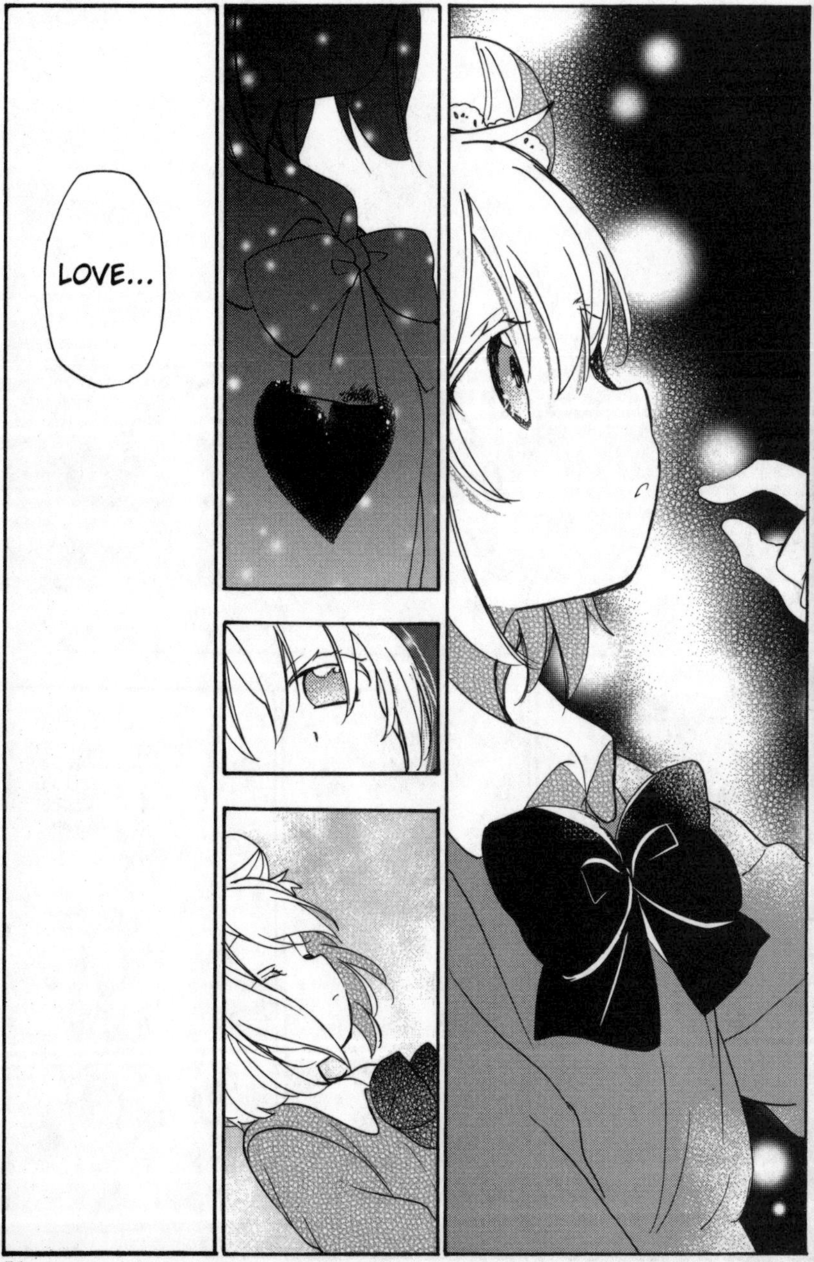
LOVE...

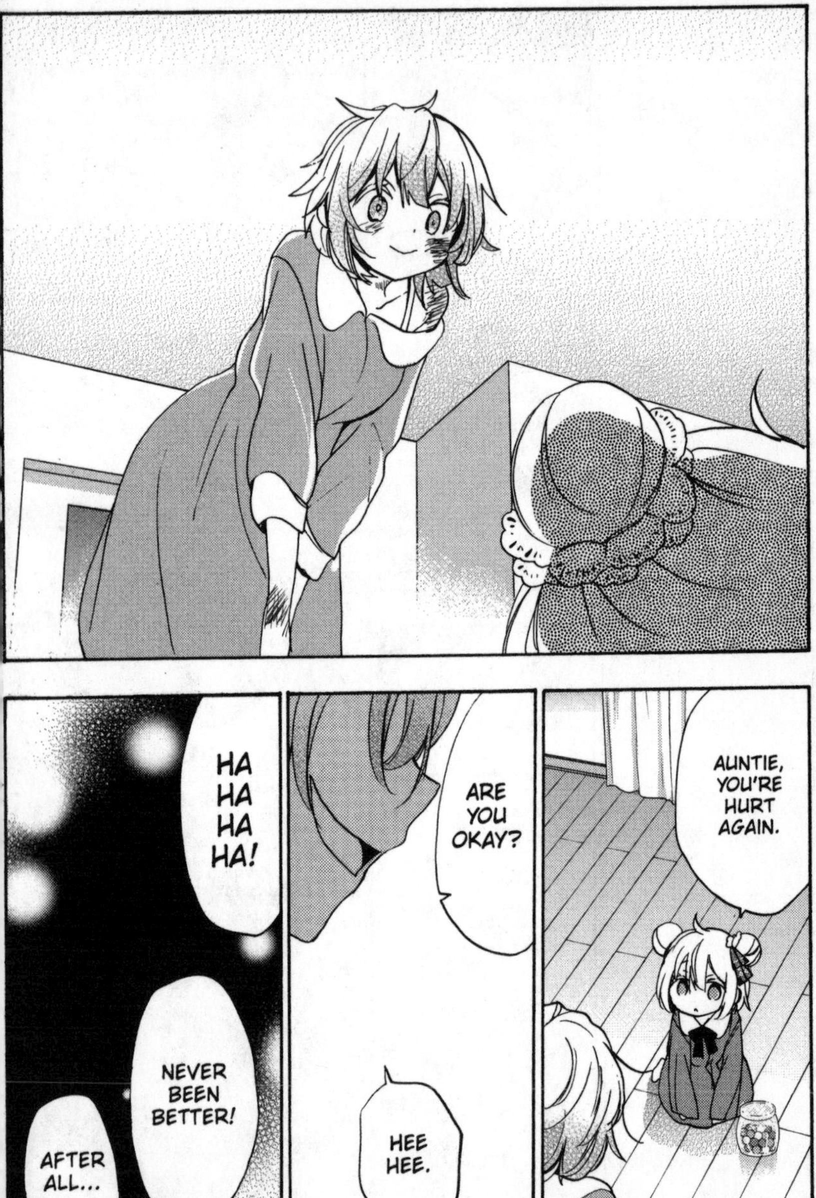
AUNTIE, YOU'RE HURT AGAIN.
ARE YOU OKAY?
HEE HEE.
HA HA HA HA!
NEVER BEEN BETTER!
AFTER ALL...

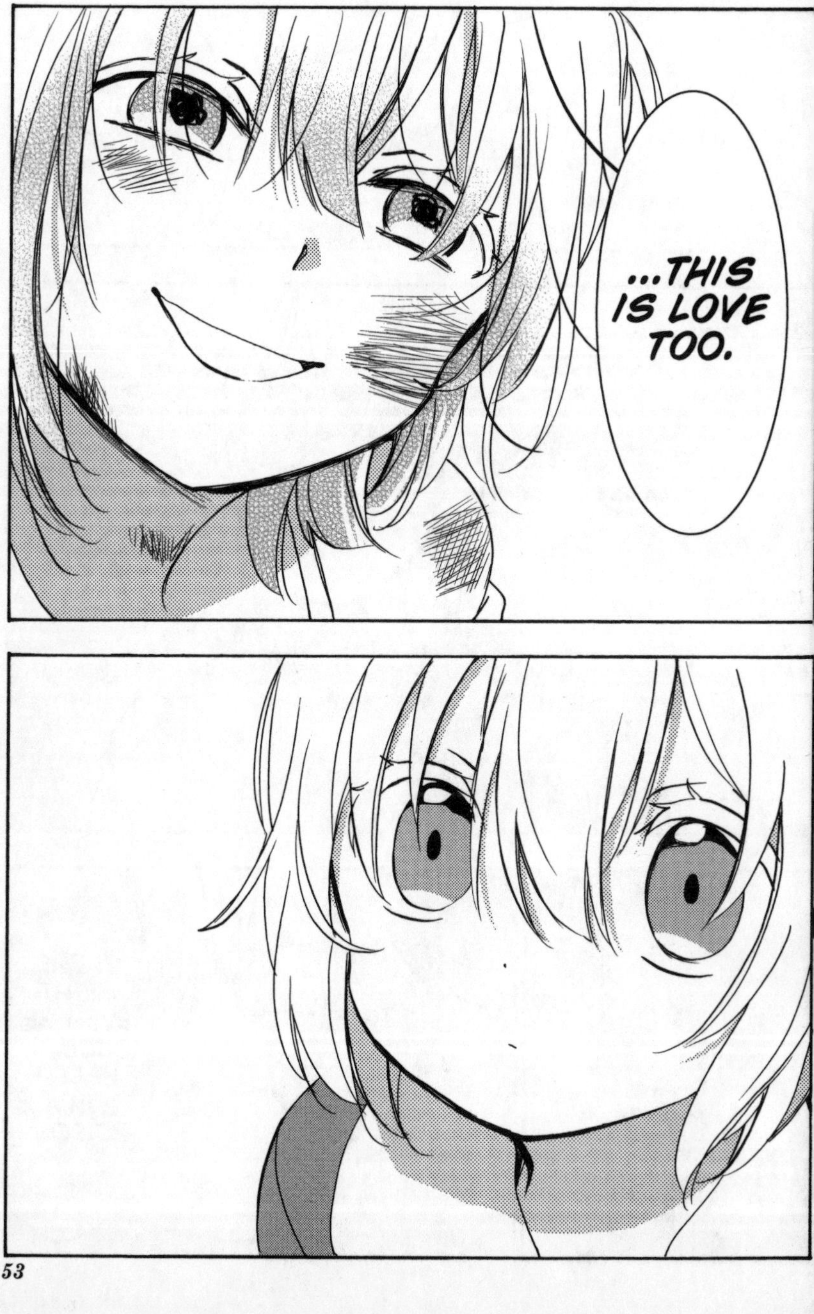
...THIS IS LOVE TOO.

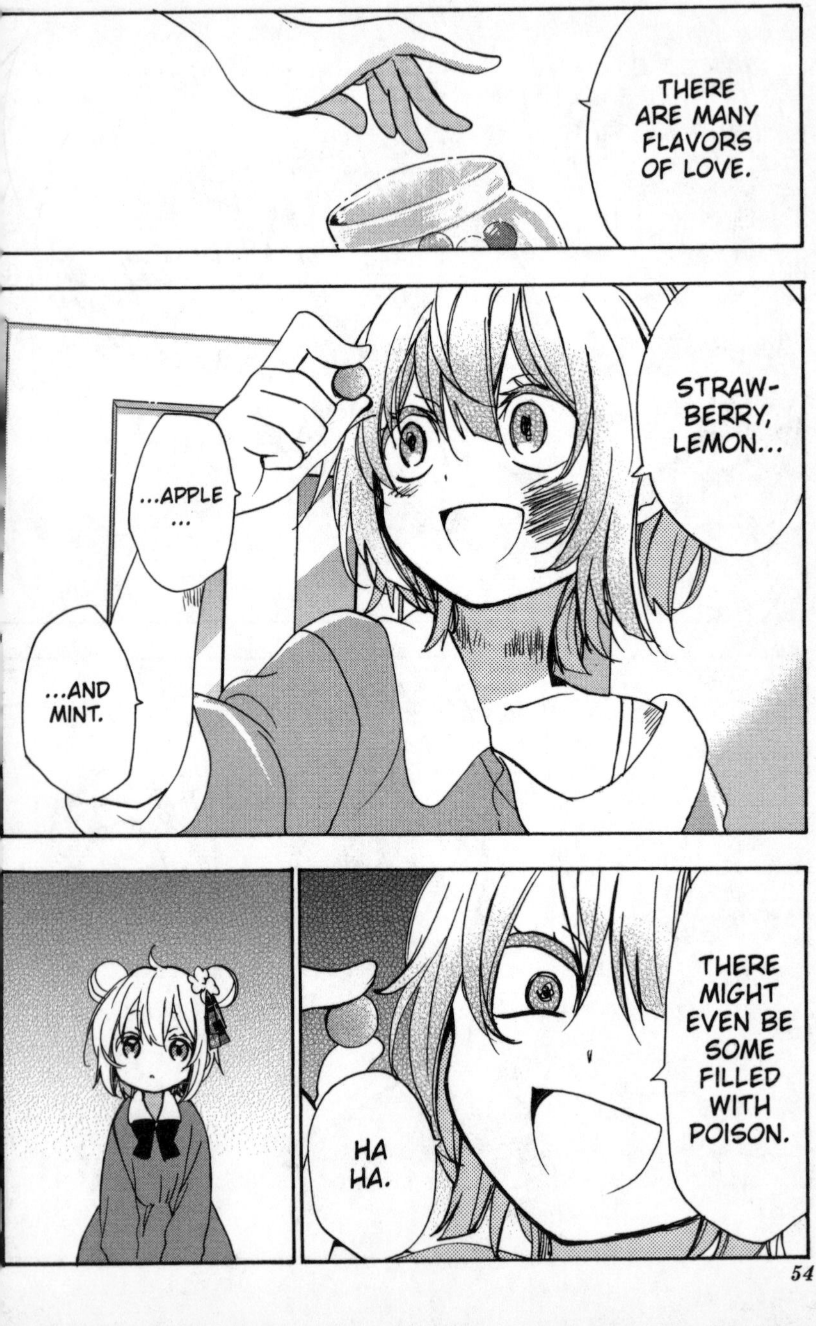
THERE ARE MANY FLAVORS OF LOVE.
STRAW-BERRY, LEMON...
...APPLE ...
...AND MINT.
THERE MIGHT EVEN BE SOME FILLED WITH POISON.
HA HA.

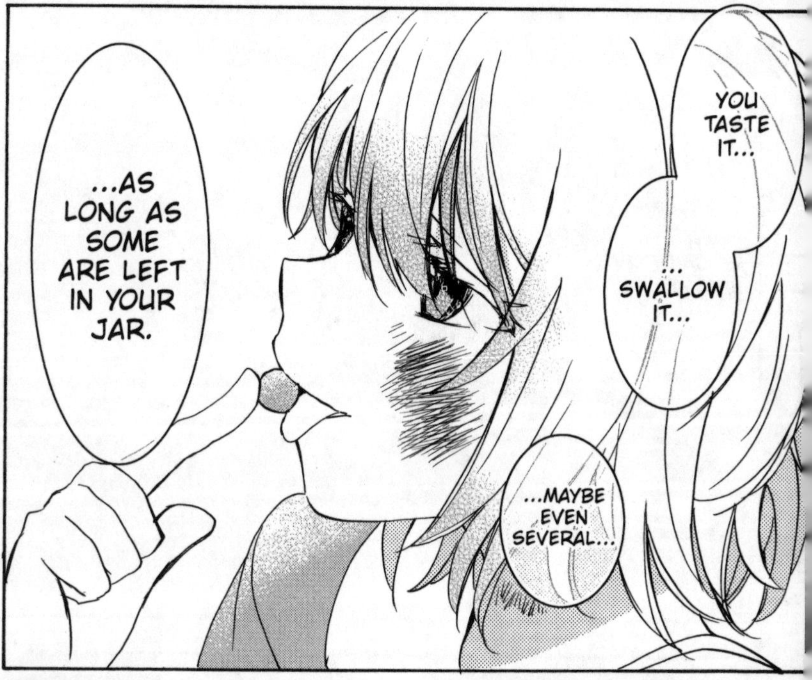
YOU TASTE IT...
...SWALLOW IT...
...MAYBE EVEN SEVERAL...
...AS LONG AS SOME ARE LEFT IN YOUR JAR.
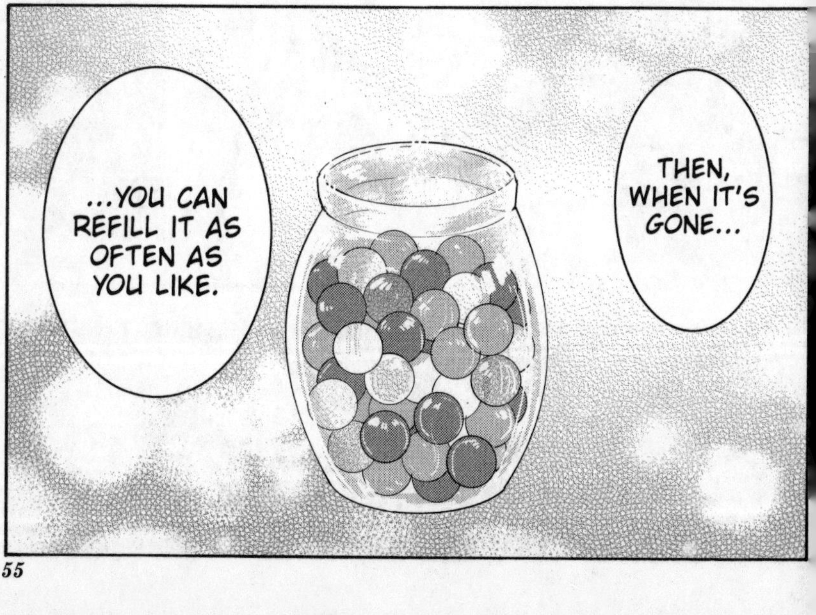
THEN, WHEN IT'S GONE...
...YOU CAN REFILL IT AS OFTEN AS YOU LIKE.

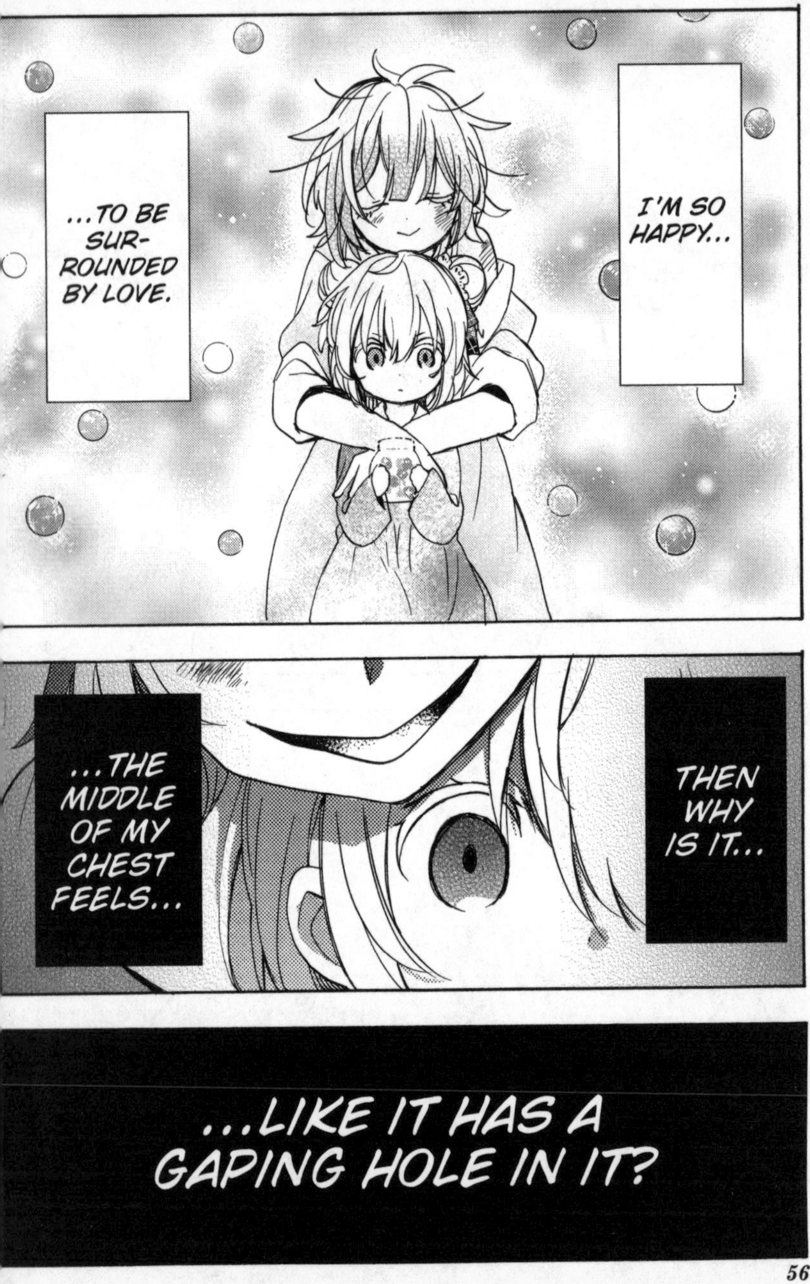
I'M SO HAPPY...
...TO BE SUR-ROUNDED BY LOVE.
THEN WHY IS IT...
...THE MIDDLE OF MY CHEST FEELS...
...LIKE IT HAS A GAPING HOLE IN IT?

Happy
Sugar
Life

{ Happy
Sugar
Life }

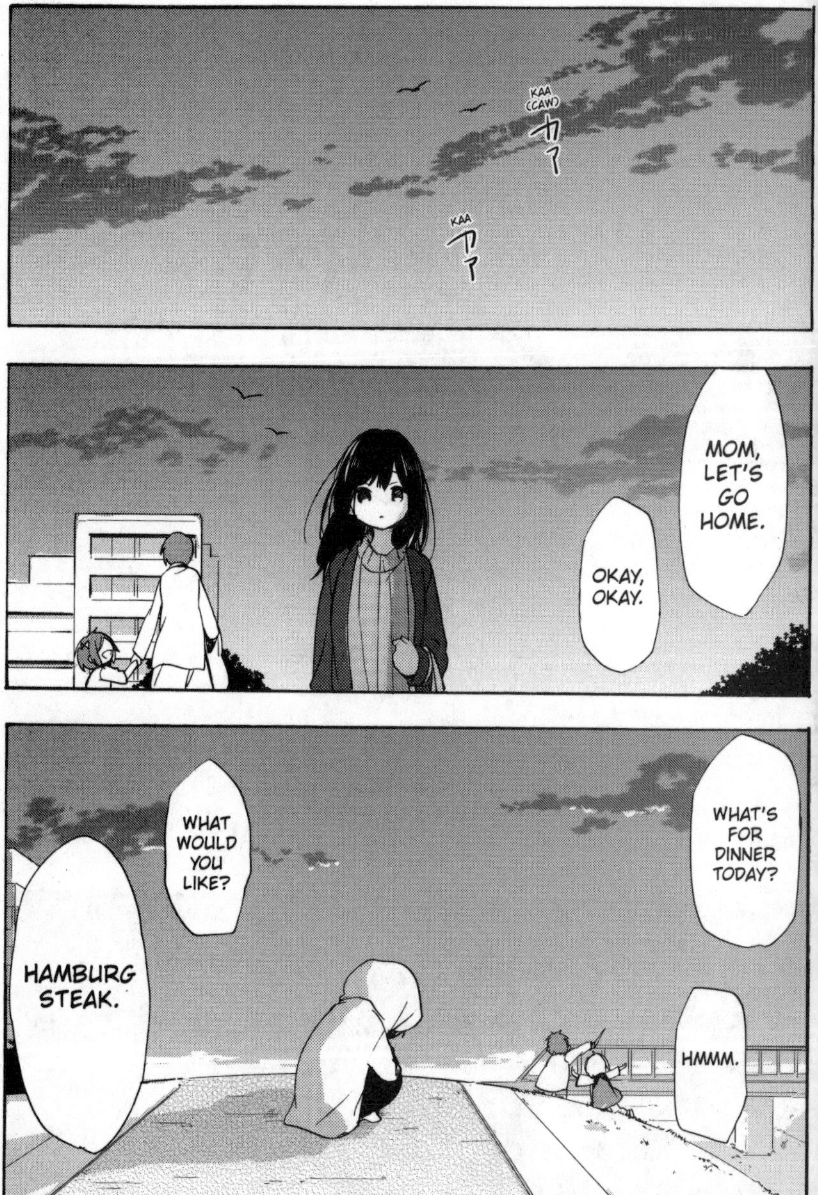
KAA (CAW)
カァ
KAA
カァ
MOM, LET'S GO HOME.
OKAY, OKAY.
WHAT'S FOR DINNER TODAY?
WHAT WOULD YOU LIKE?
HMMM.
HAMBURG STEAK.

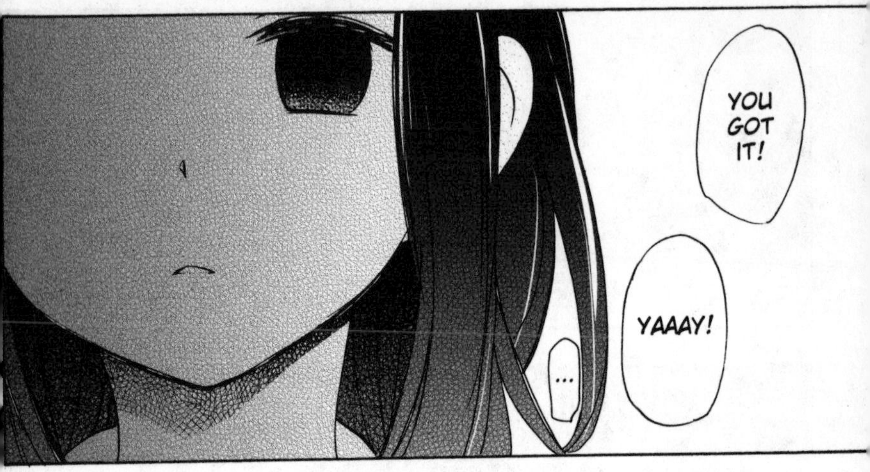
YOU GOT IT!
YAAAY!
...

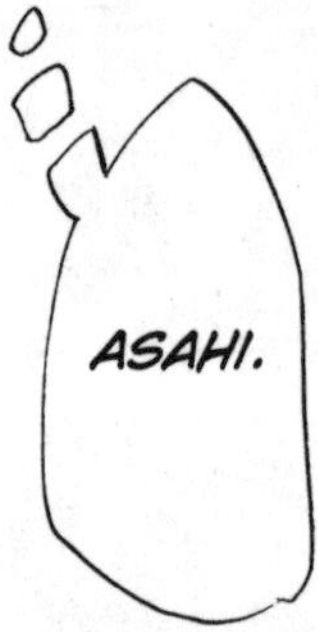
ASAHI.

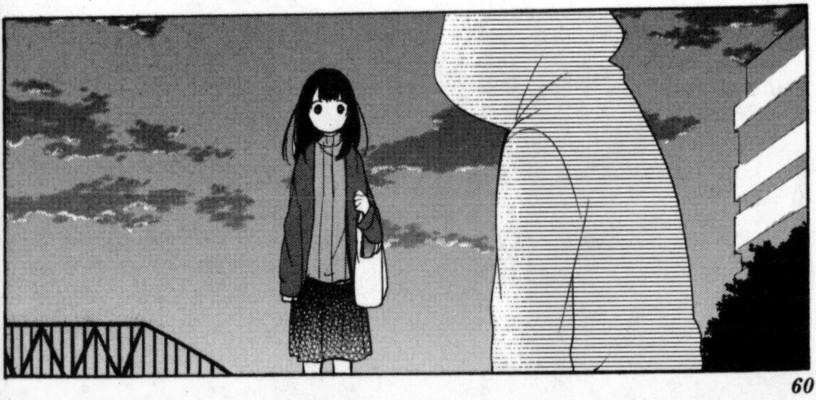

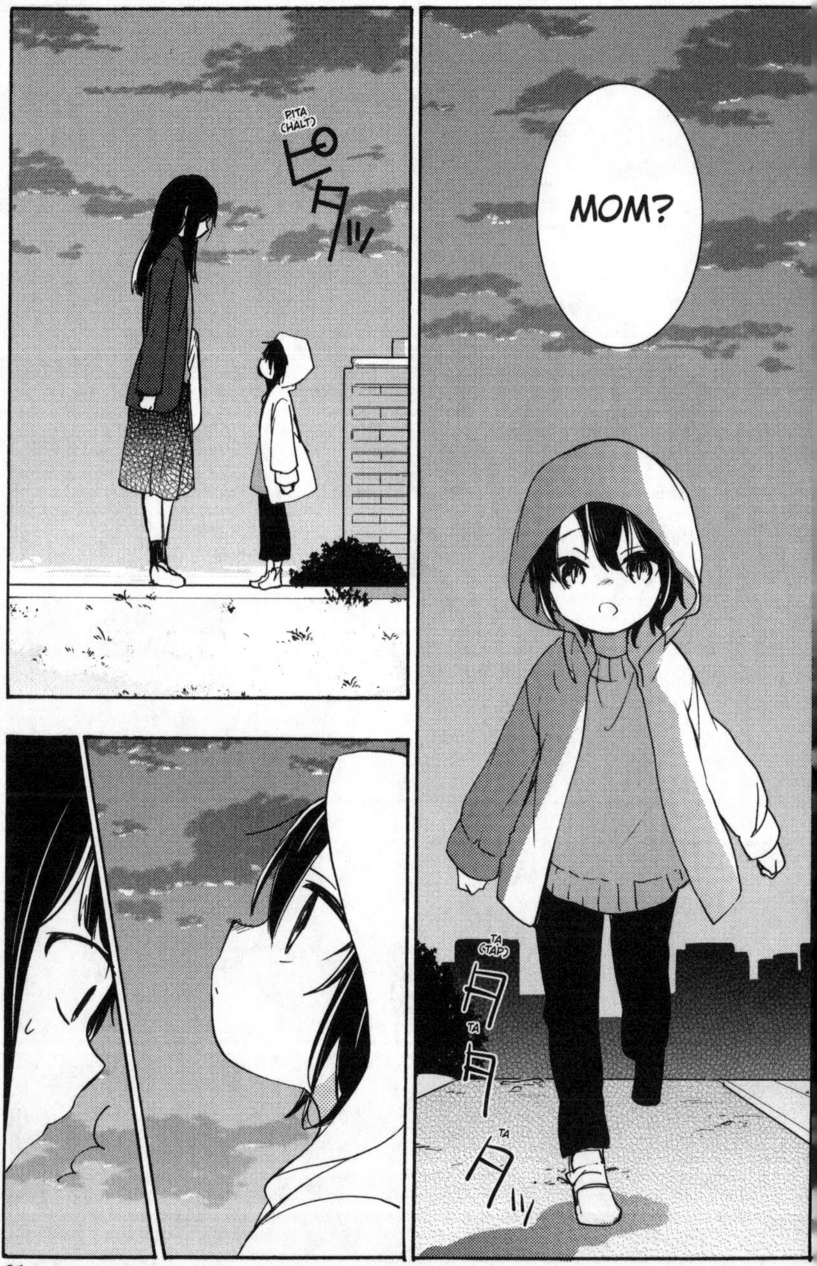
MOM?
TA (TAP)
TA
TA
PITA (HALT)

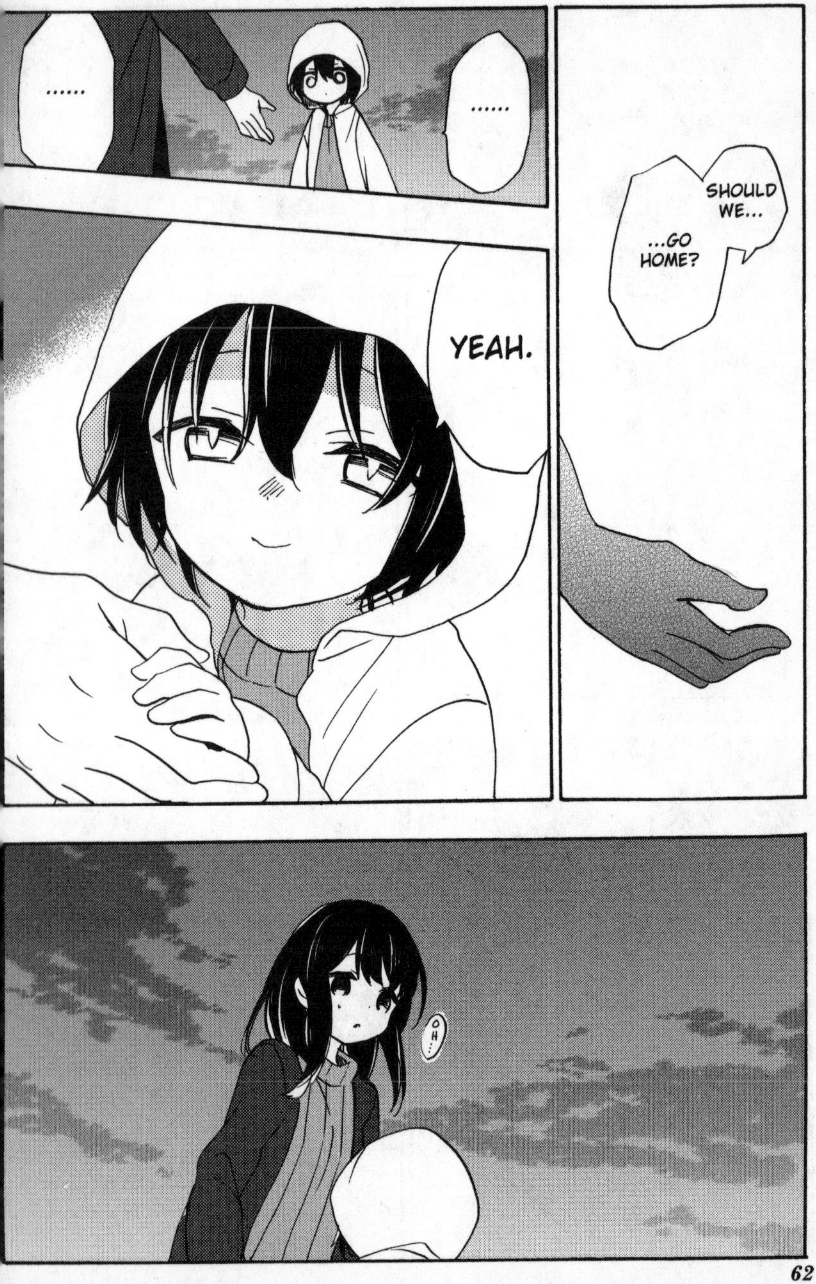
SHOULD WE... ...GO HOME?
......
......
YEAH.
OH...

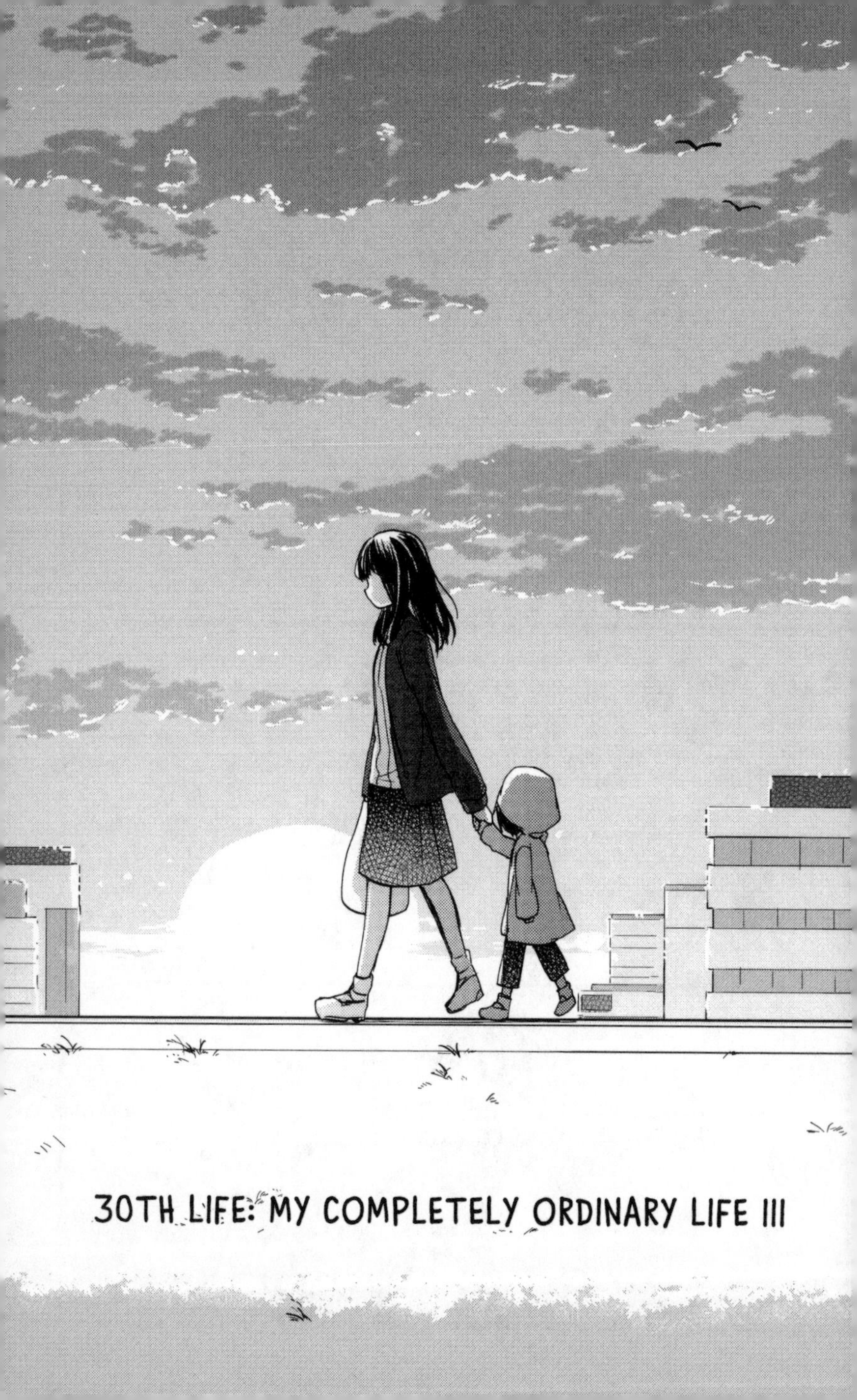
30TH LIFE: MY COMPLETELY ORDINARY LIFE III

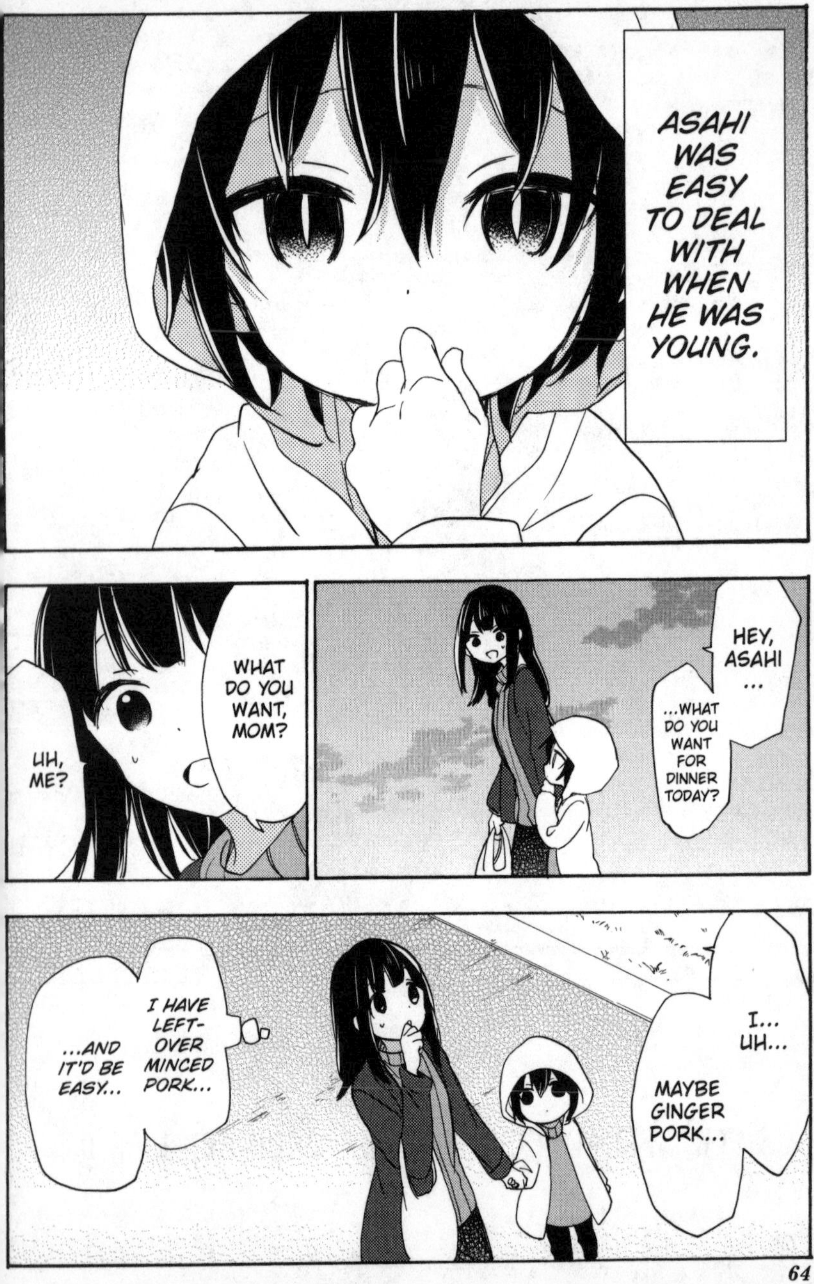
ASAHI WAS EASY TO DEAL WITH WHEN HE WAS YOUNG.
HEY, ASAHI ...
...WHAT DO YOU WANT FOR DINNER TODAY?
WHAT DO YOU WANT, MOM?
UH, ME?
I... UH...
MAYBE GINGER PORK...
I HAVE LEFT-OVER MINCED PORK...
...AND IT'D BE EASY...

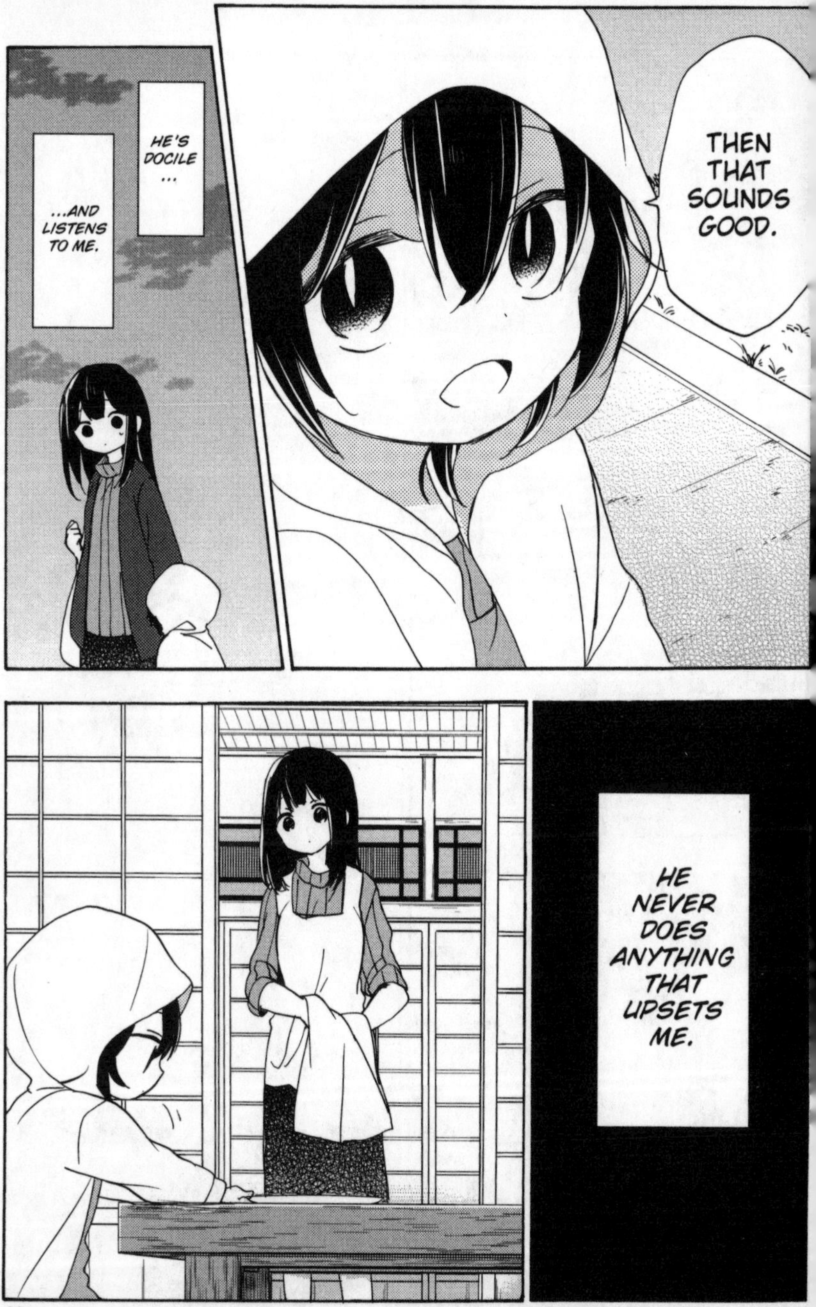
THEN THAT SOUNDS GOOD.
HE'S DOCILE ...
...AND LISTENS TO ME.
HE NEVER DOES ANYTHING THAT UPSETS ME.

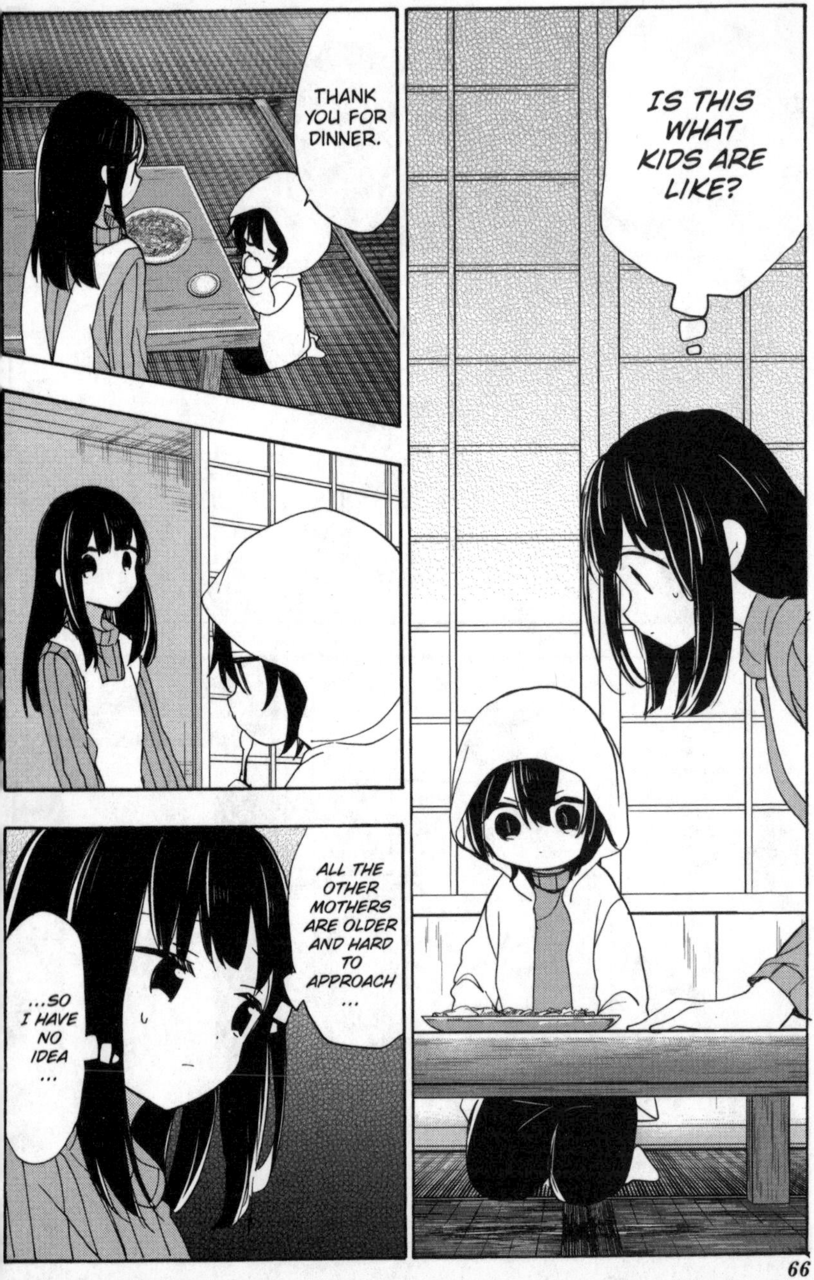
IS THIS WHAT KIDS ARE LIKE?
THANK YOU FOR DINNER.
ALL THE OTHER MOTHERS ARE OLDER AND HARD TO APPROACH...
...SO I HAVE NO IDEA...

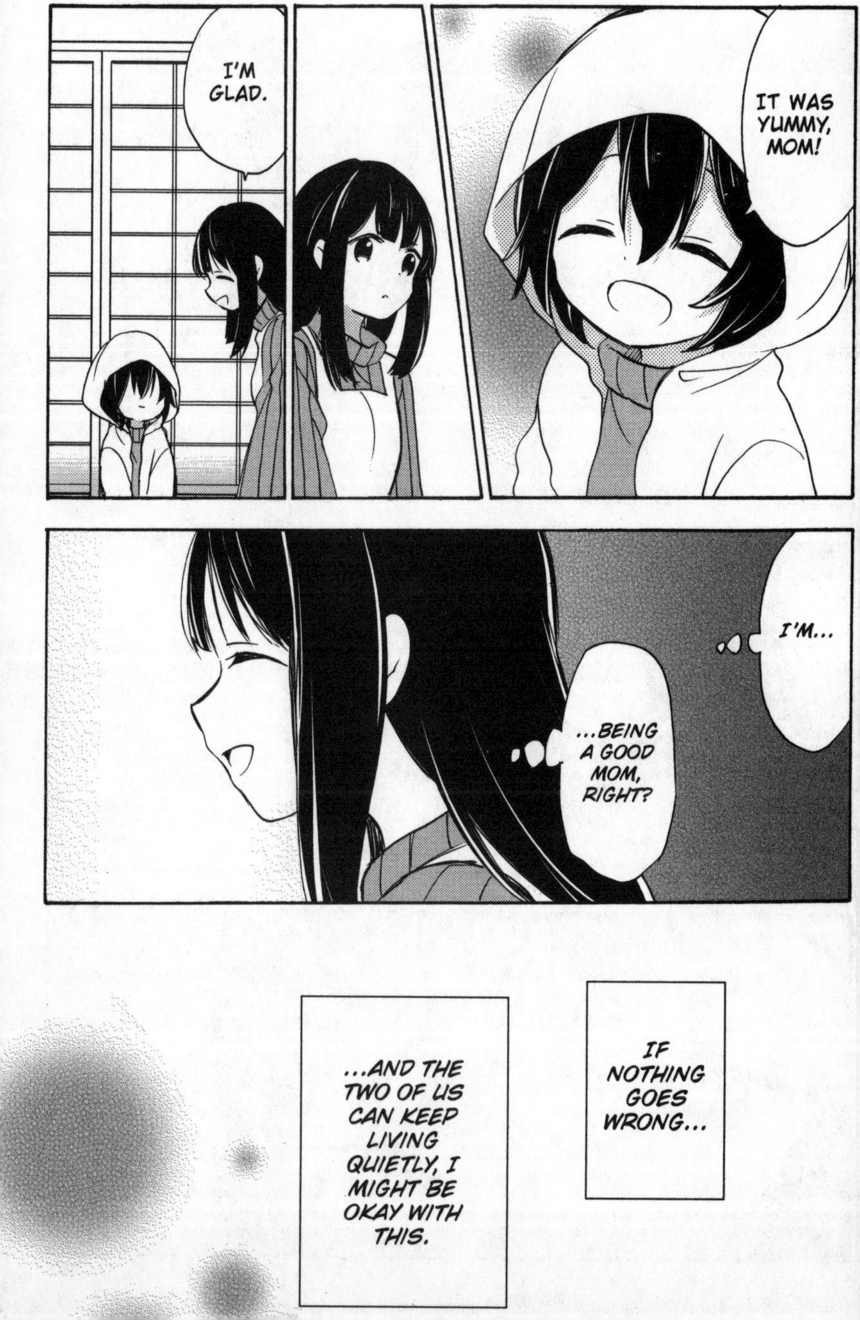
IT WAS YUMMY, MOM!
I'M GLAD.
I'M...
...BEING A GOOD MOM, RIGHT?
IF NOTHING GOES WRONG...
...AND THE TWO OF US CAN KEEP LIVING QUIETLY, I MIGHT BE OKAY WITH THIS.

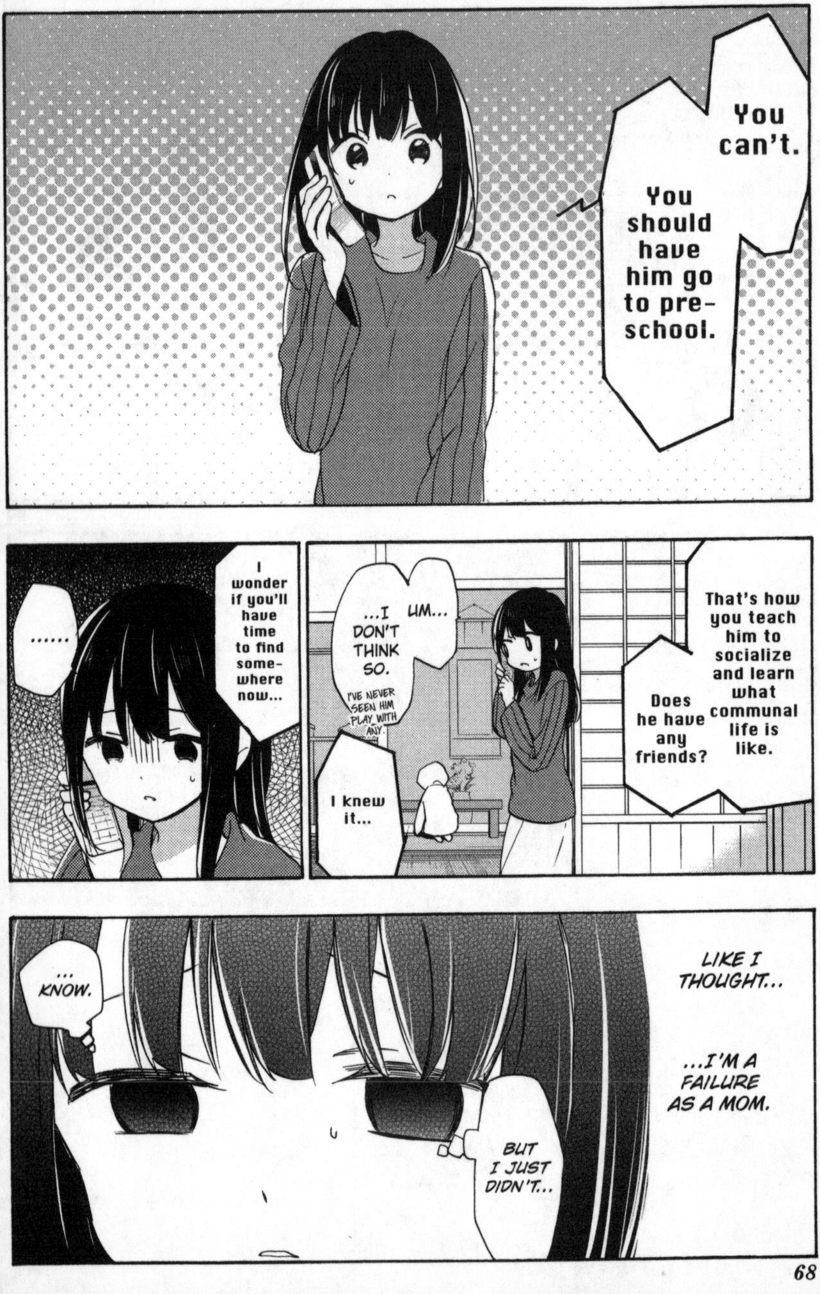
You can't.
You should have him go to pre-school.
That's how you teach him to socialize and learn what communal life is like.
Does he have any friends?
UM...
...I DON'T THINK SO.
I'VE NEVER SEEN HIM PLAY WITH ANY.
I knew it...
I wonder if you'll have time to find some-where now...
......
LIKE I THOUGHT...
...I'M A FAILURE AS A MOM.
BUT I JUST DIDN'T...
...KNOW.

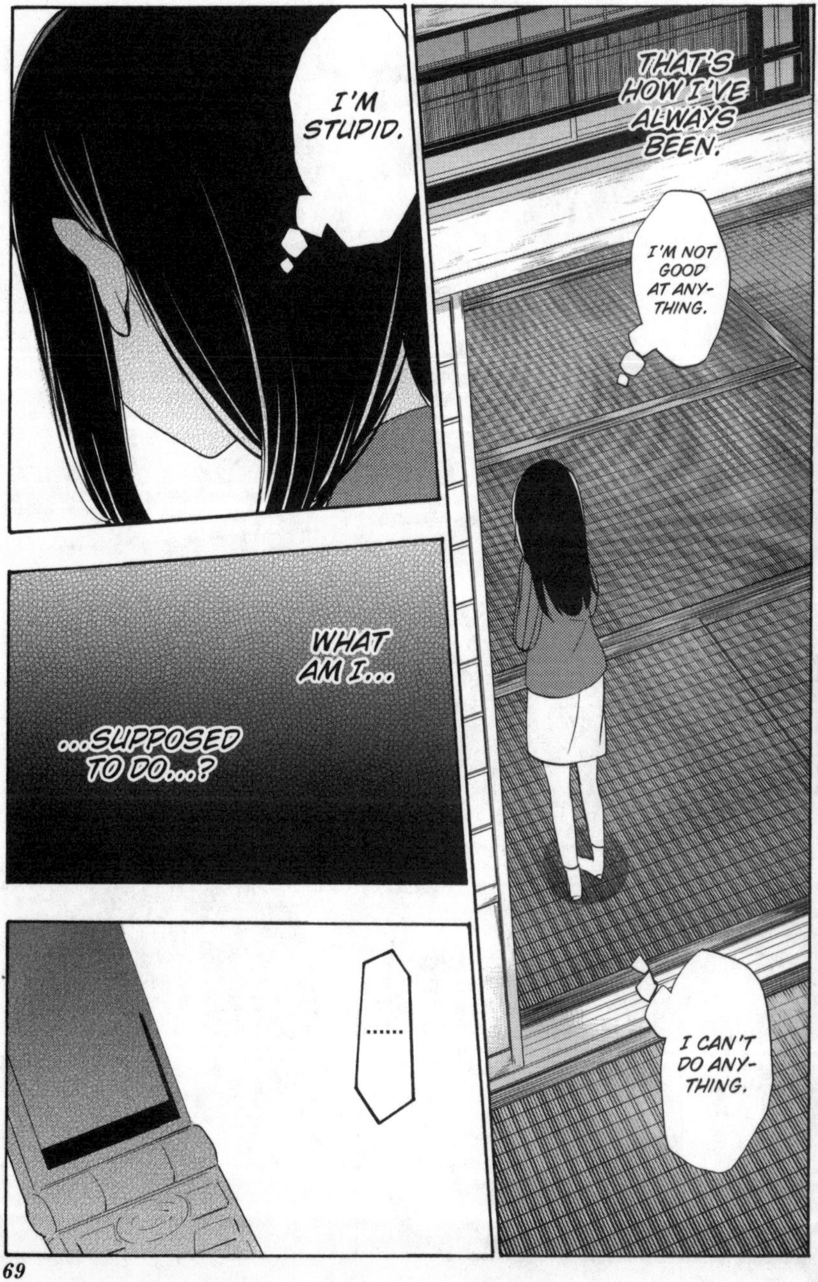
THAT'S HOW I'VE ALWAYS BEEN.
I'M NOT GOOD AT ANY-THING.
I CAN'T DO ANY-THING.
I'M STUPID.
WHAT AM I...
...SUPPOSED TO DO...?
......

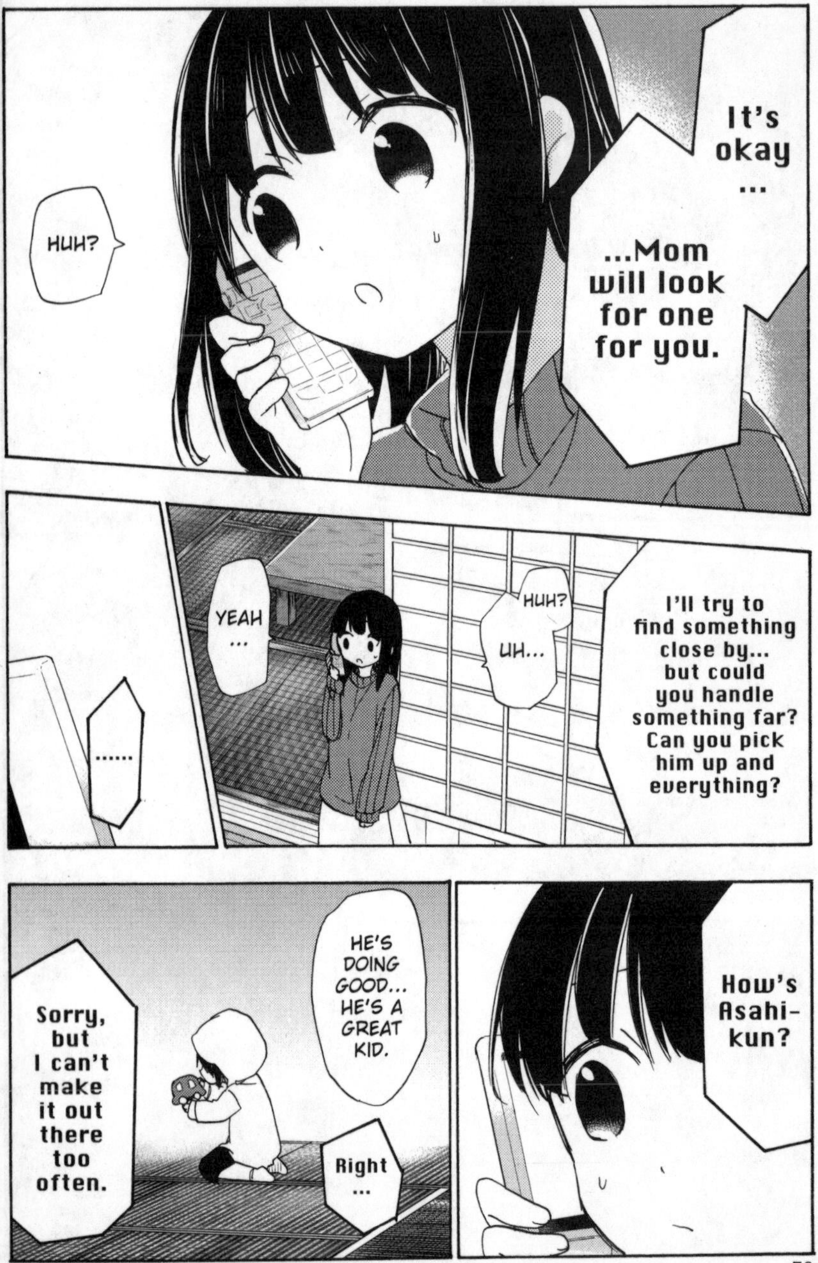
It's okay ...
...Mom will look for one for you.
HUH?
I'll try to find something close by... but could you handle something far? Can you pick him up and everything?
HUH?
UH...
YEAH ...
......
How's Asahi-kun?
HE'S DOING GOOD... HE'S A GREAT KID.
Right ...
Sorry, but I can't make it out there too often.

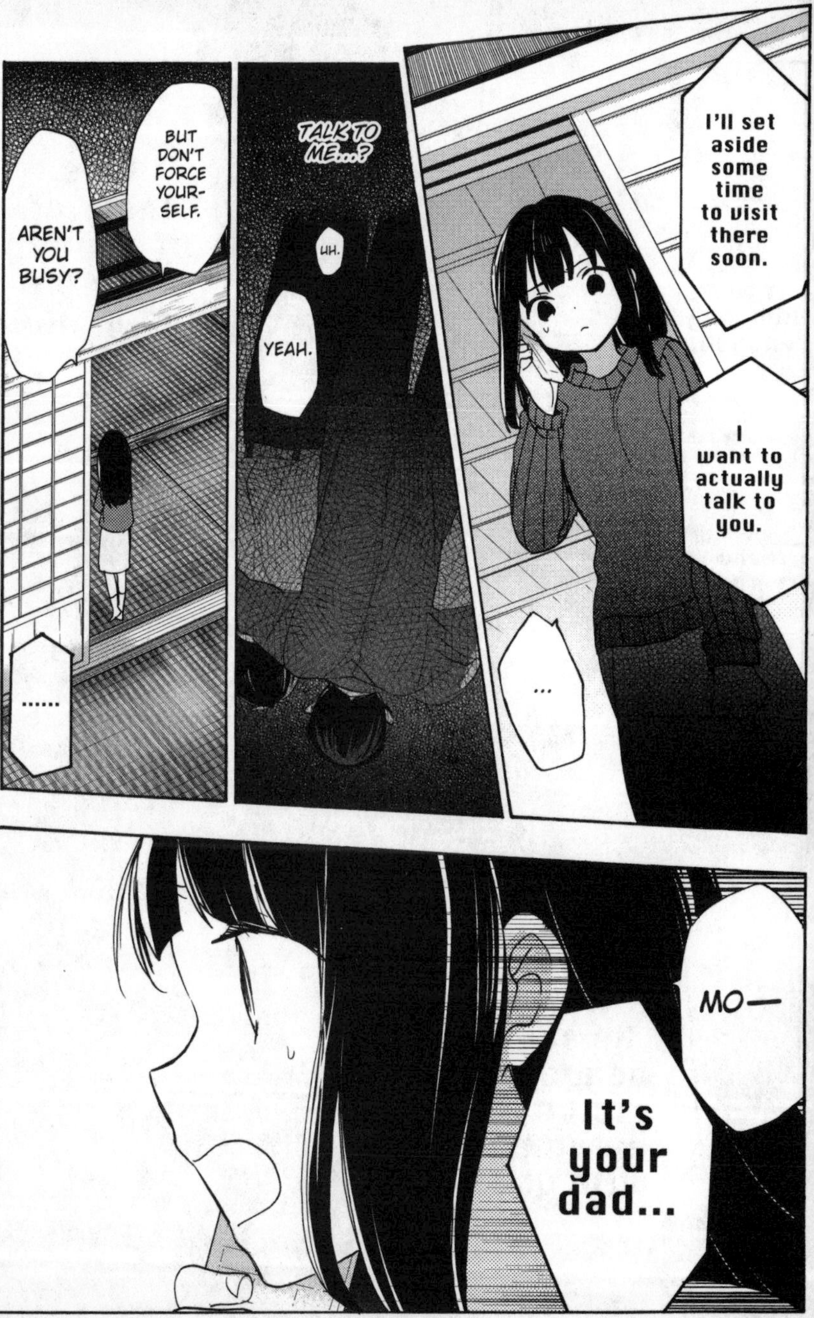
I'll set aside some time to visit there soon.
I want to actually talk to you.
...
TALK TO ME...?
UH.
YEAH.
BUT DON'T FORCE YOURSELF.
AREN'T YOU BUSY?
......
MO—
It's your dad...

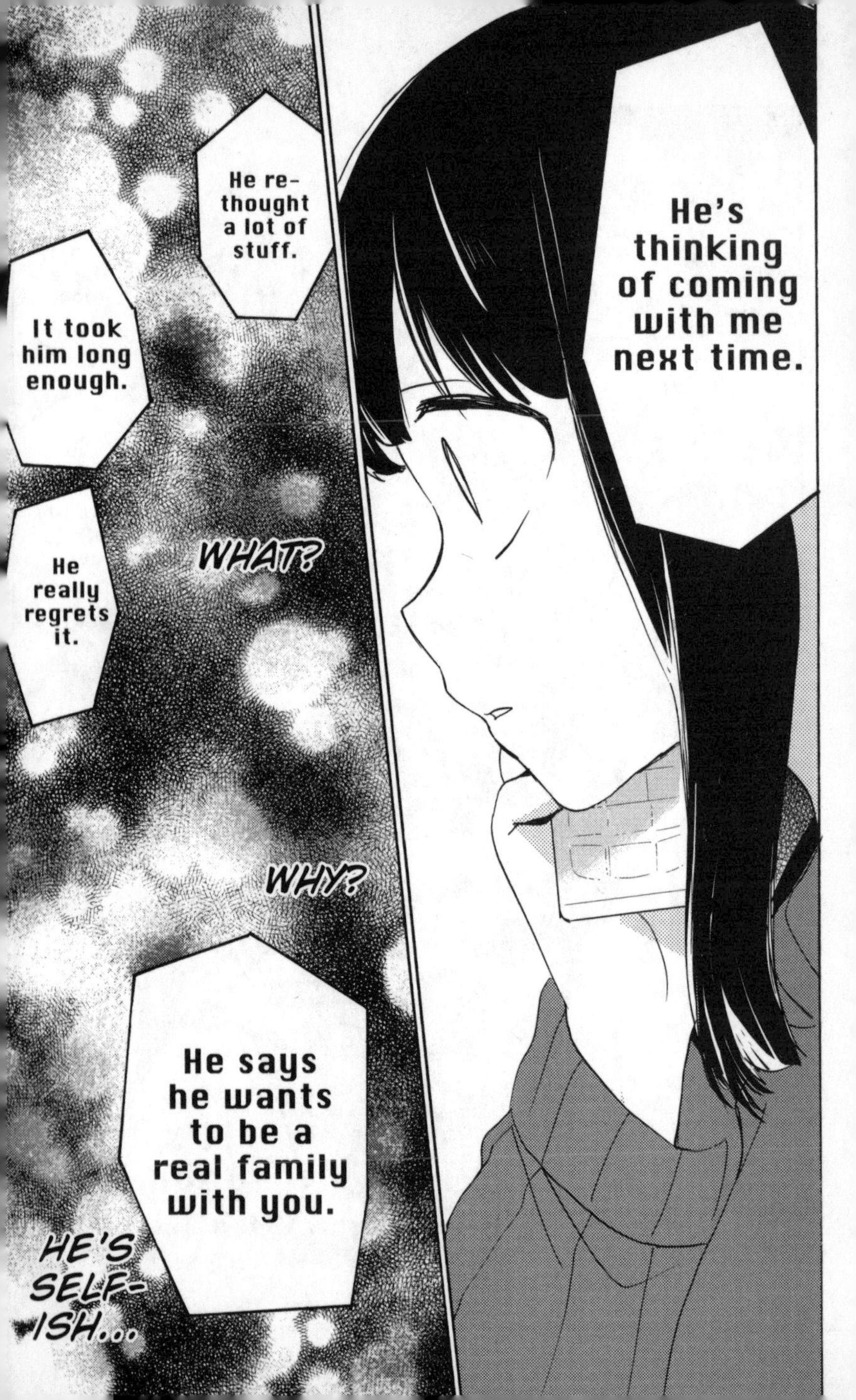
He's thinking of coming with me next time.
He re-thought a lot of stuff.
It took him long enough.
He really regrets it.
WHAT?
WHY?
He says he wants to be a real family with you.
HE'S SELF-ISH...

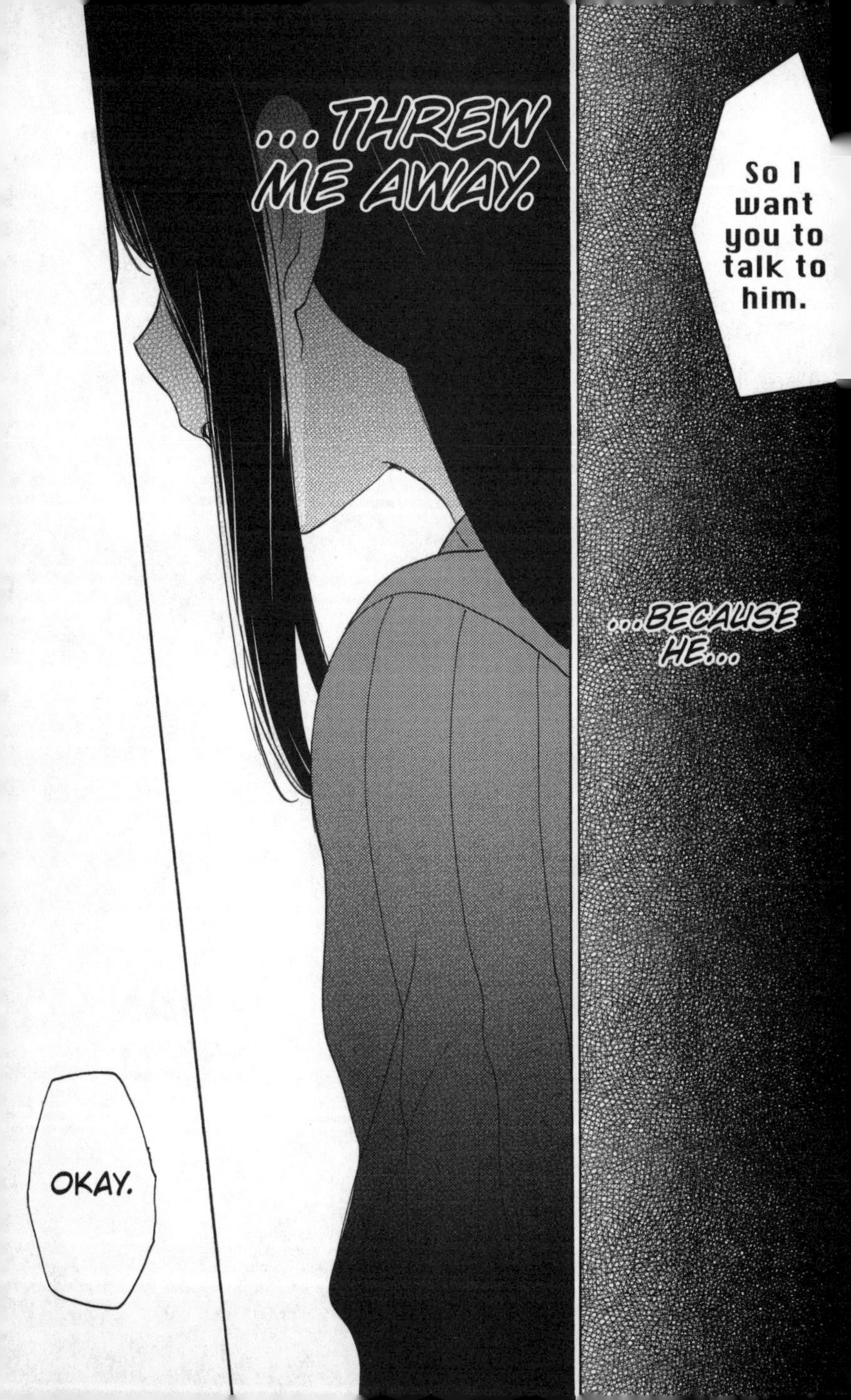
So I want you to talk to him.
...BECAUSE HE...
...THREW ME AWAY.
OKAY.

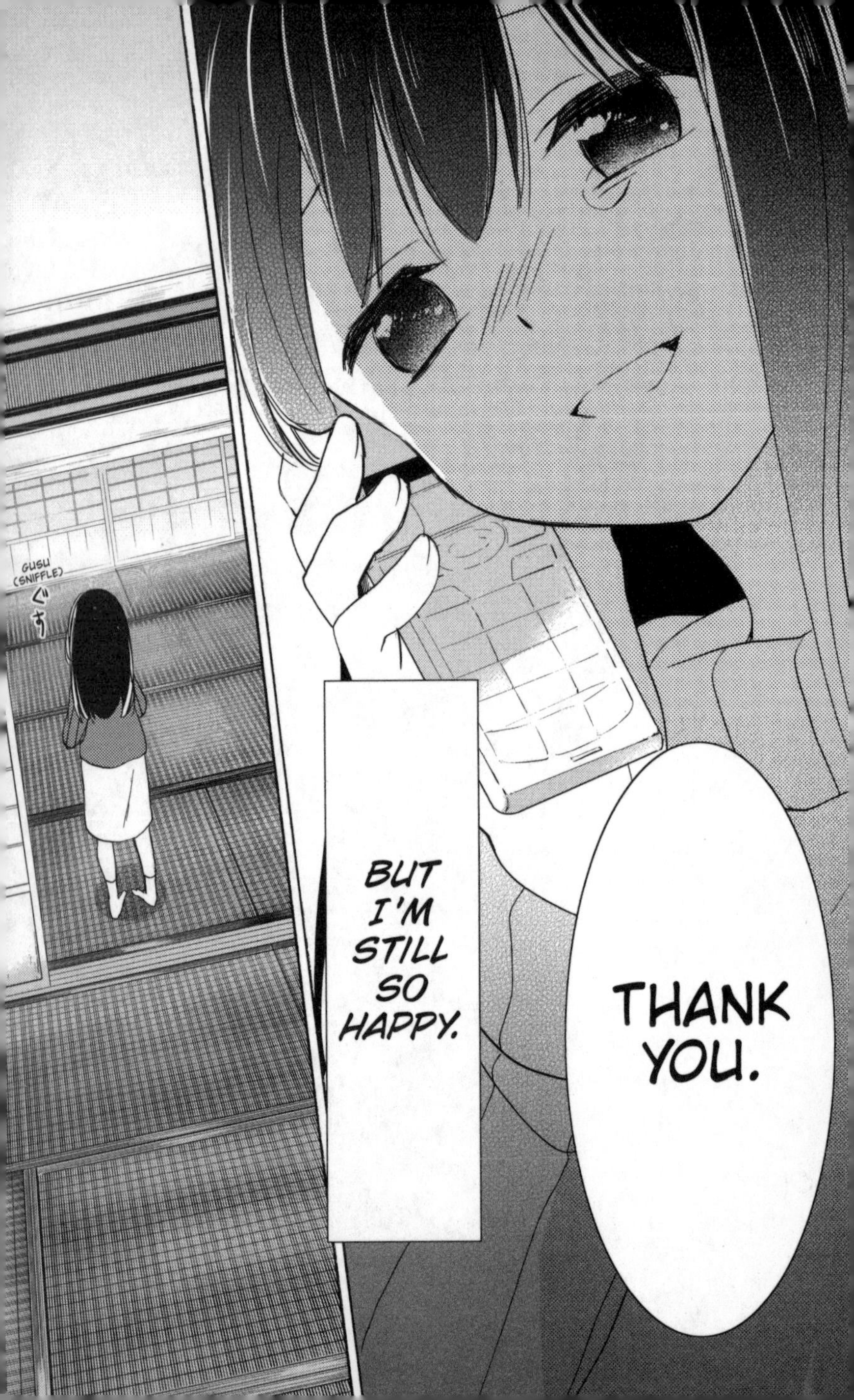
THANK YOU.
BUT I'M STILL SO HAPPY.
GUSU (SNIFFLE)
ぐす

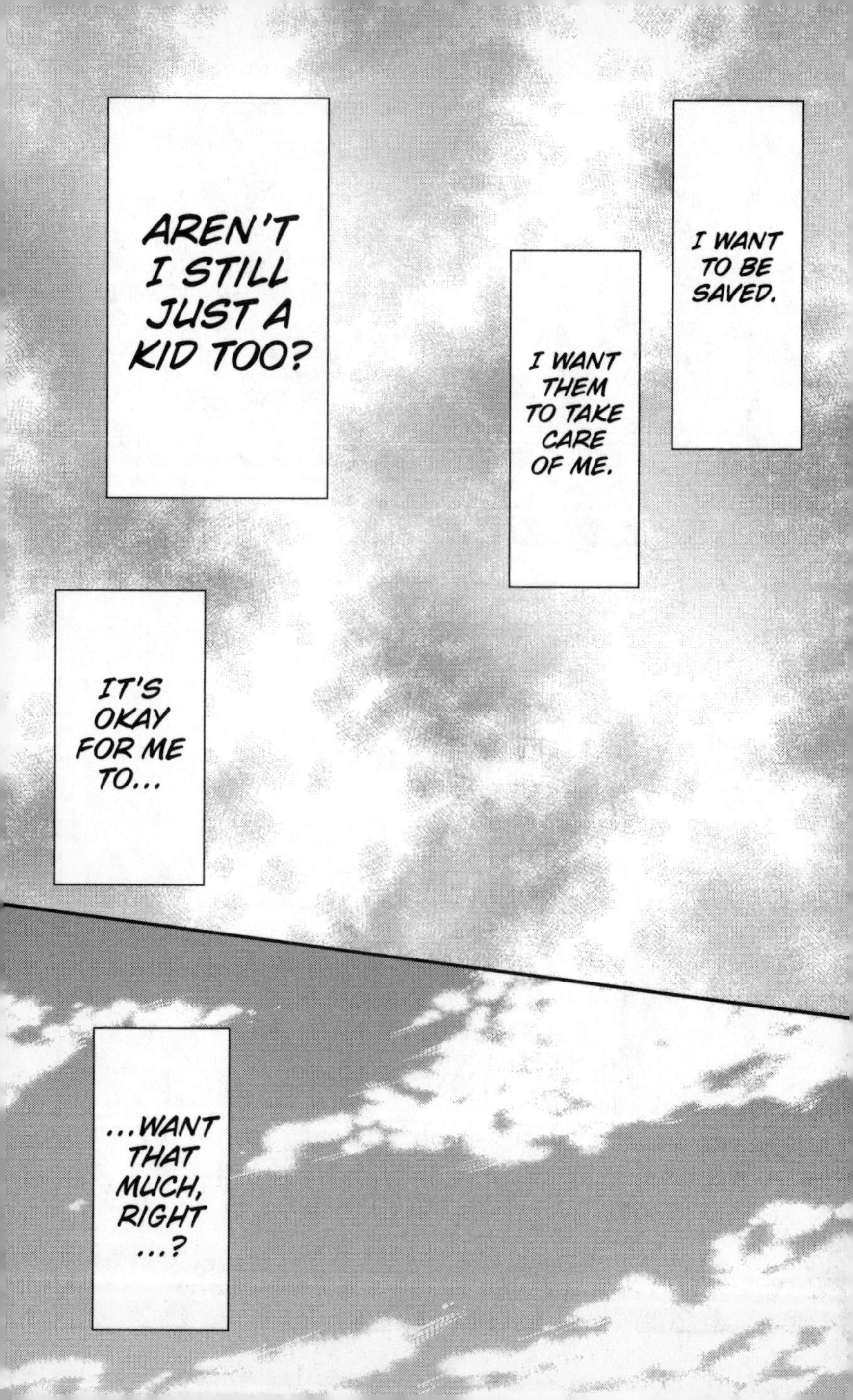
I WANT TO BE SAVED.
I WANT THEM TO TAKE CARE OF ME.
AREN'T I STILL JUST A KID TOO?
IT'S OKAY FOR ME TO...
...WANT THAT MUCH, RIGHT...?

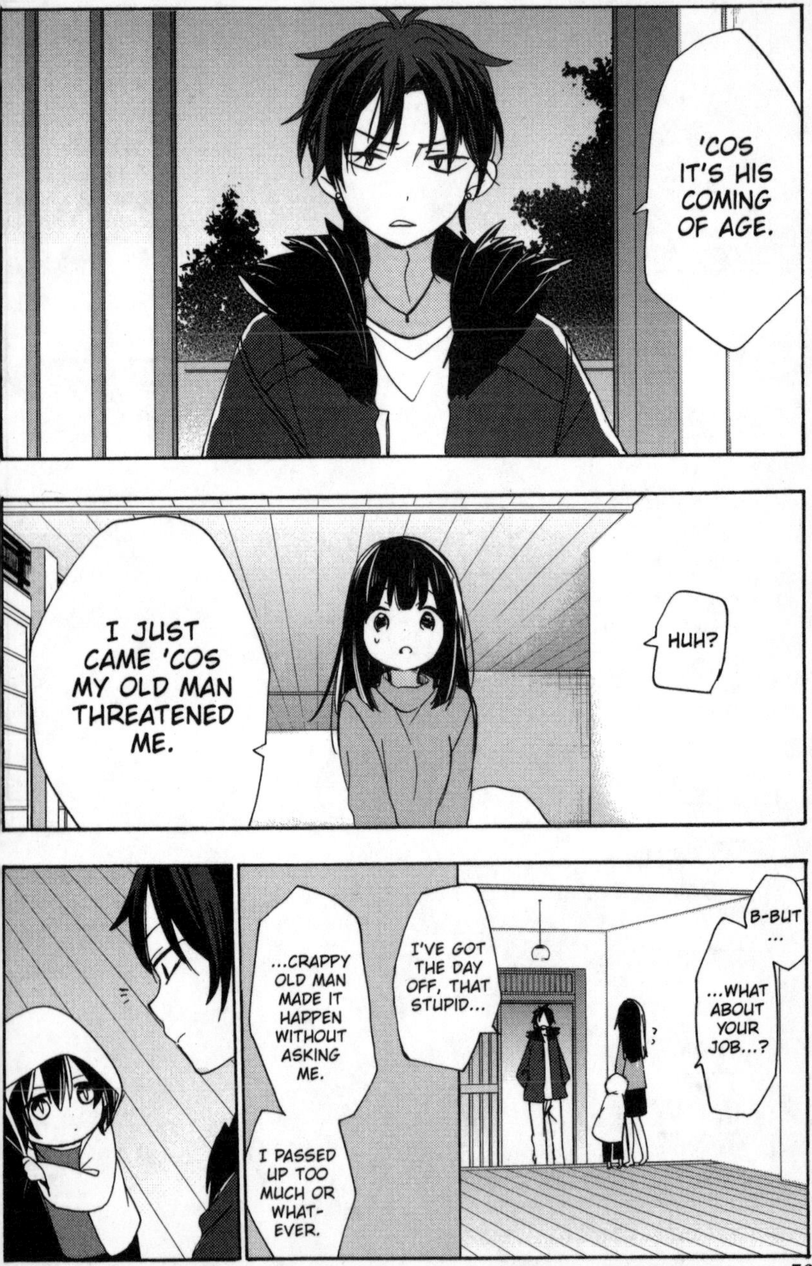
'COS IT'S HIS COMING OF AGE.
HUH?
I JUST CAME 'COS MY OLD MAN THREATENED ME.
B-BUT ...
...WHAT ABOUT YOUR JOB...?
I'VE GOT THE DAY OFF, THAT STUPID...
...CRAPPY OLD MAN MADE IT HAPPEN WITHOUT ASKING ME.
I PASSED UP TOO MUCH OR WHATEVER.

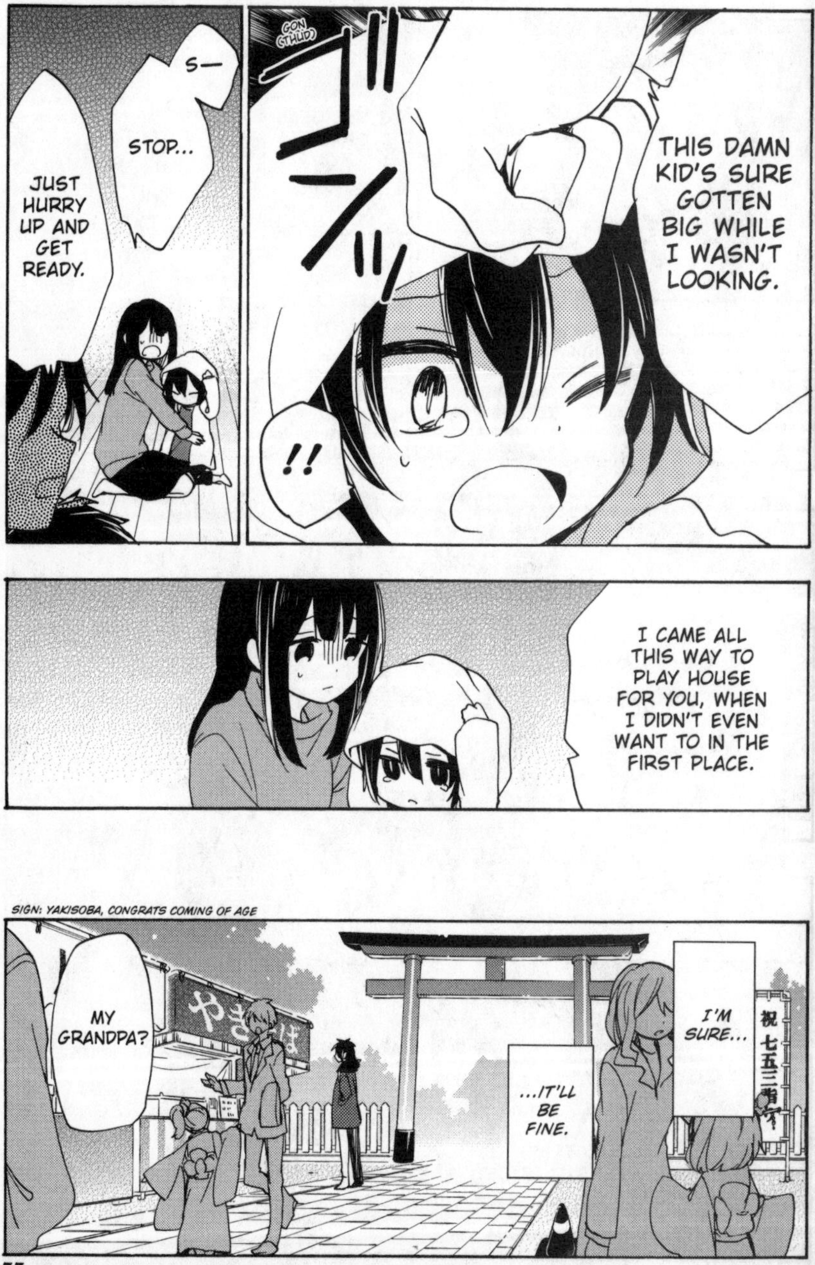
THIS DAMN KID'S SURE GOTTEN BIG WHILE I WASN'T LOOKING.
GON (THUD)
!!
S—
STOP...
JUST HURRY UP AND GET READY.
I CAME ALL THIS WAY TO PLAY HOUSE FOR YOU, WHEN I DIDN'T EVEN WANT TO IN THE FIRST PLACE.
祝 七五三
I'M SURE...
...IT'LL BE FINE.
MY GRANDPA?

SIGN: YAKISOBA, CONGRATS COMING OF AGE

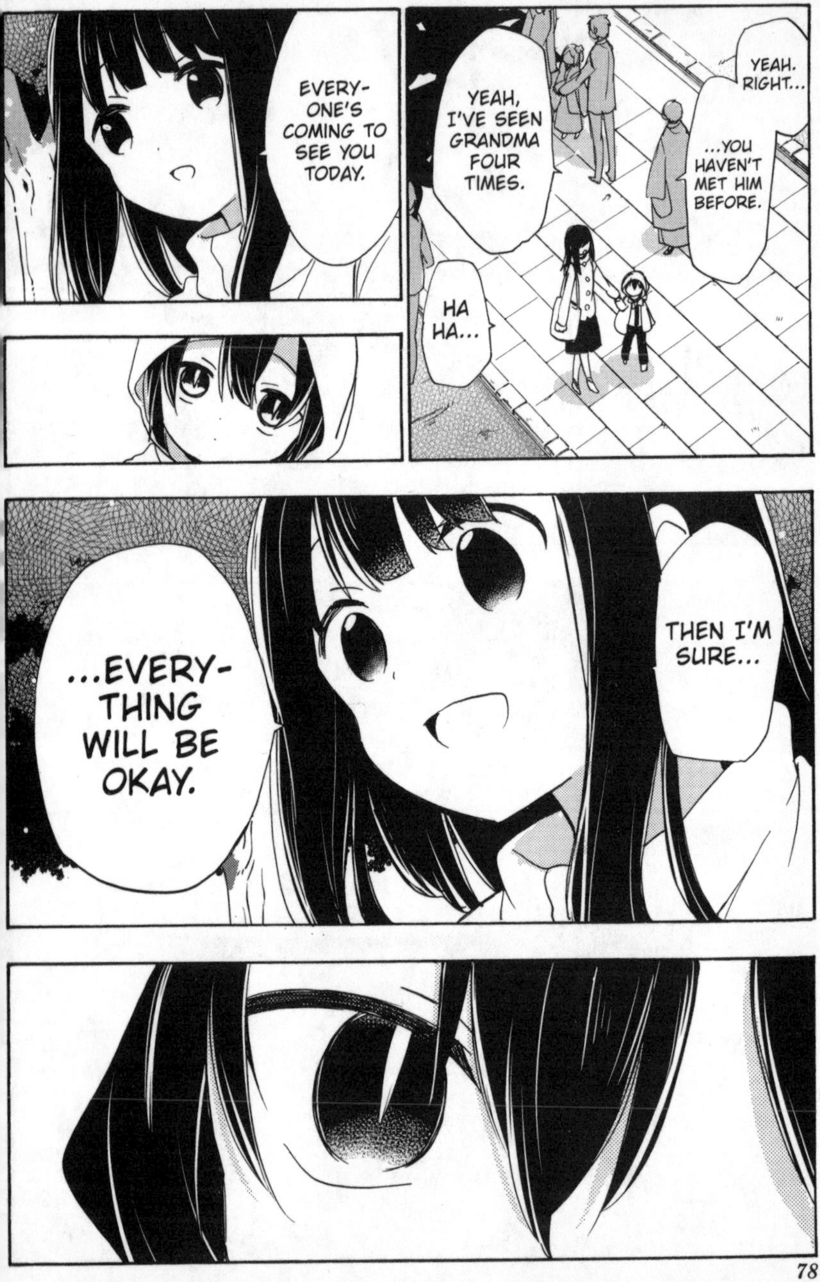
YEAH. RIGHT...
...YOU HAVEN'T MET HIM BEFORE.
YEAH, I'VE SEEN GRANDMA FOUR TIMES.
HA HA...
EVERY-ONE'S COMING TO SEE YOU TODAY.
THEN I'M SURE...
...EVERY-THING WILL BE OKAY.

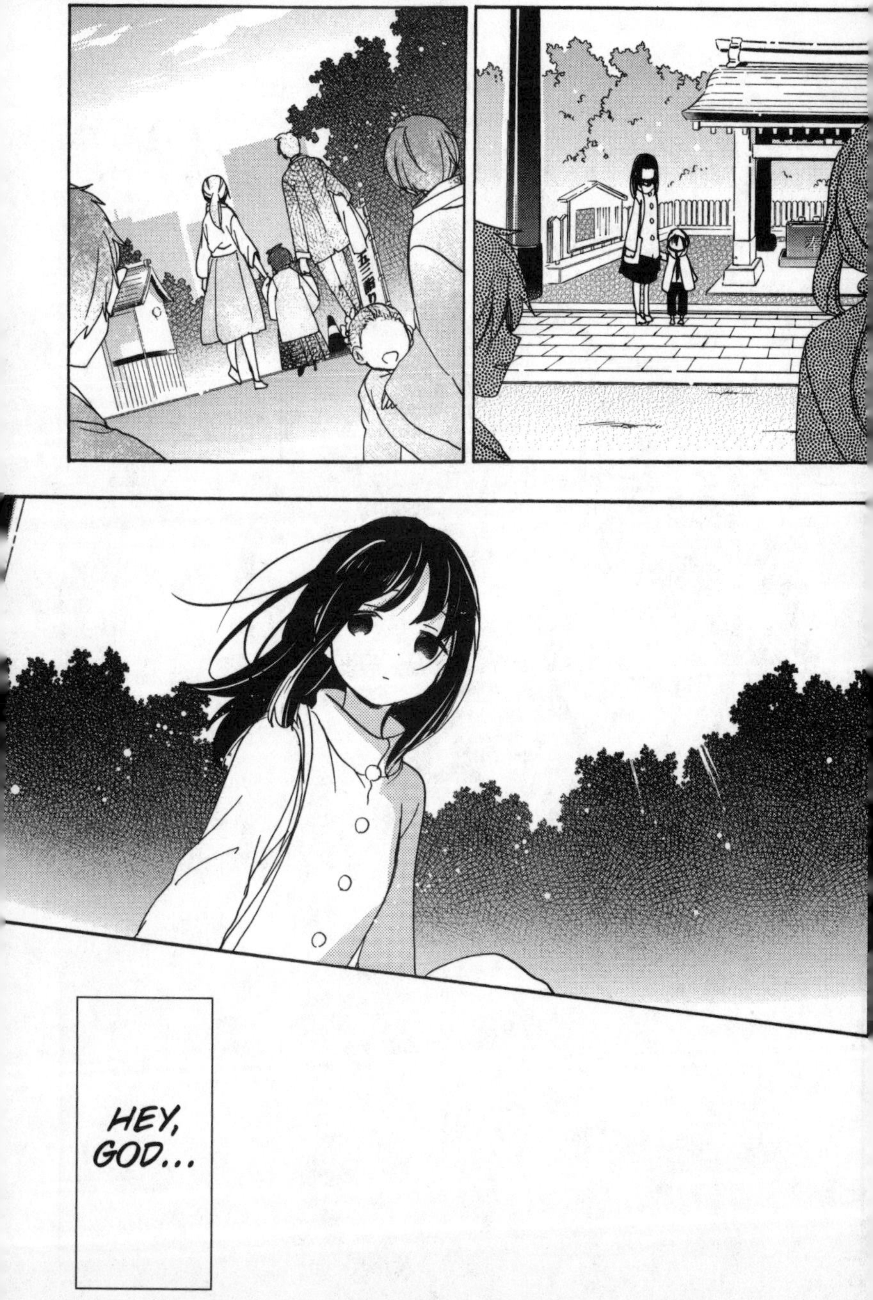
HEY, GOD...

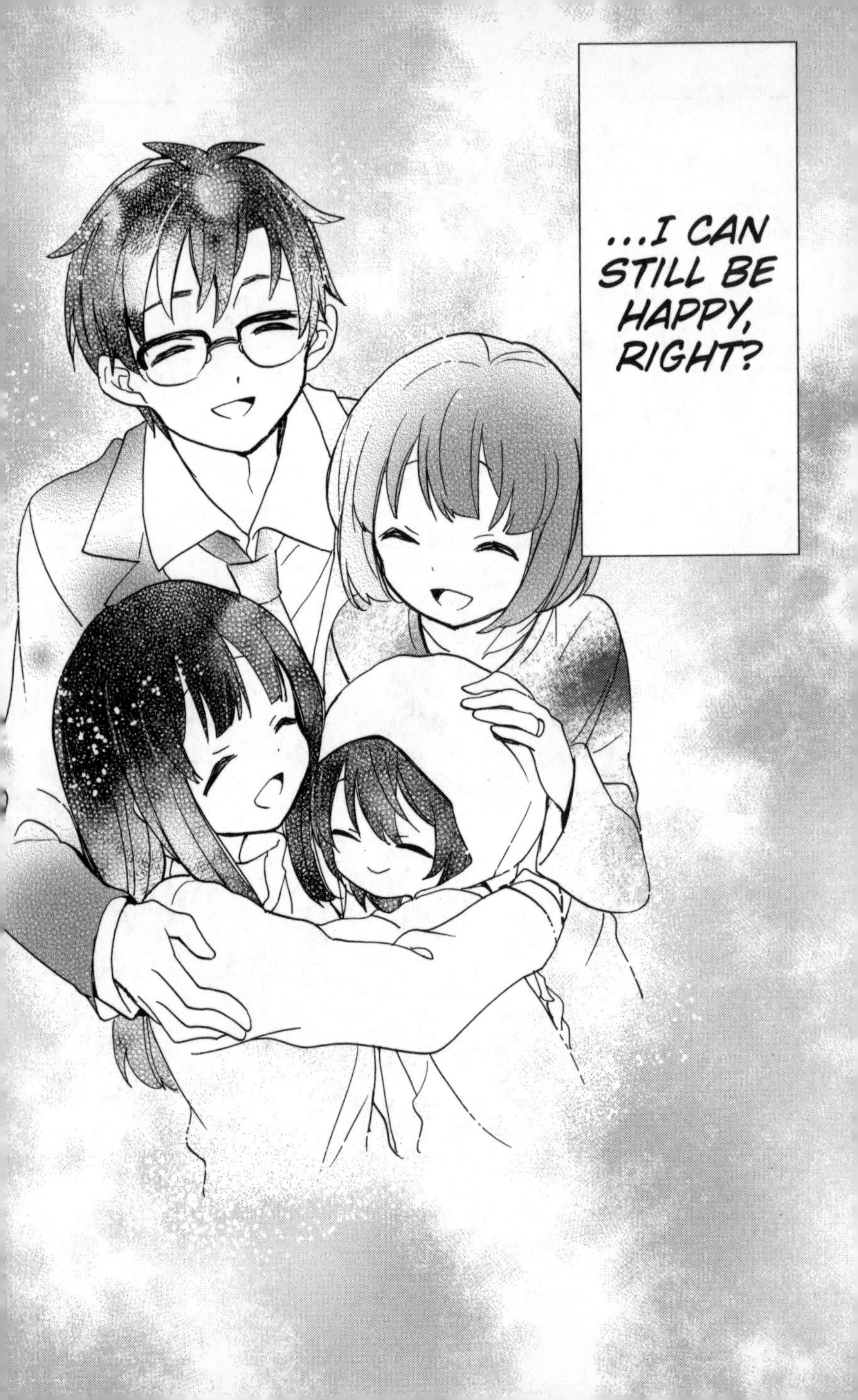
...I CAN STILL BE HAPPY, RIGHT?

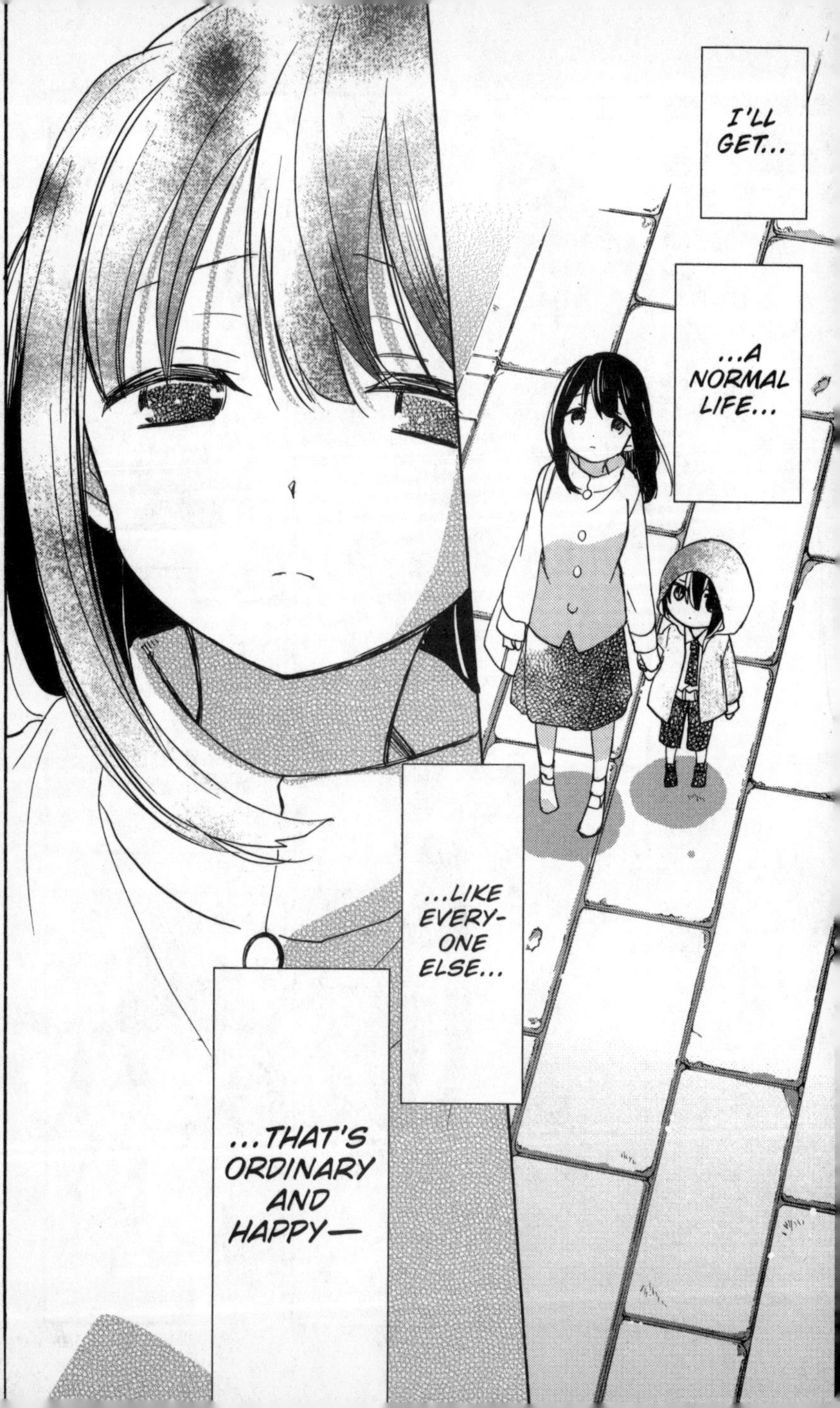
I'LL GET...
...A NORMAL LIFE...
...LIKE EVERY-ONE ELSE...
...THAT'S ORDINARY AND HAPPY—

♫
...?
I DON'T KNOW THIS NUMBER.
HELLO.
やきそば
400 エン

STREET SIGN: YAKISOBA

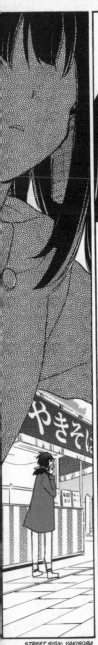

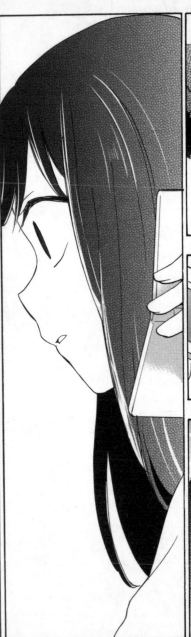

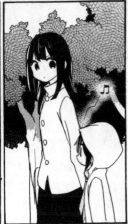

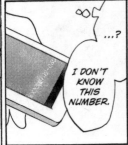

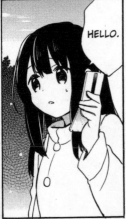

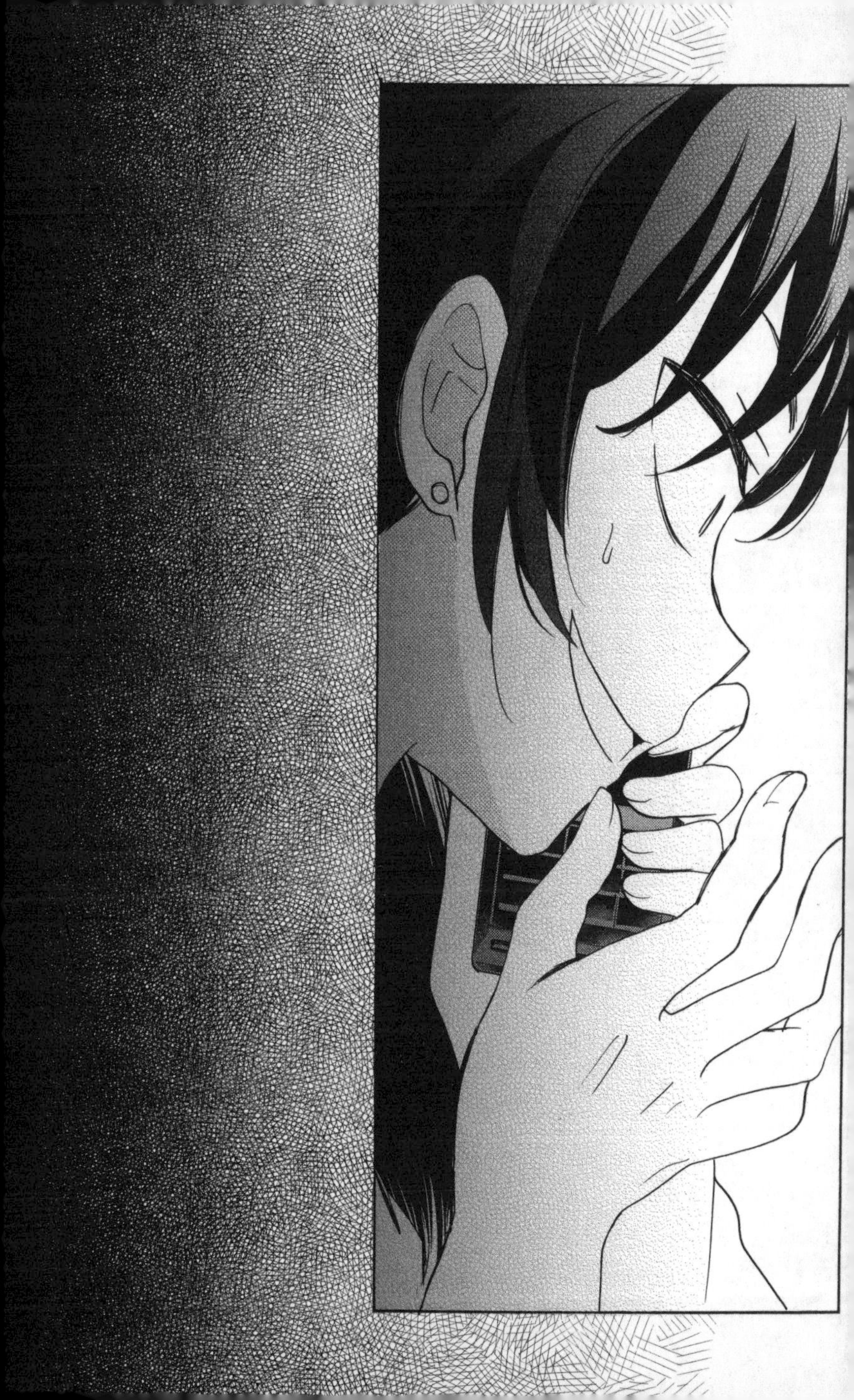

MY CONDOLENCES FOR YOUR LOSS IN THIS TIME.

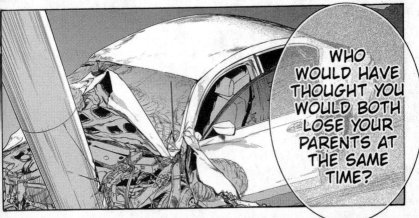

WHO WOULD HAVE THOUGHT YOU WOULD BOTH LOSE YOUR PARENTS AT THE SAME TIME?

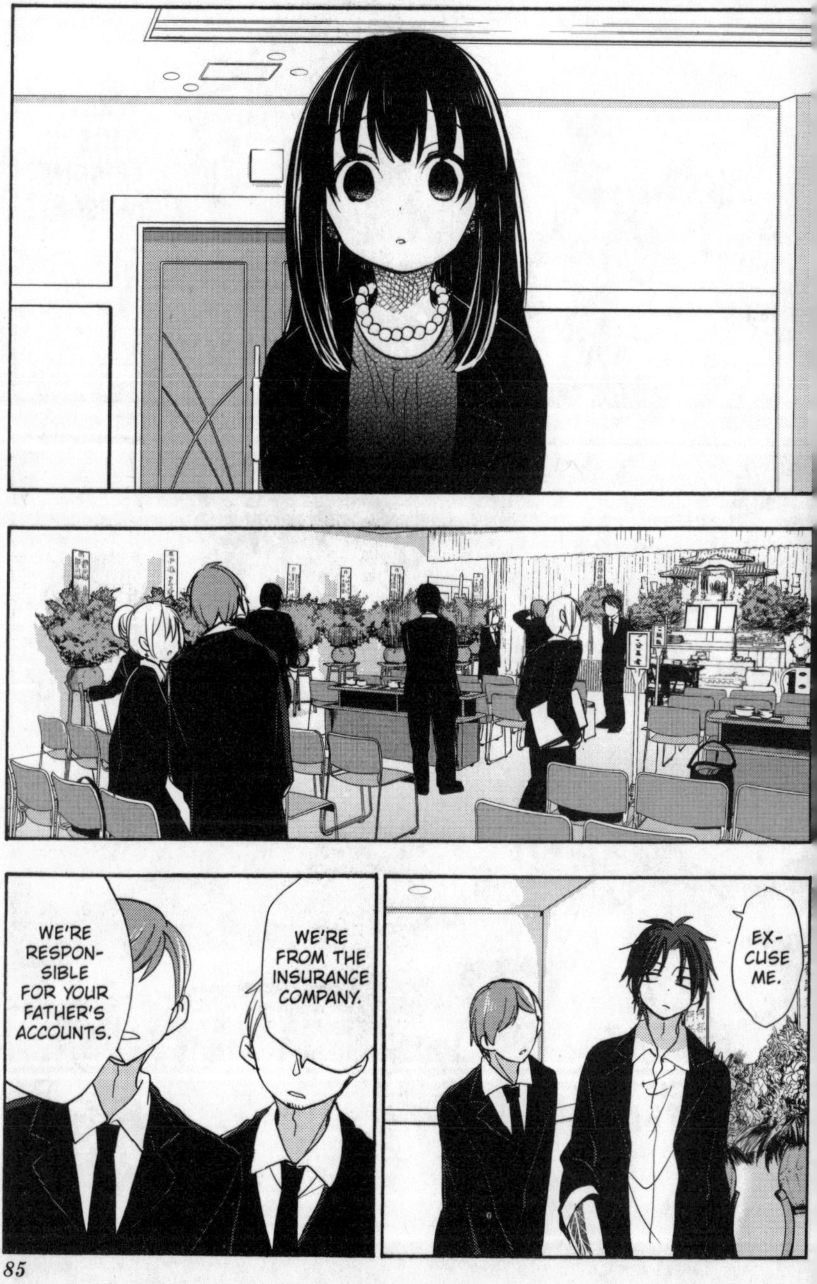
EXCUSE ME.
WE'RE FROM THE INSURANCE COMPANY.
WE'RE RESPONSIBLE FOR YOUR FATHER'S ACCOUNTS.

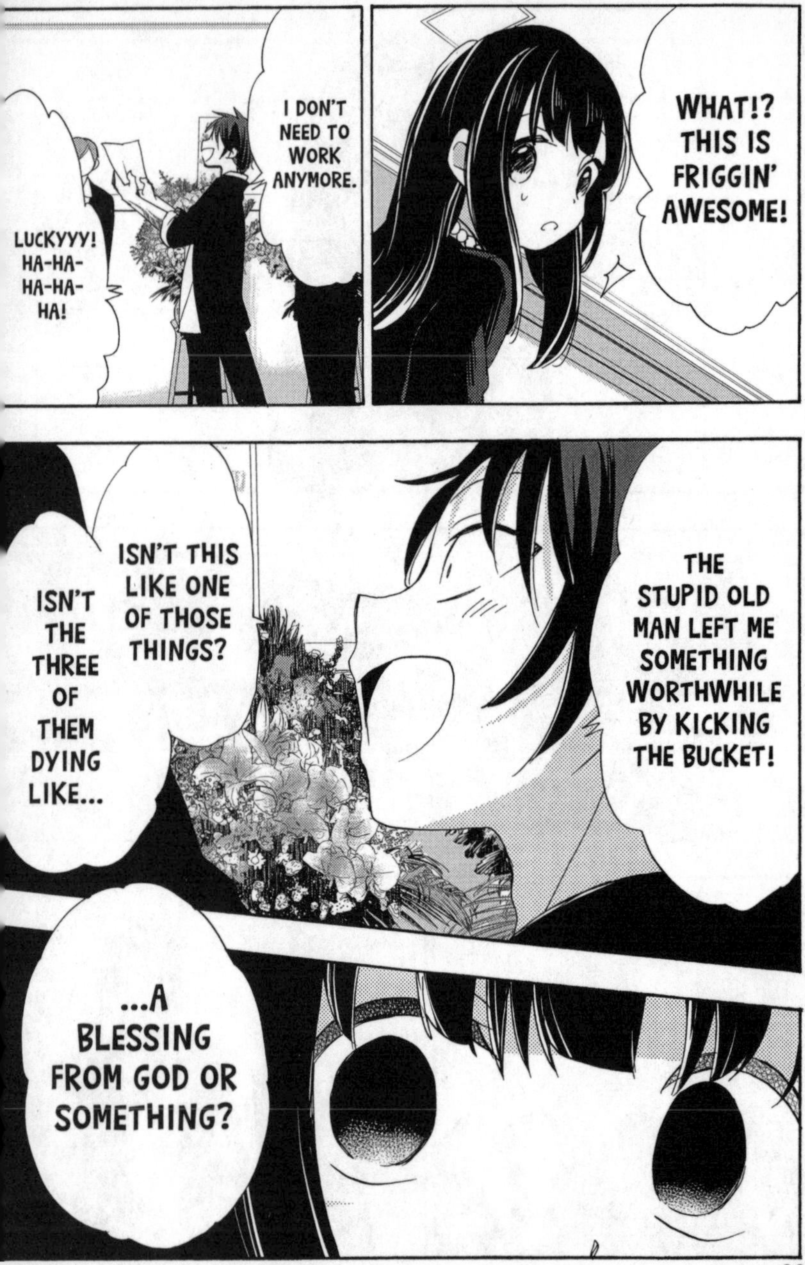
WHAT!? THIS IS FRIGGIN' AWESOME!
I DON'T NEED TO WORK ANYMORE.
LUCKYYY! HA-HA-HA-HA-HA!
THE STUPID OLD MAN LEFT ME SOMETHING WORTHWHILE BY KICKING THE BUCKET!
ISN'T THIS LIKE ONE OF THOSE THINGS?
ISN'T THE THREE OF THEM DYING LIKE...
...A BLESSING FROM GOD OR SOMETHING?

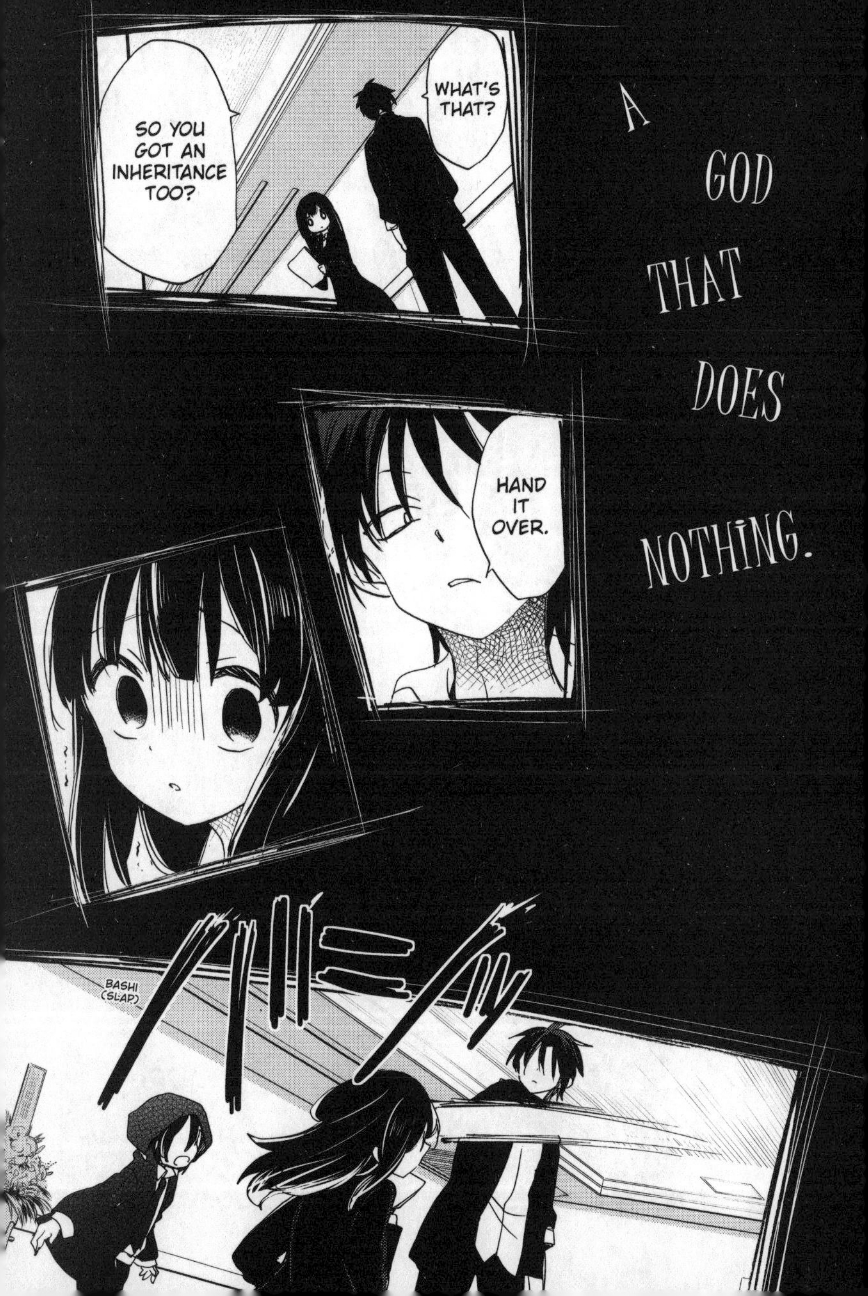
A GOD THAT DOES NOTHING.
WHAT'S THAT?
SO YOU GOT AN INHERITANCE TOO?
HAND IT OVER.
BASHI (SLAP)

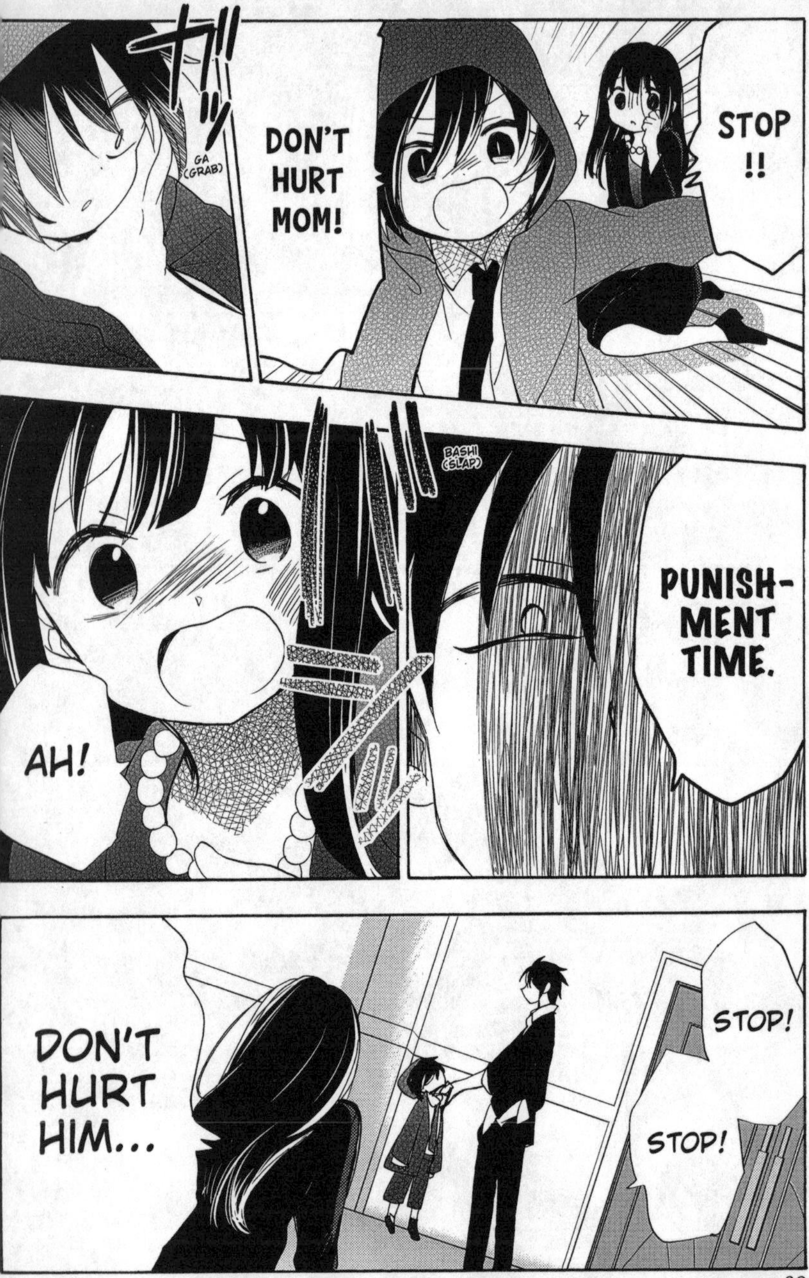
STOP !!
DON'T HURT MOM!
GA (GRAB)
BASHI (SLAP)
PUNISH-MENT TIME.
AH!
STOP!
STOP!
DON'T HURT HIM...

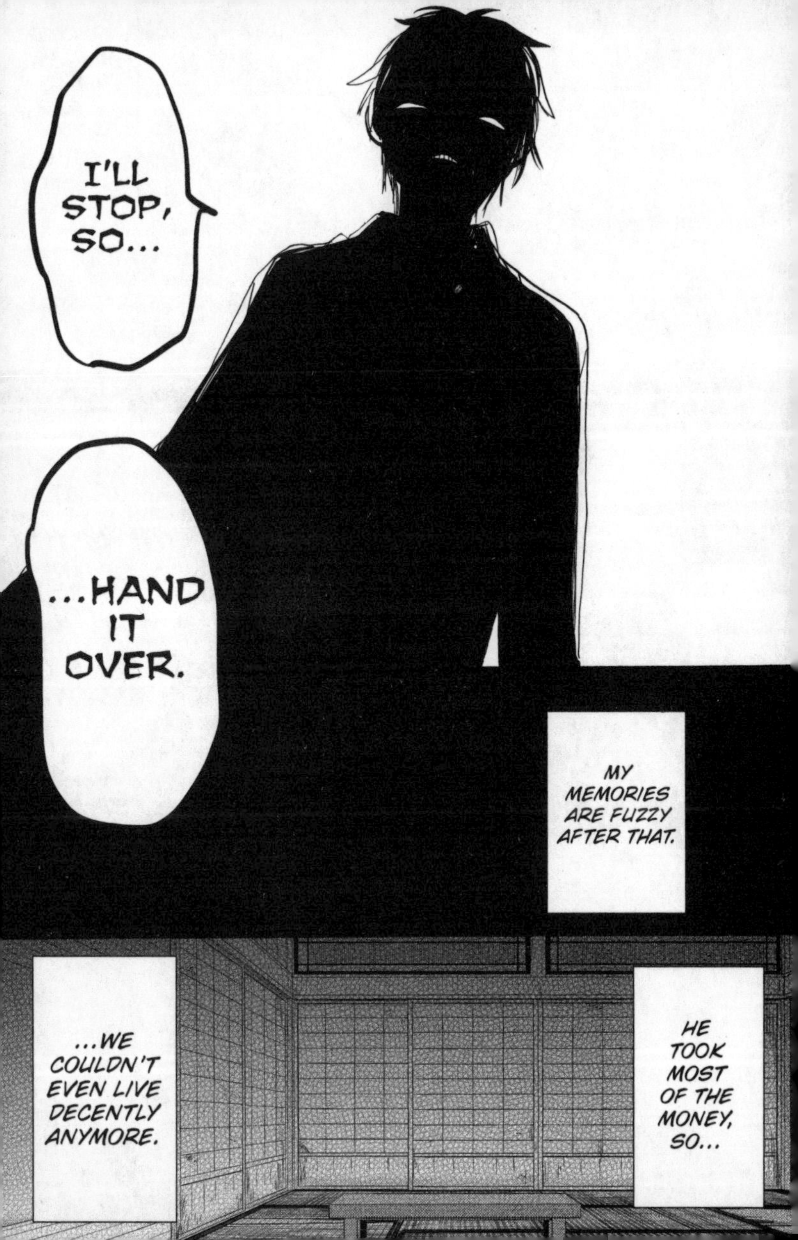
I'LL STOP, SO...
...HAND IT OVER.
MY MEMORIES ARE FUZZY AFTER THAT.
HE TOOK MOST OF THE MONEY, SO...
...WE COULDN'T EVEN LIVE DECENTLY ANYMORE.

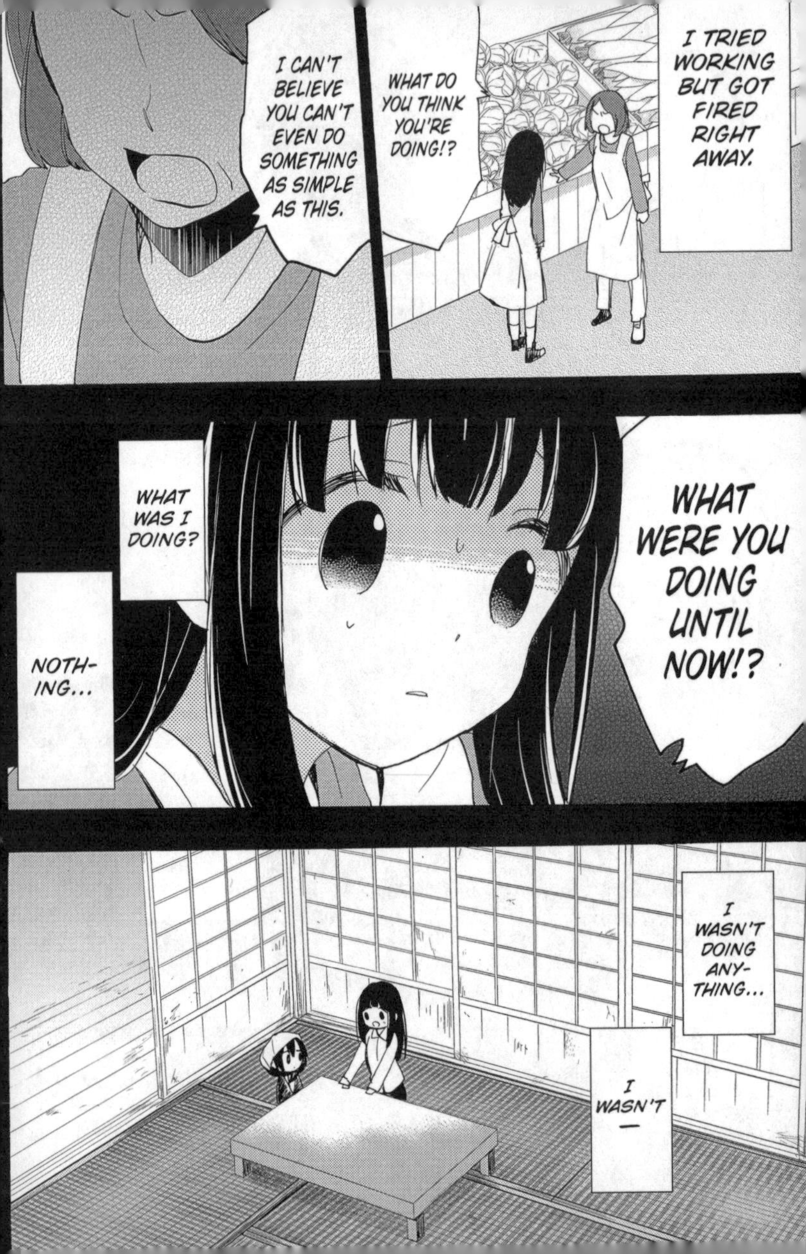
I TRIED WORKING BUT GOT FIRED RIGHT AWAY.
WHAT DO YOU THINK YOU'RE DOING!?
I CAN'T BELIEVE YOU CAN'T EVEN DO SOMETHING AS SIMPLE AS THIS.
WHAT WERE YOU DOING UNTIL NOW!?
WHAT WAS I DOING?
NOTH-ING...
I WASN'T DOING ANY-THING...
I WASN'T —

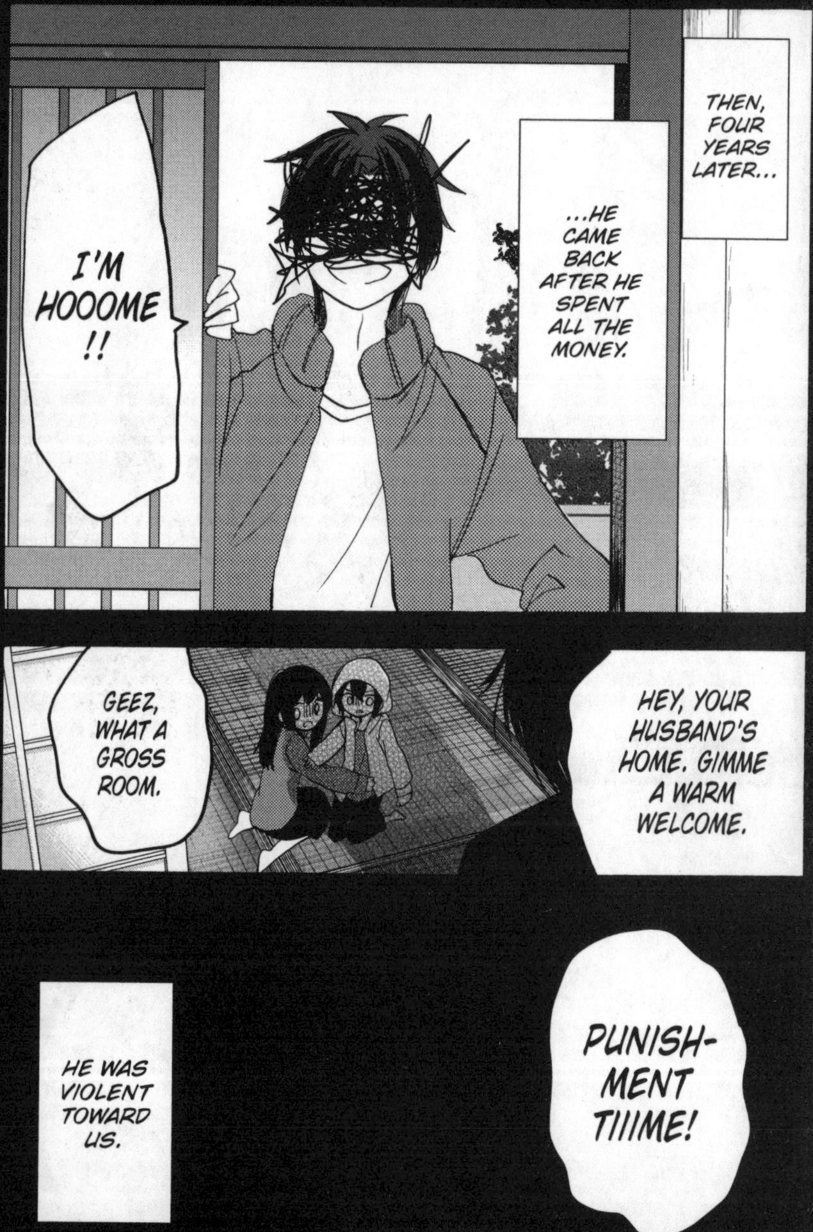
THEN, FOUR YEARS LATER...
...HE CAME BACK AFTER HE SPENT ALL THE MONEY.
I'M HOOOME!!
HEY, YOUR HUSBAND'S HOME. GIMME A WARM WELCOME.
GEEZ, WHAT A GROSS ROOM.
PUNISH-MENT TIIIME!
HE WAS VIOLENT TOWARD US.

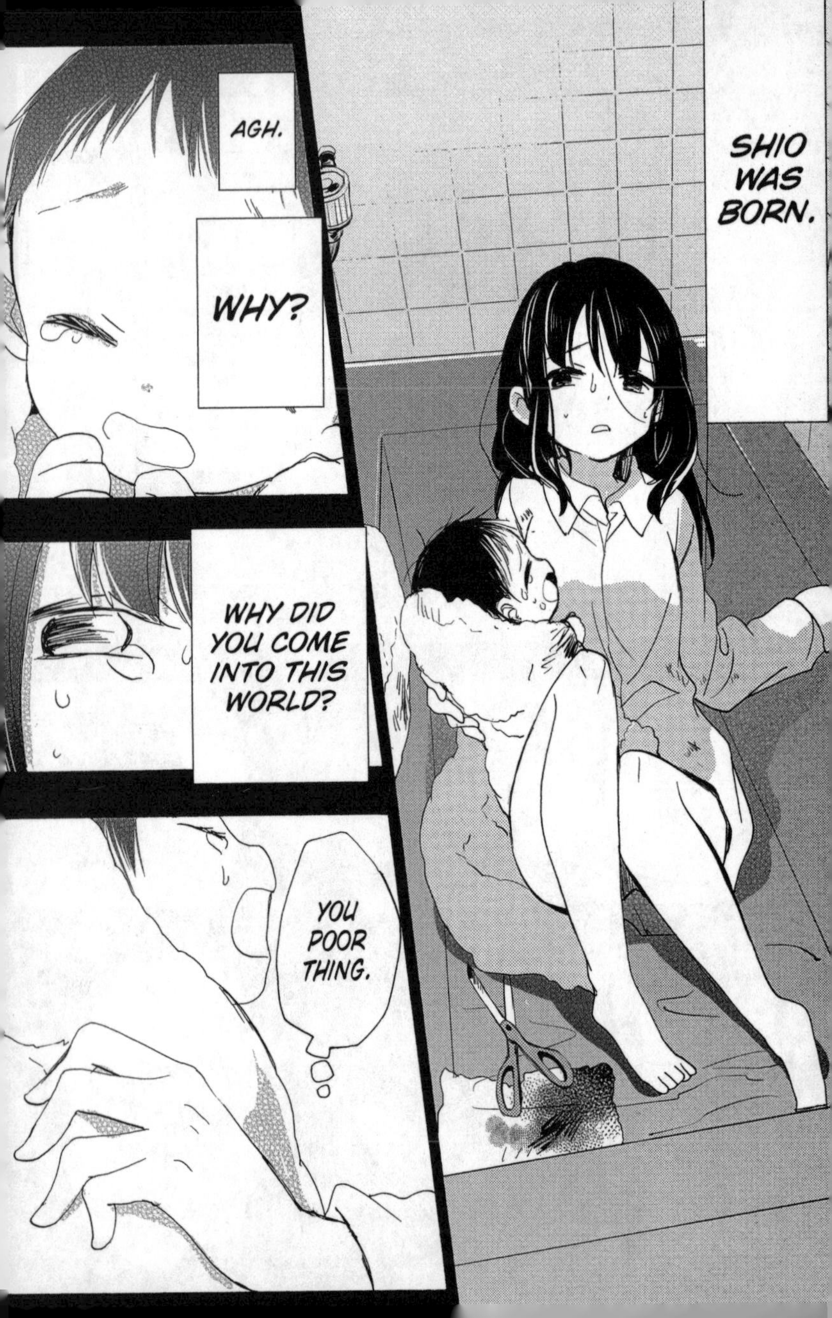
SHIO WAS BORN.
AGH.
WHY?
WHY DID YOU COME INTO THIS WORLD?
YOU POOR THING.

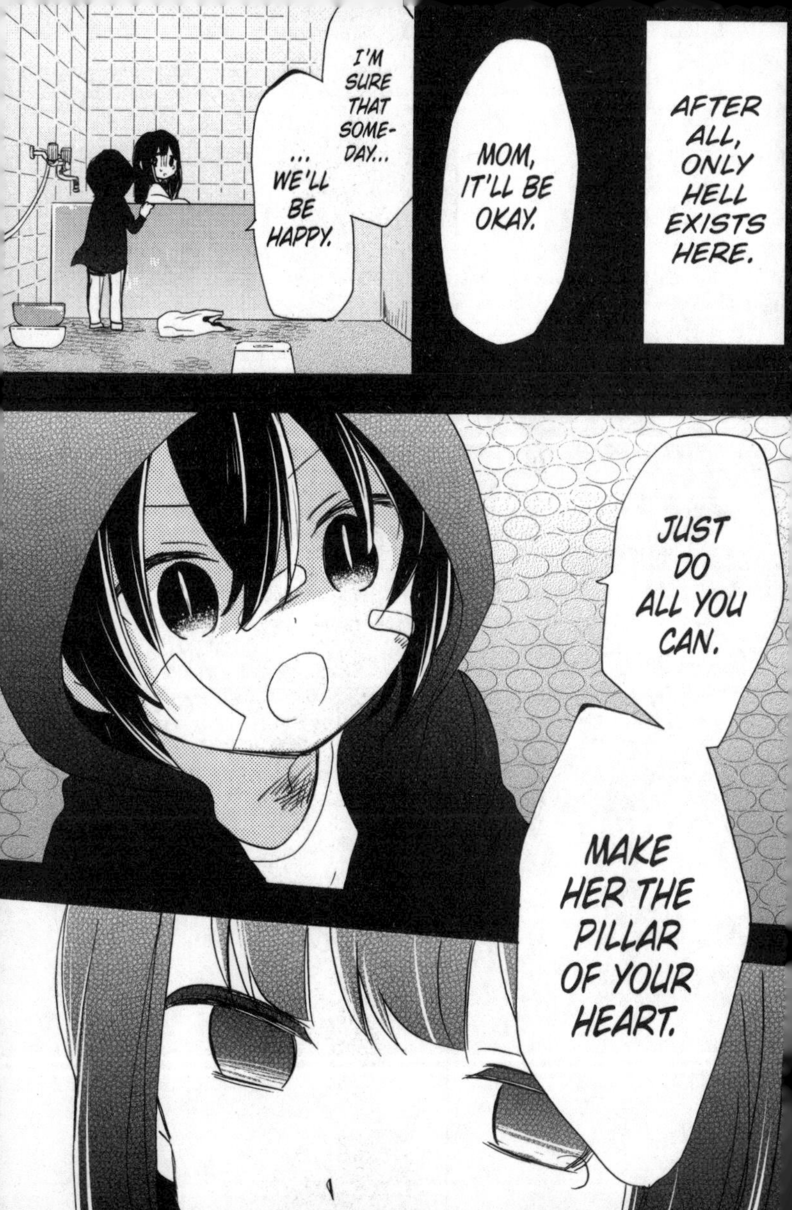
AFTER ALL, ONLY HELL EXISTS HERE.
MOM, IT'LL BE OKAY.
I'M SURE THAT SOME-DAY...
...WE'LL BE HAPPY.
JUST DO ALL YOU CAN.
MAKE HER THE PILLAR OF YOUR HEART.

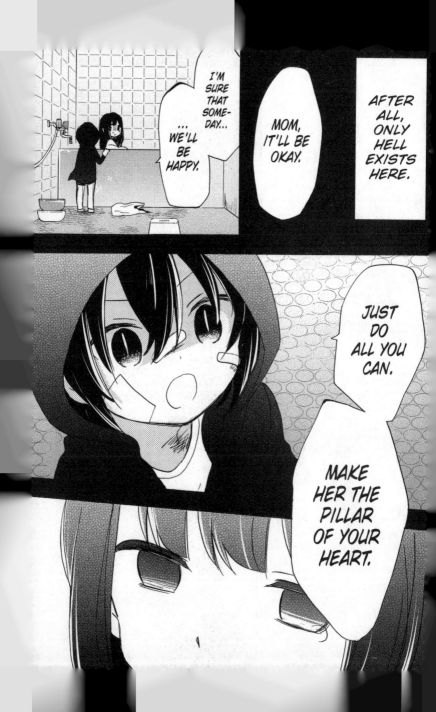

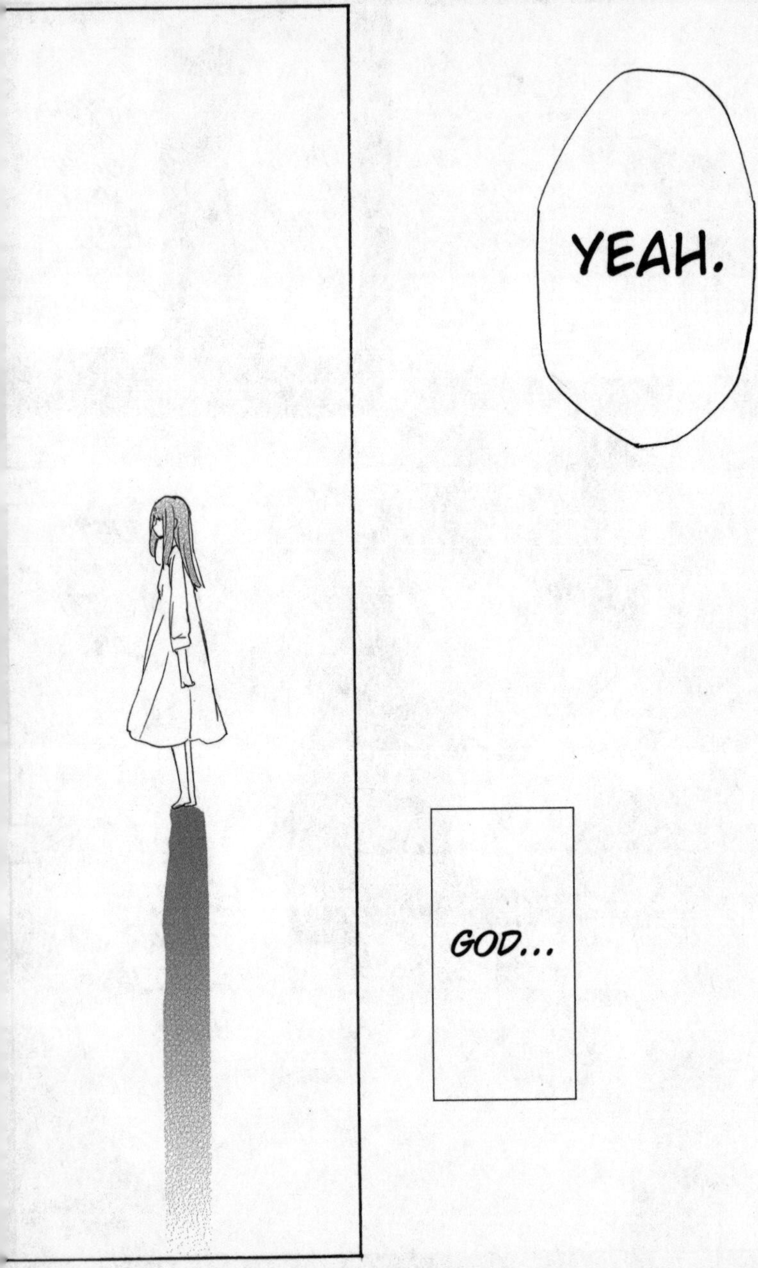
YEAH.
GOD...

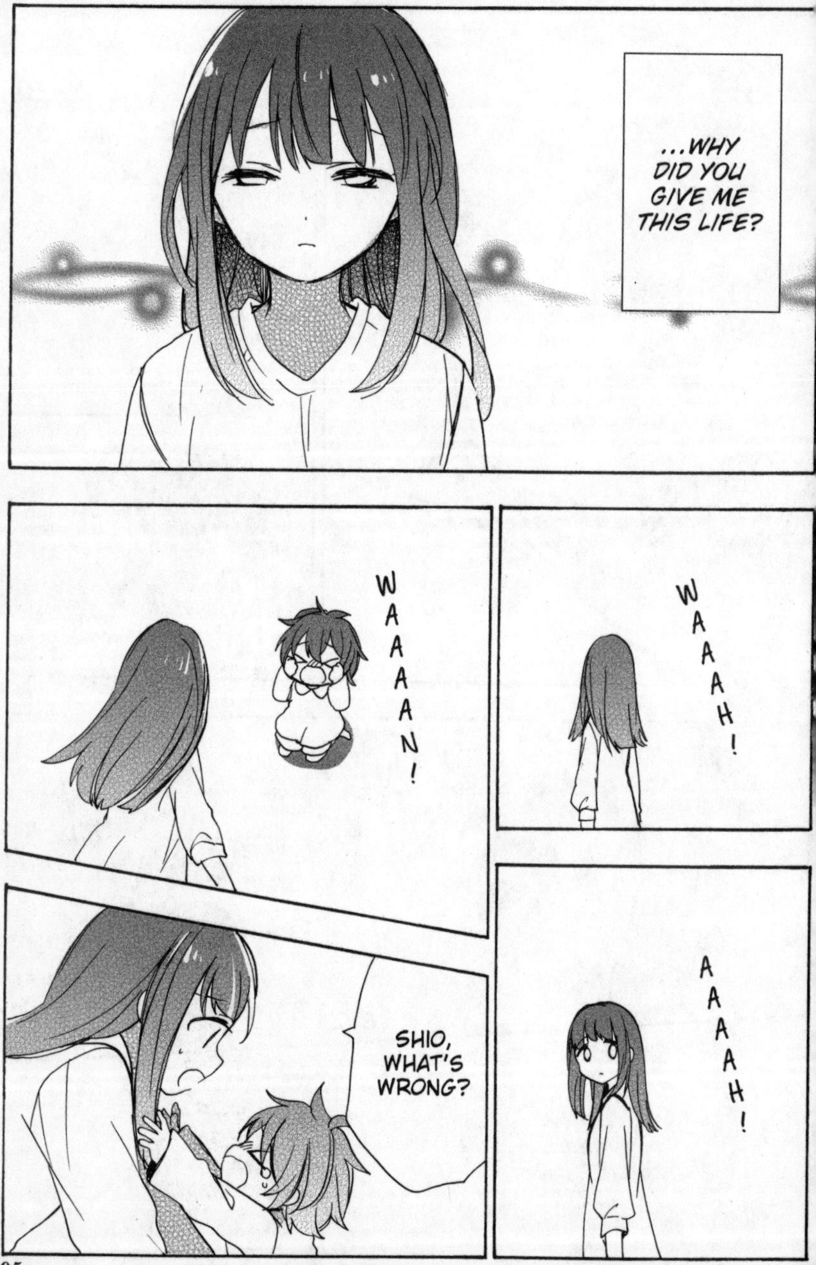
...WHY DID YOU GIVE ME THIS LIFE?
WAAAAH!
WAAAAN!
AAAAH!
SHIO, WHAT'S WRONG?

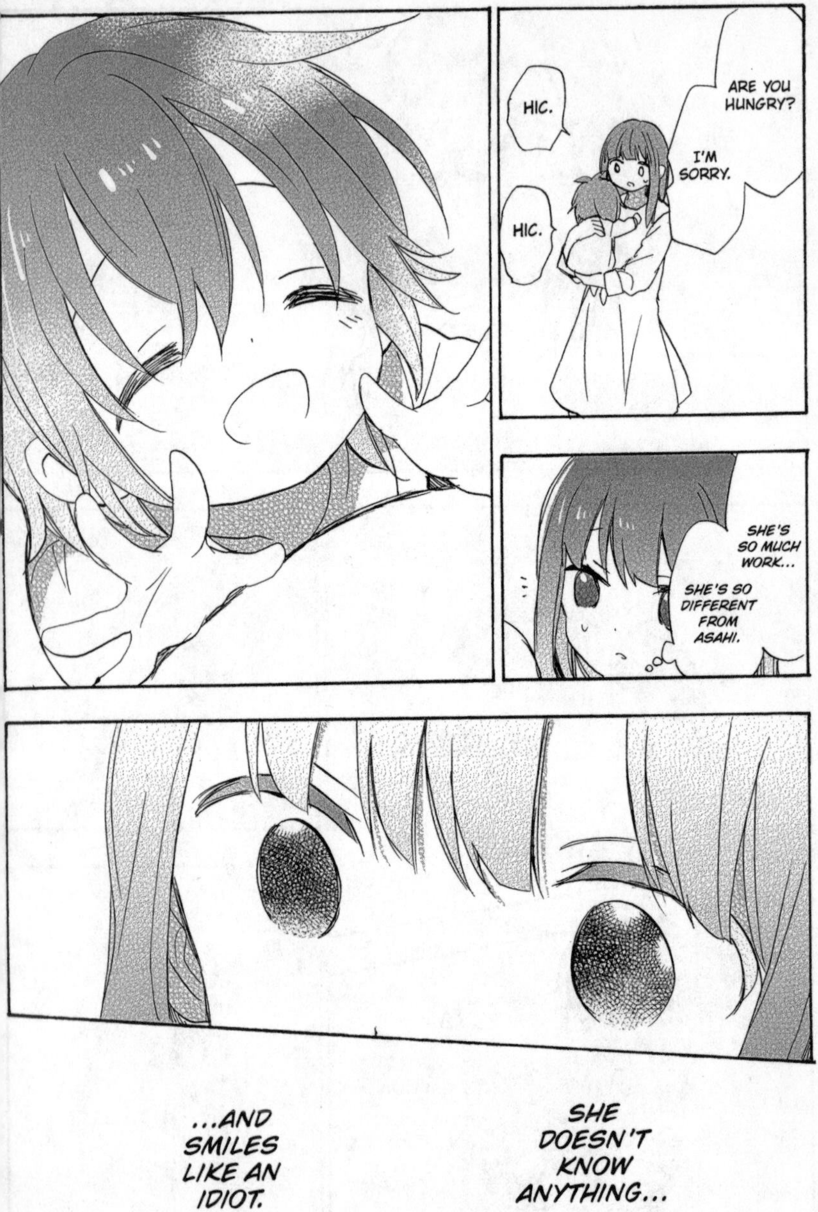
ARE YOU HUNGRY?
I'M SORRY.
HIC.
HIC.
SHE'S SO MUCH WORK...
SHE'S SO DIFFERENT FROM ASAHI.
SHE DOESN'T KNOW ANYTHING...
...AND SMILES LIKE AN IDIOT.

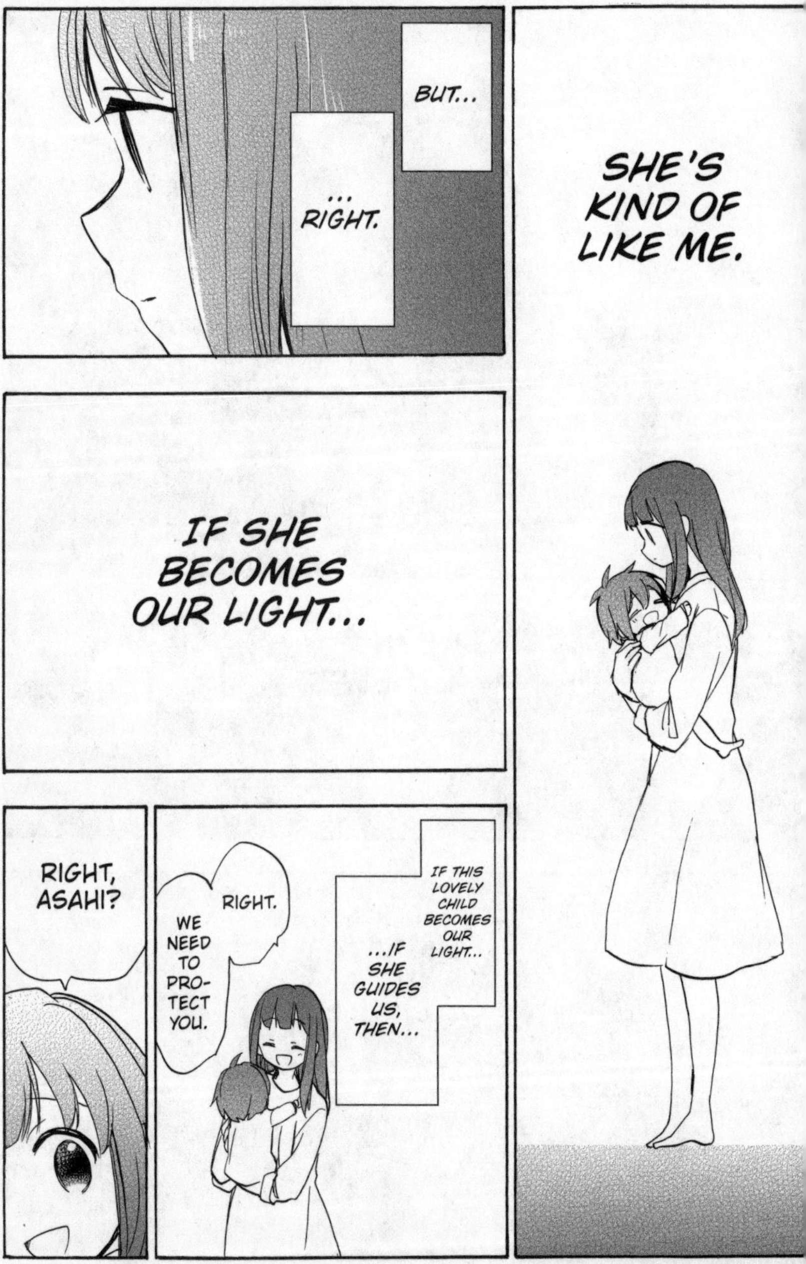
SHE'S KIND OF LIKE ME.
BUT...
...RIGHT.
IF SHE BECOMES OUR LIGHT...
IF THIS LOVELY CHILD BECOMES OUR LIGHT...
...IF SHE GUIDES US, THEN...
RIGHT.
WE NEED TO PROTECT YOU.
RIGHT, ASAHI?

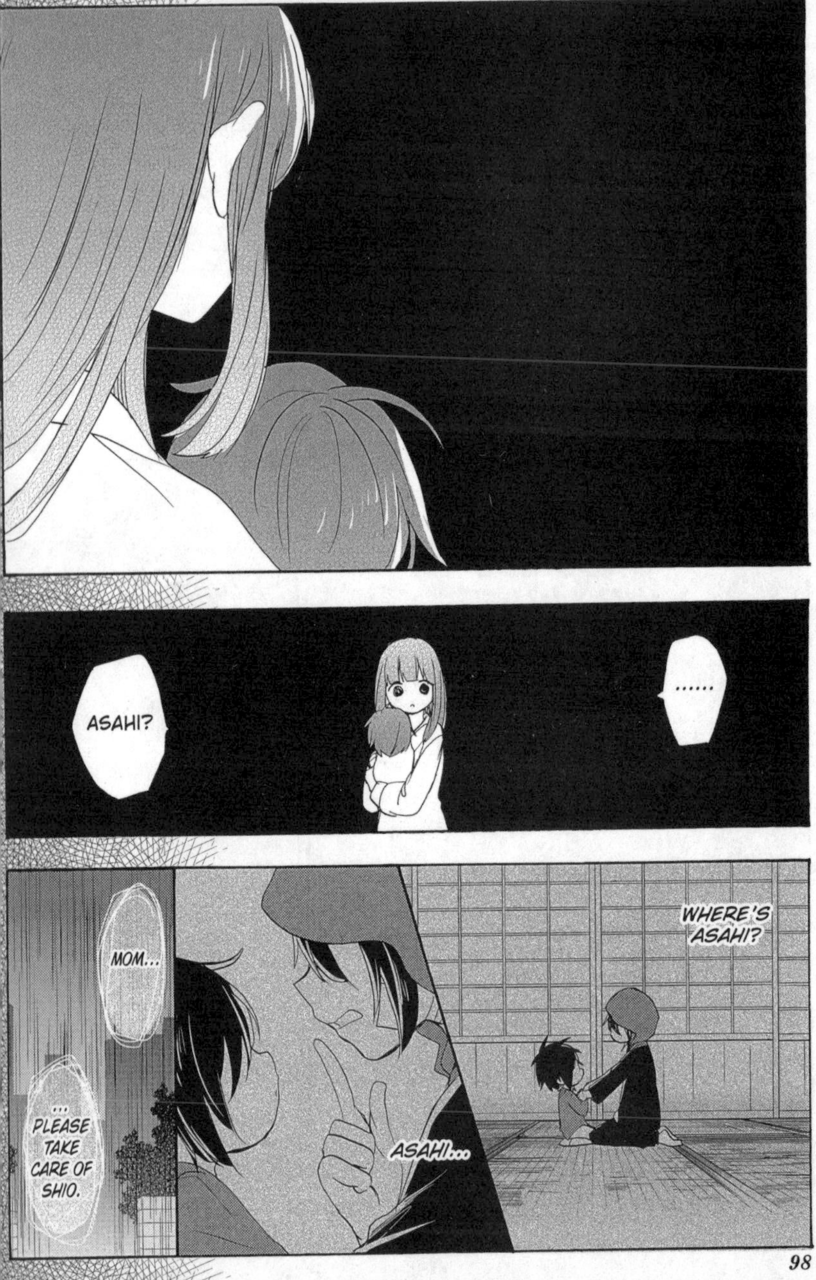
......
ASAHI?
WHERE'S ASAHI?
ASAHI...
MOM...
... PLEASE TAKE CARE OF SHIO.

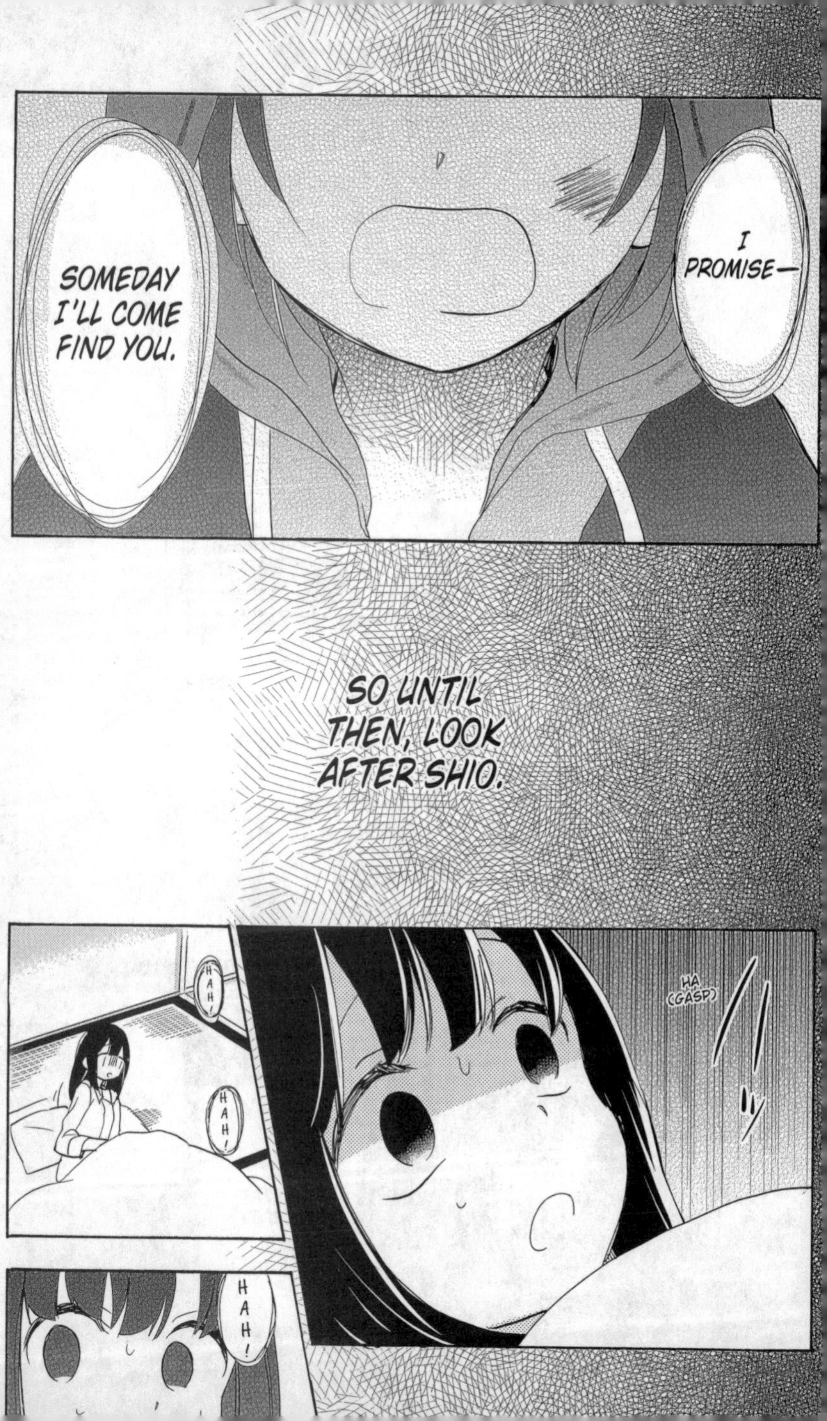
I PROMISE—
SOMEDAY I'LL COME FIND YOU.
SO UNTIL THEN, LOOK AFTER SHIO.
HA (GASP)
HAH!
HAH!
HAH!

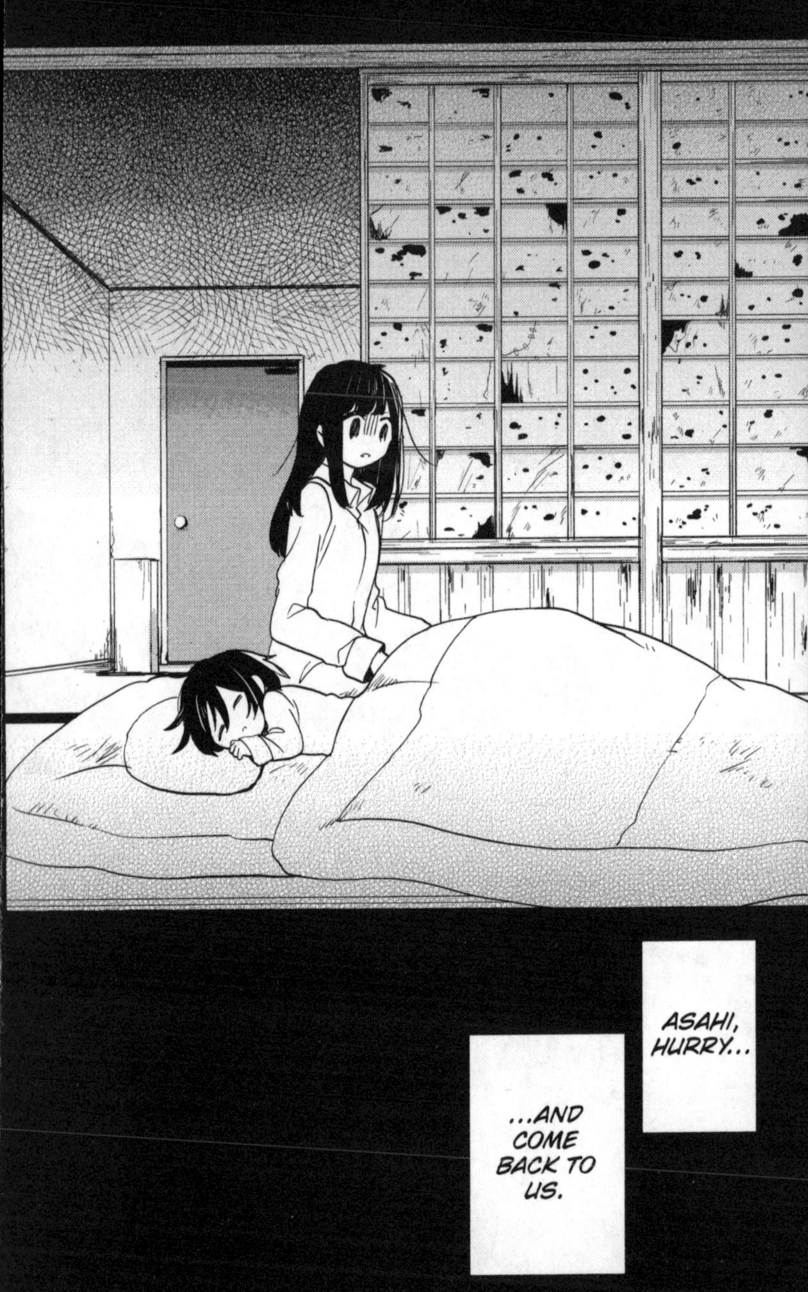
ASAHI, HURRY...
...AND COME BACK TO US.

Happy
Sugar
Life

Happy
Sugar
Life

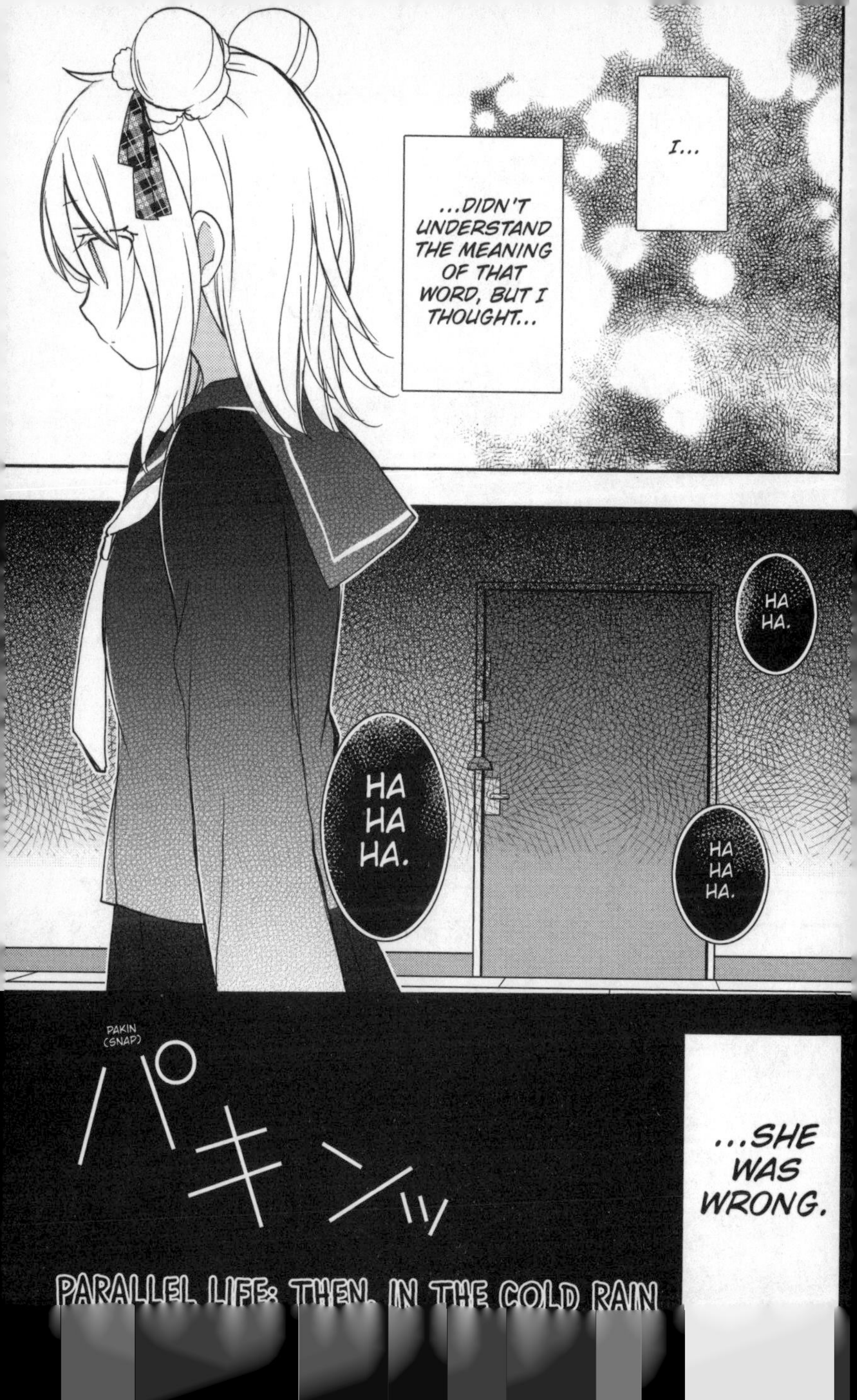
I...
...DIDN'T UNDERSTAND THE MEANING OF THAT WORD, BUT I THOUGHT...
HA HA.
HA HA HA.
HA HA HA.
...SHE WAS WRONG.
パキンッ
PAKIN (SNAP)
PARALLEL LIFE: THEN, IN THE COLD RAIN

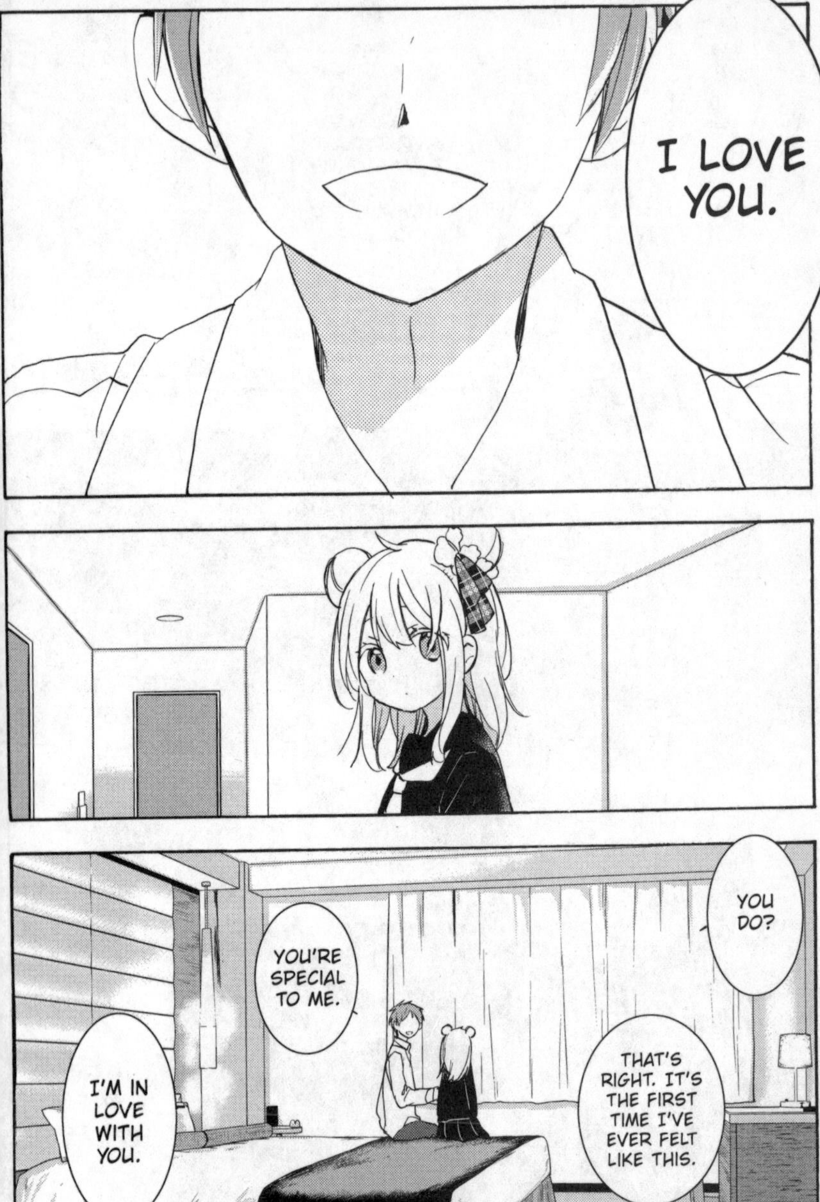
I LOVE YOU.
YOU DO?
THAT'S RIGHT. IT'S THE FIRST TIME I'VE EVER FELT LIKE THIS.
YOU'RE SPECIAL TO ME.
I'M IN LOVE WITH YOU.

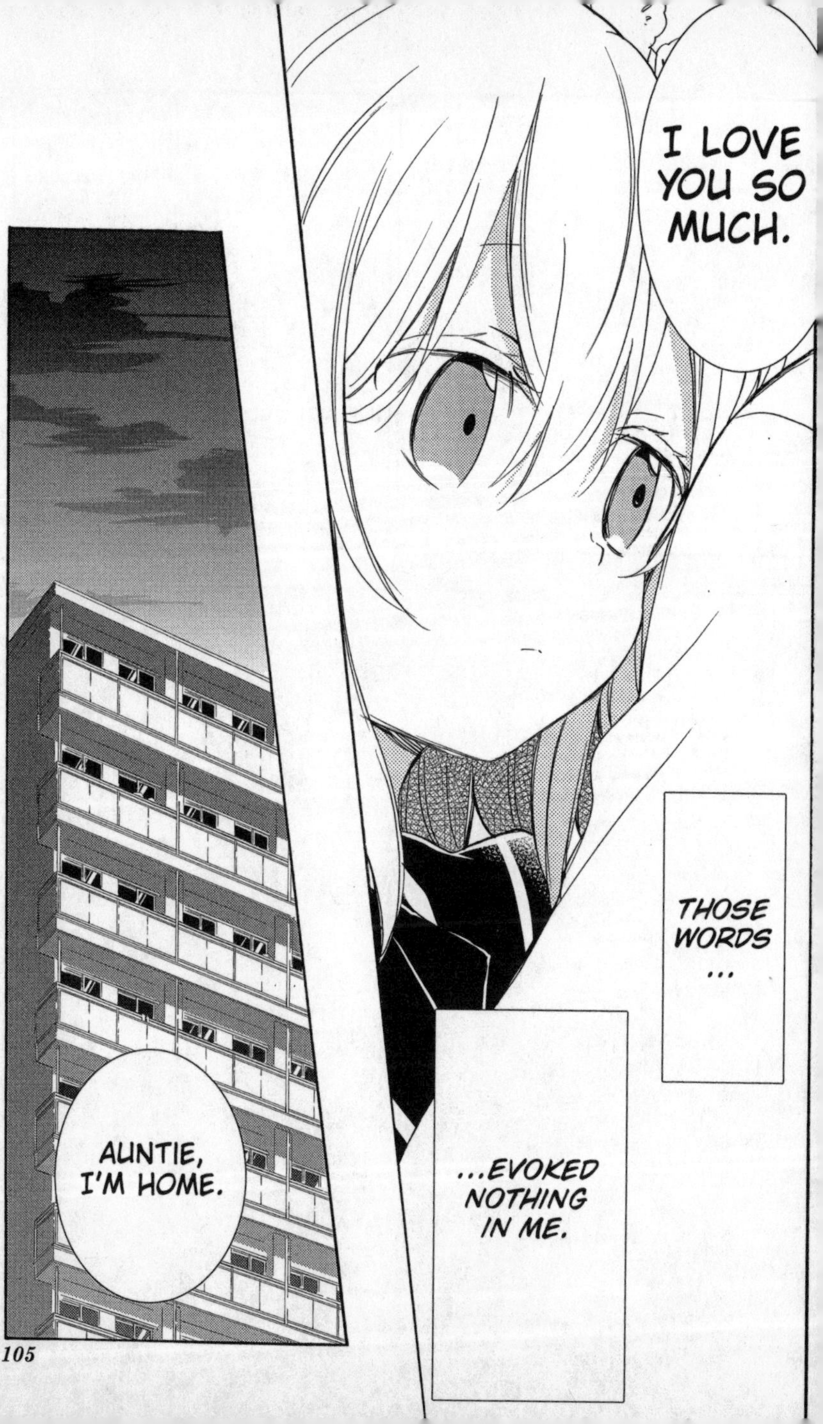
I LOVE YOU SO MUCH.
THOSE WORDS ...
...EVOKED NOTHING IN ME.
AUNTIE, I'M HOME.

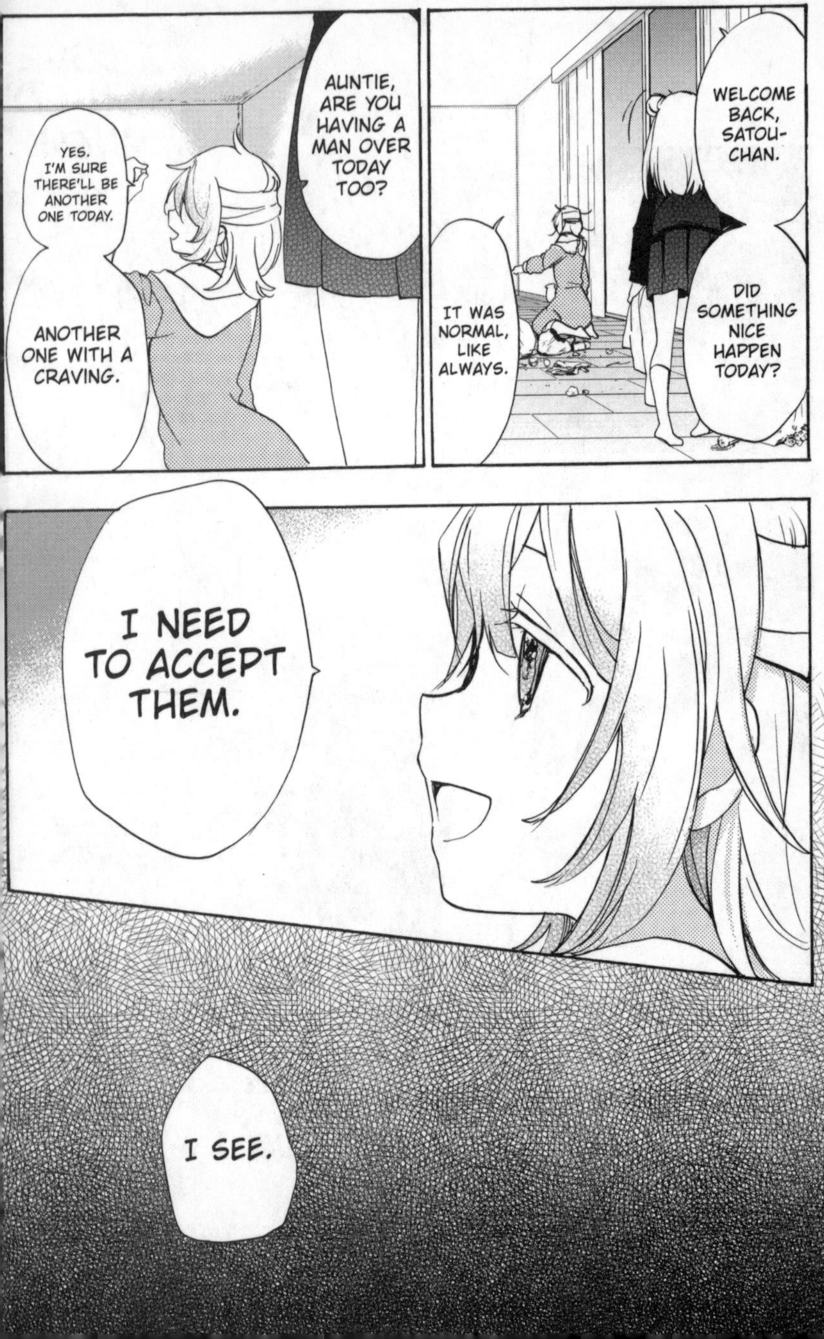
WELCOME BACK, SATOU-CHAN.
DID SOMETHING NICE HAPPEN TODAY?
IT WAS NORMAL, LIKE ALWAYS.
AUNTIE, ARE YOU HAVING A MAN OVER TODAY TOO?
YES. I'M SURE THERE'LL BE ANOTHER ONE TODAY.
ANOTHER ONE WITH A CRAVING.
I NEED TO ACCEPT THEM.
I SEE.

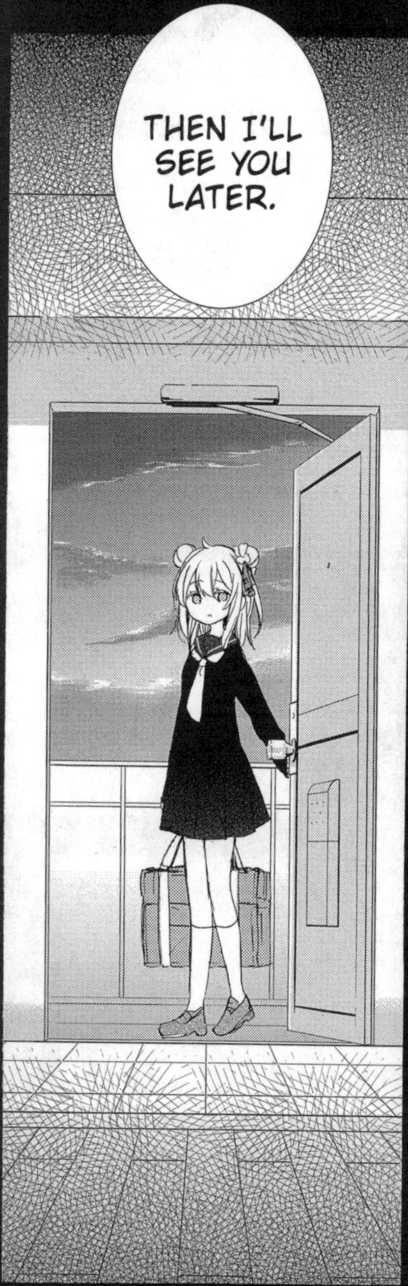
THEN I'LL SEE YOU LATER.

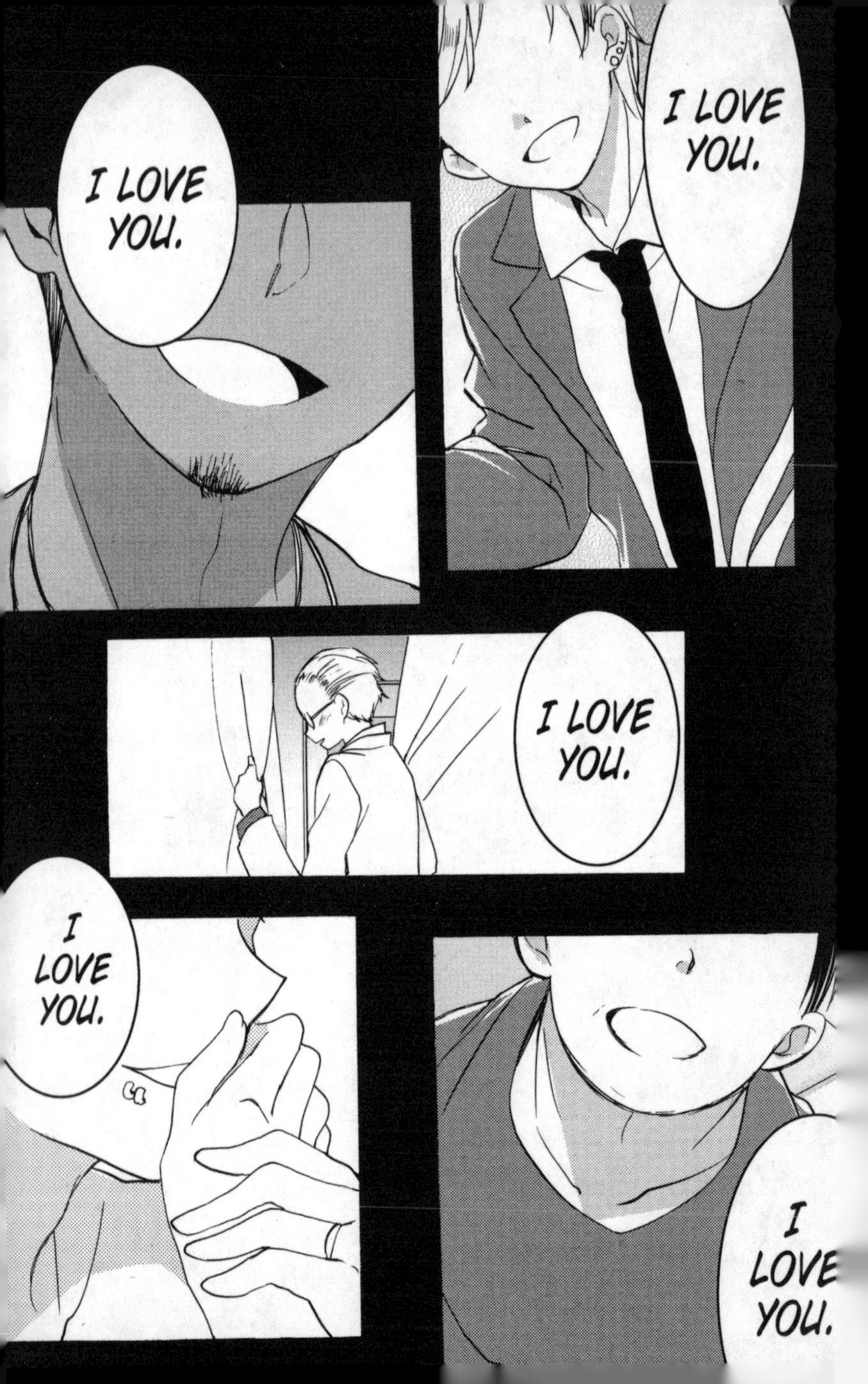
I LOVE YOU.
I LOVE YOU.
I LOVE YOU.
I LOVE YOU.
I LOVE YOU.

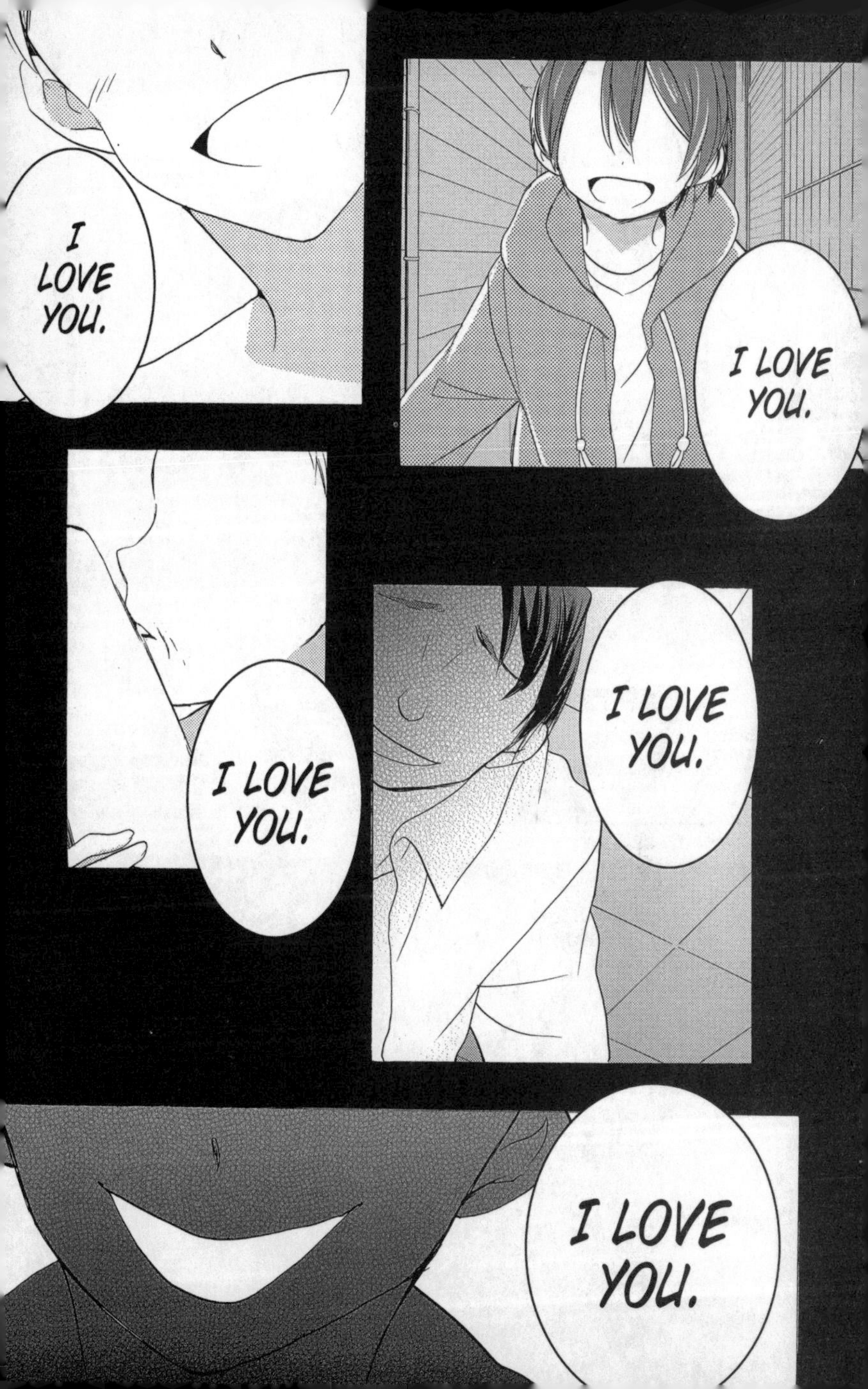
I LOVE YOU.
I LOVE YOU.
I LOVE YOU.
I LOVE YOU.
I LOVE YOU.

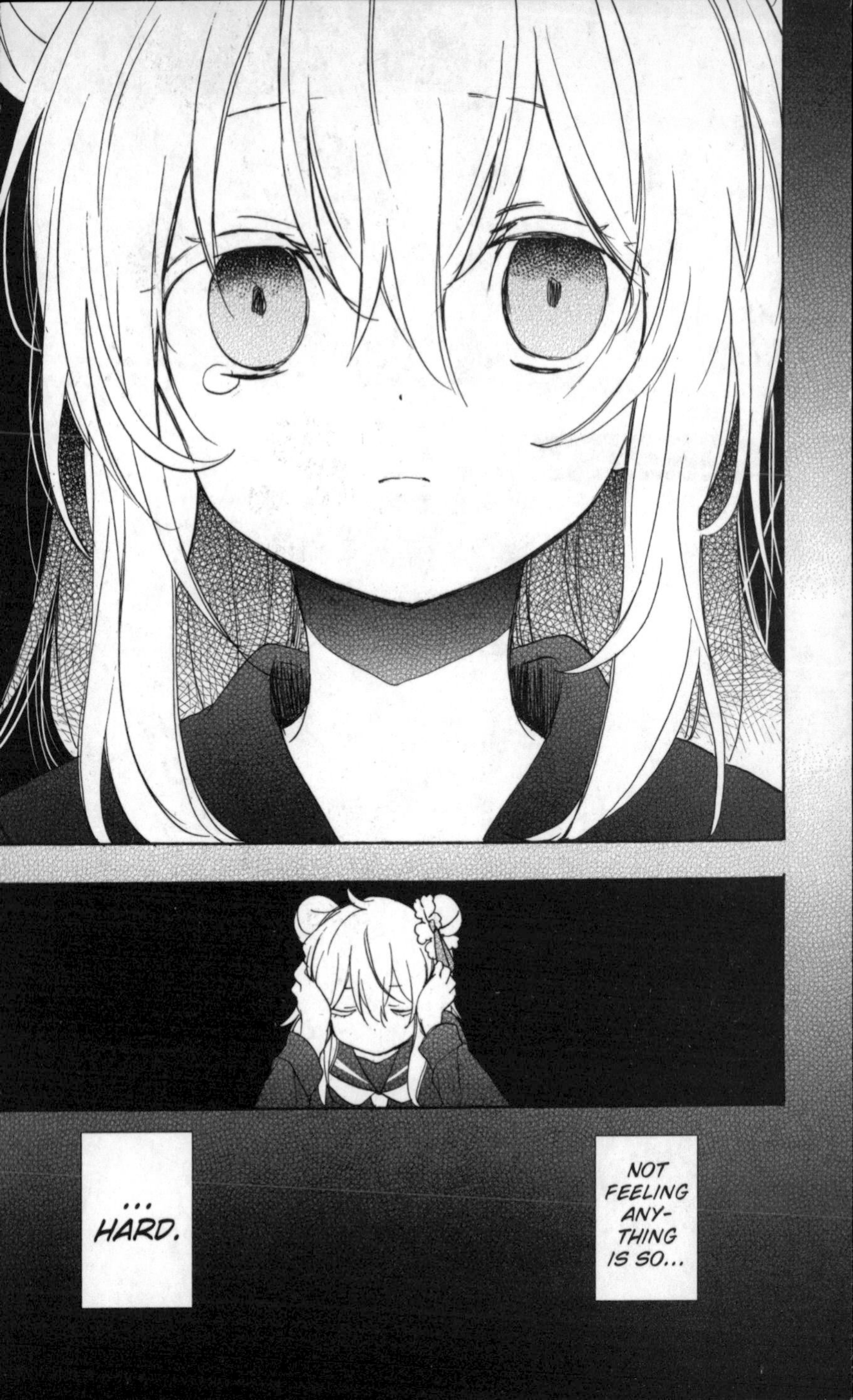
NOT FEELING ANY-THING IS SO...
...HARD.

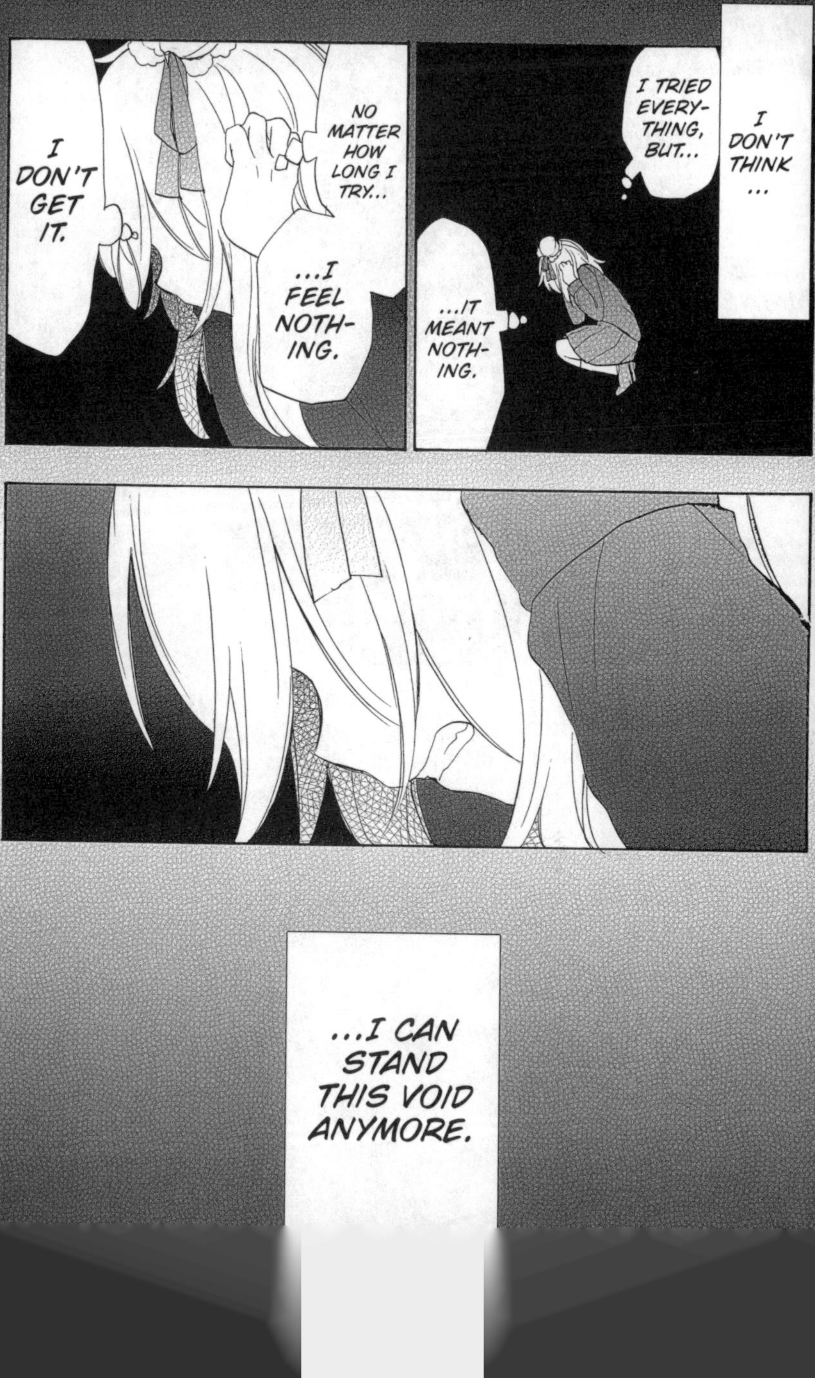
I DON'T THINK ...
I TRIED EVERY-THING, BUT...
...IT MEANT NOTH-ING.
NO MATTER HOW LONG I TRY...
...I FEEL NOTH-ING.
I DON'T GET IT.
...I CAN STAND THIS VOID ANYMORE.

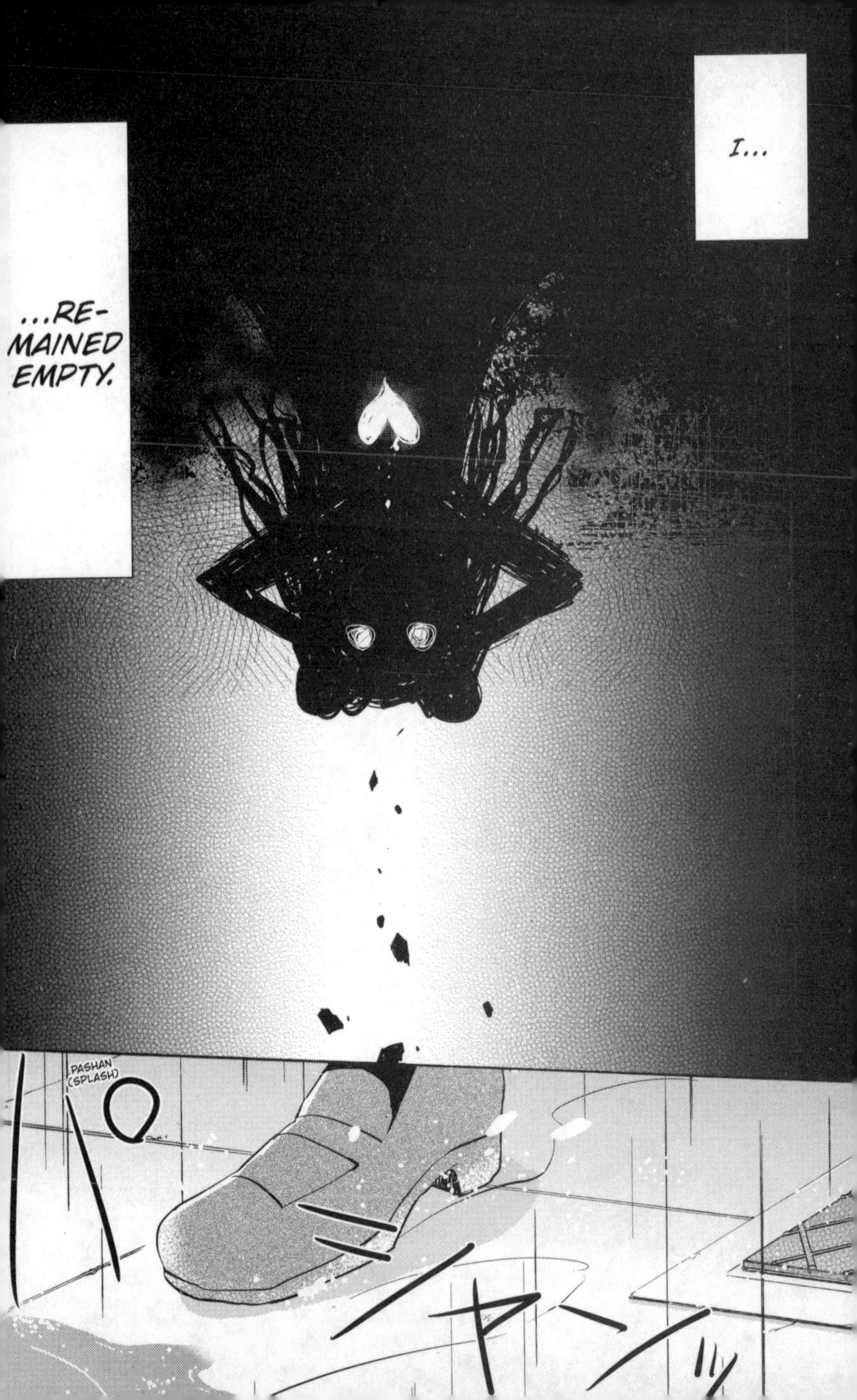
I...
...RE-MAINED EMPTY.
PASHAN (SPLASH)

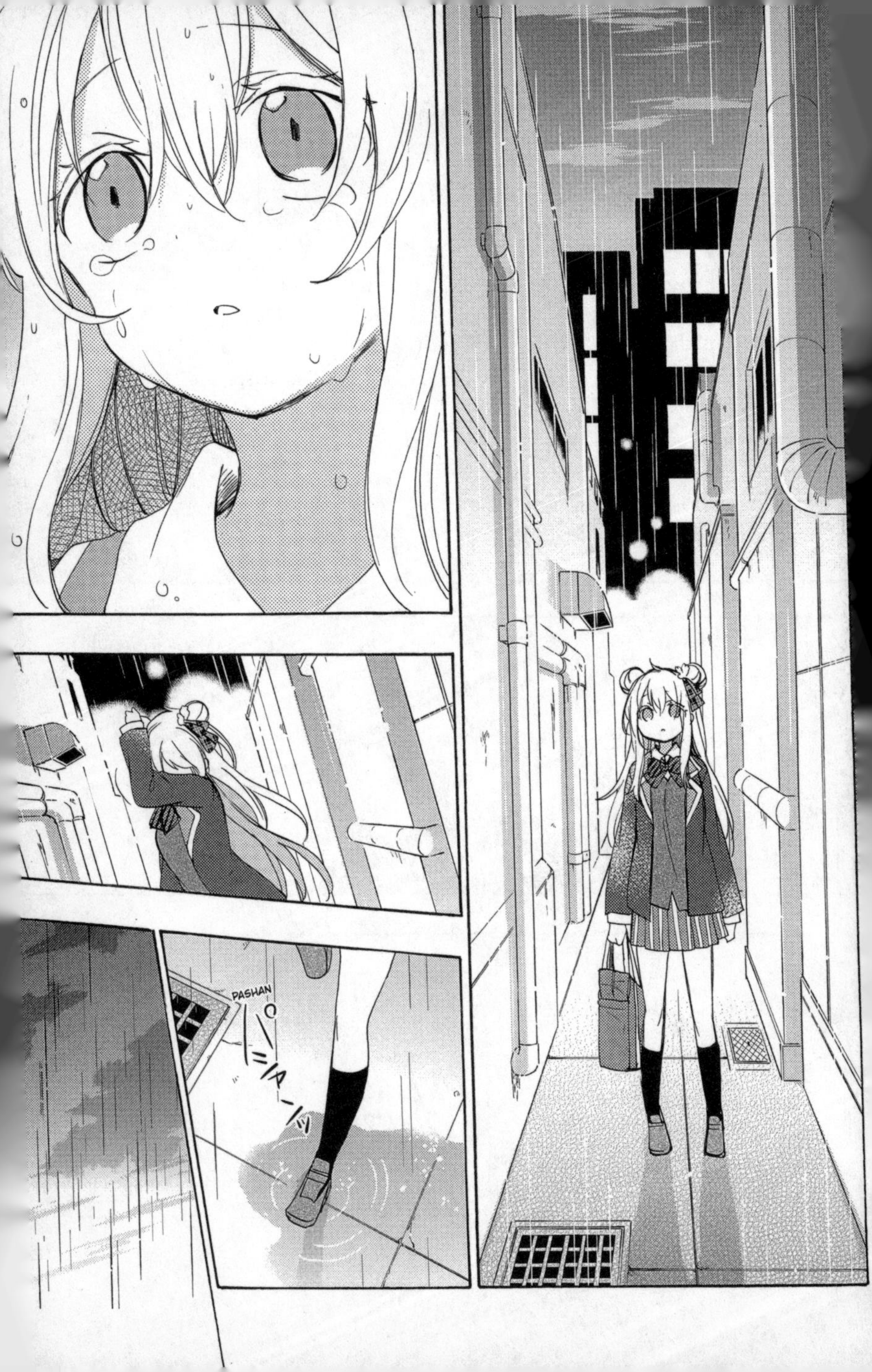
PASHAN
パシャーンッ

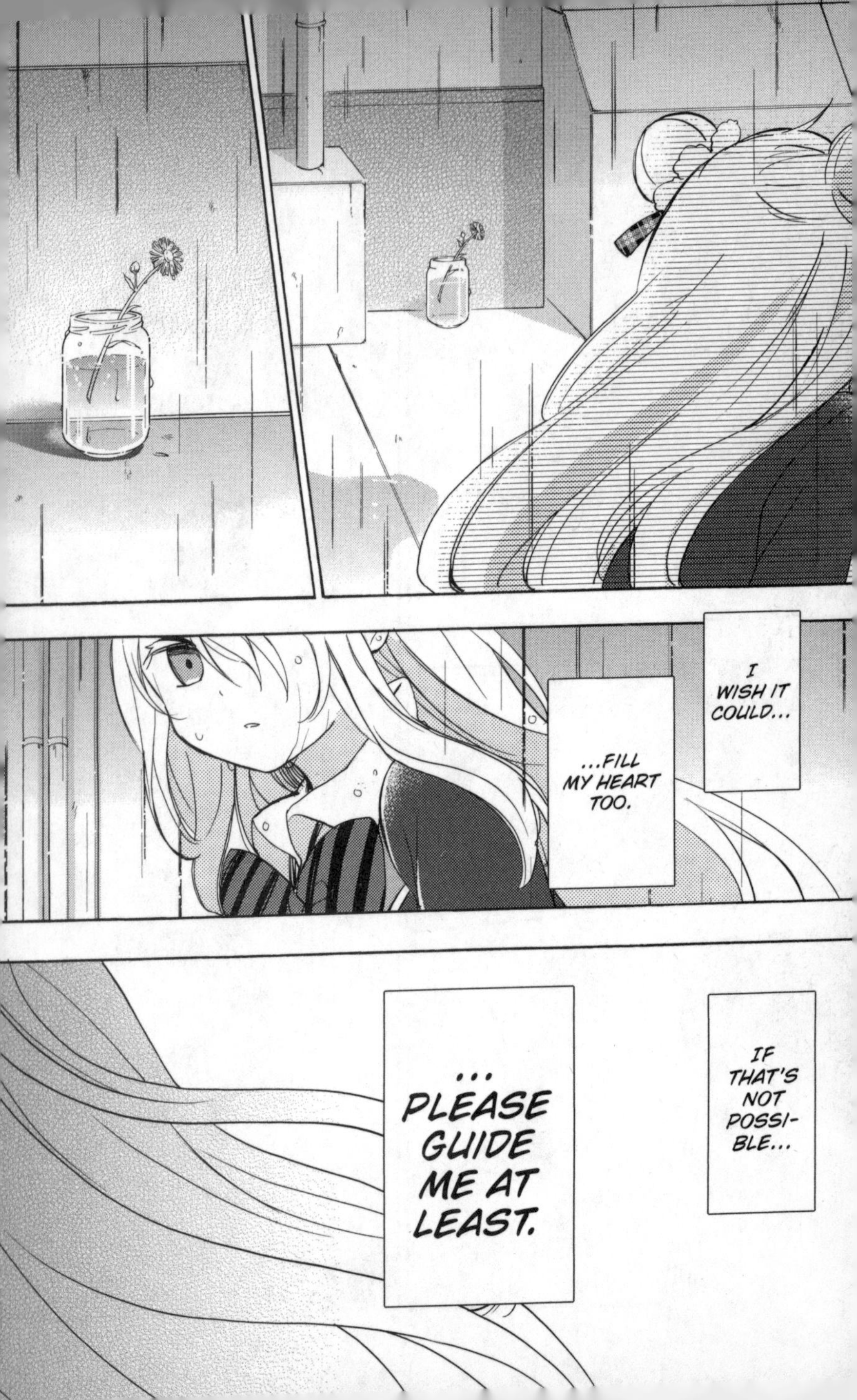
I WISH IT COULD...
...FILL MY HEART TOO.
IF THAT'S NOT POSSI- BLE...
... PLEASE GUIDE ME AT LEAST.

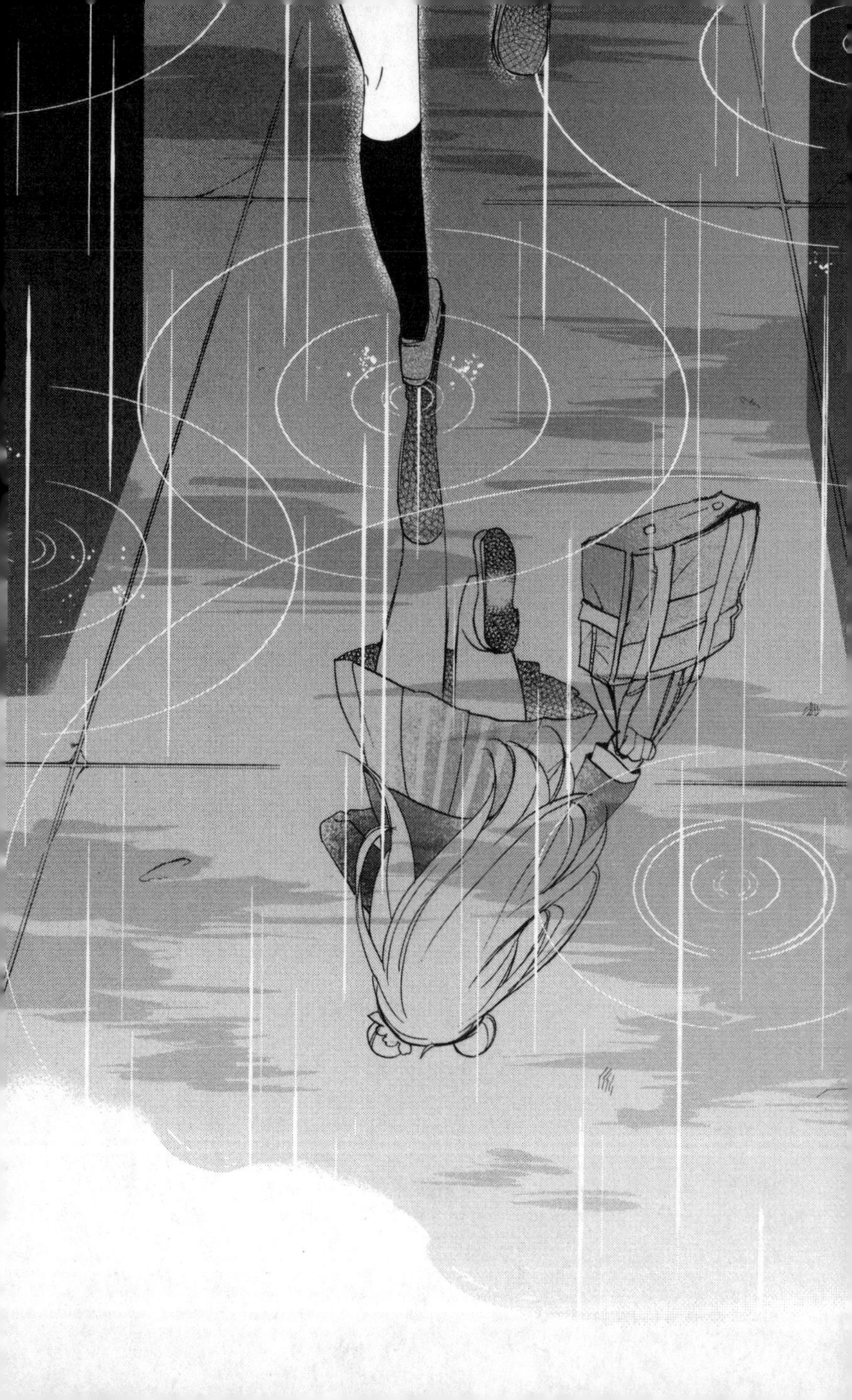

Happy
Sugar
Life

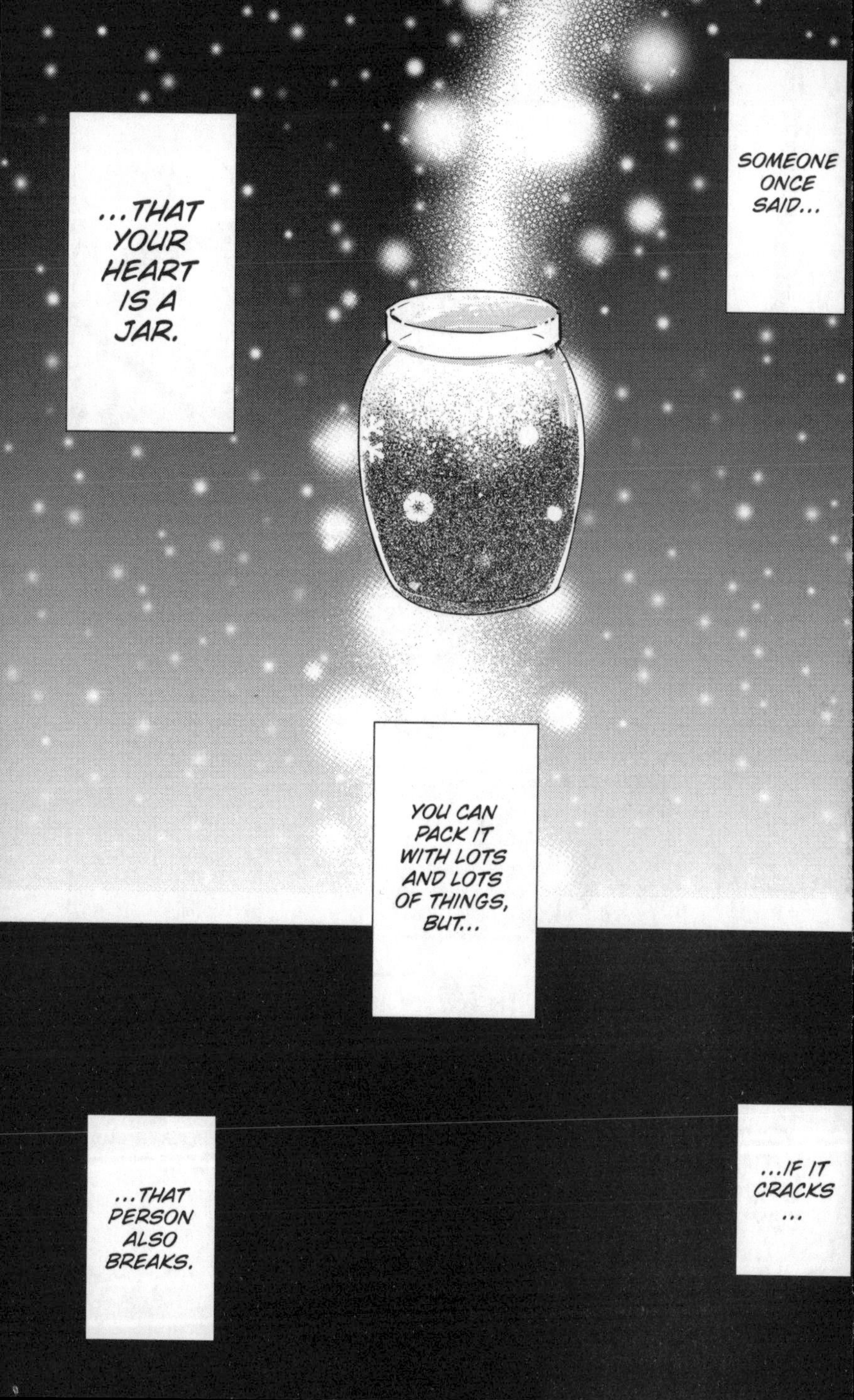
SOMEONE ONCE SAID...
...THAT YOUR HEART IS A JAR.
YOU CAN PACK IT WITH LOTS AND LOTS OF THINGS, BUT...
...IF IT CRACKS...
...THAT PERSON ALSO BREAKS.

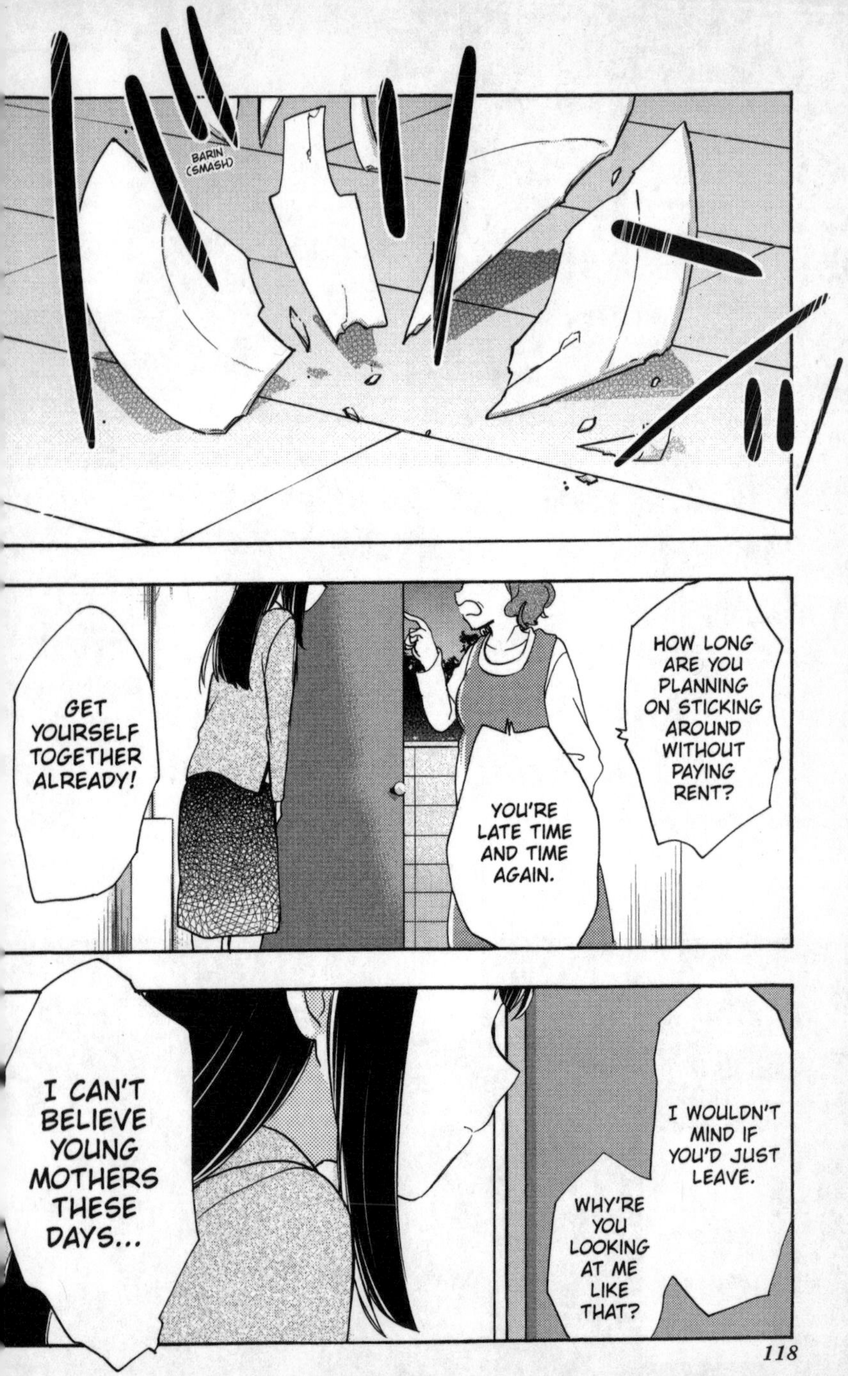
BARIN (SMASH)
HOW LONG ARE YOU PLANNING ON STICKING AROUND WITHOUT PAYING RENT?
YOU'RE LATE TIME AND TIME AGAIN.
GET YOURSELF TOGETHER ALREADY!
I WOULDN'T MIND IF YOU'D JUST LEAVE.
WHY'RE YOU LOOKING AT ME LIKE THAT?
I CAN'T BELIEVE YOUNG MOTHERS THESE DAYS...

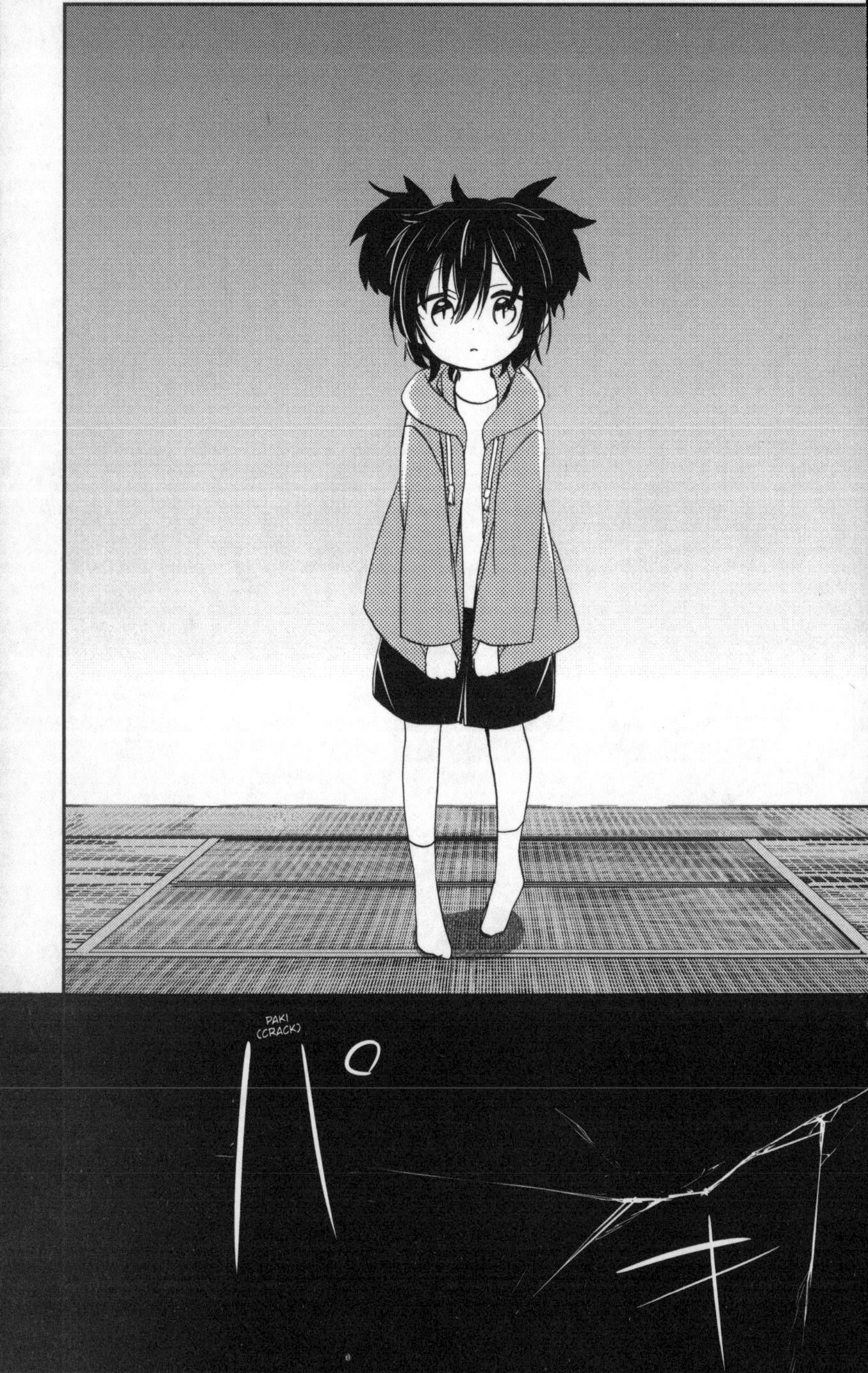
PAKI
(CRACK)
パキ

31ST LIFE: IN THE JAR, ONE DROP OF LOVE

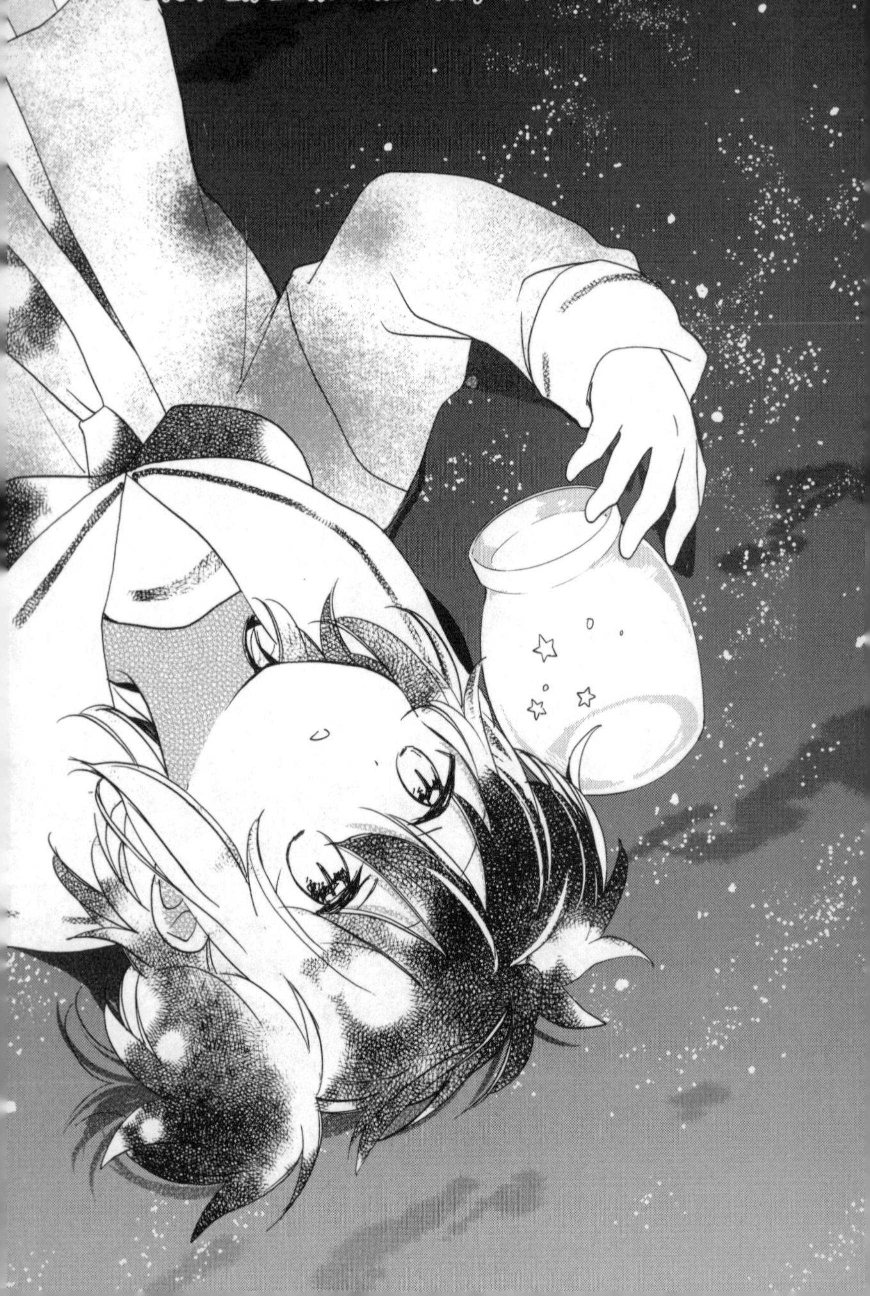

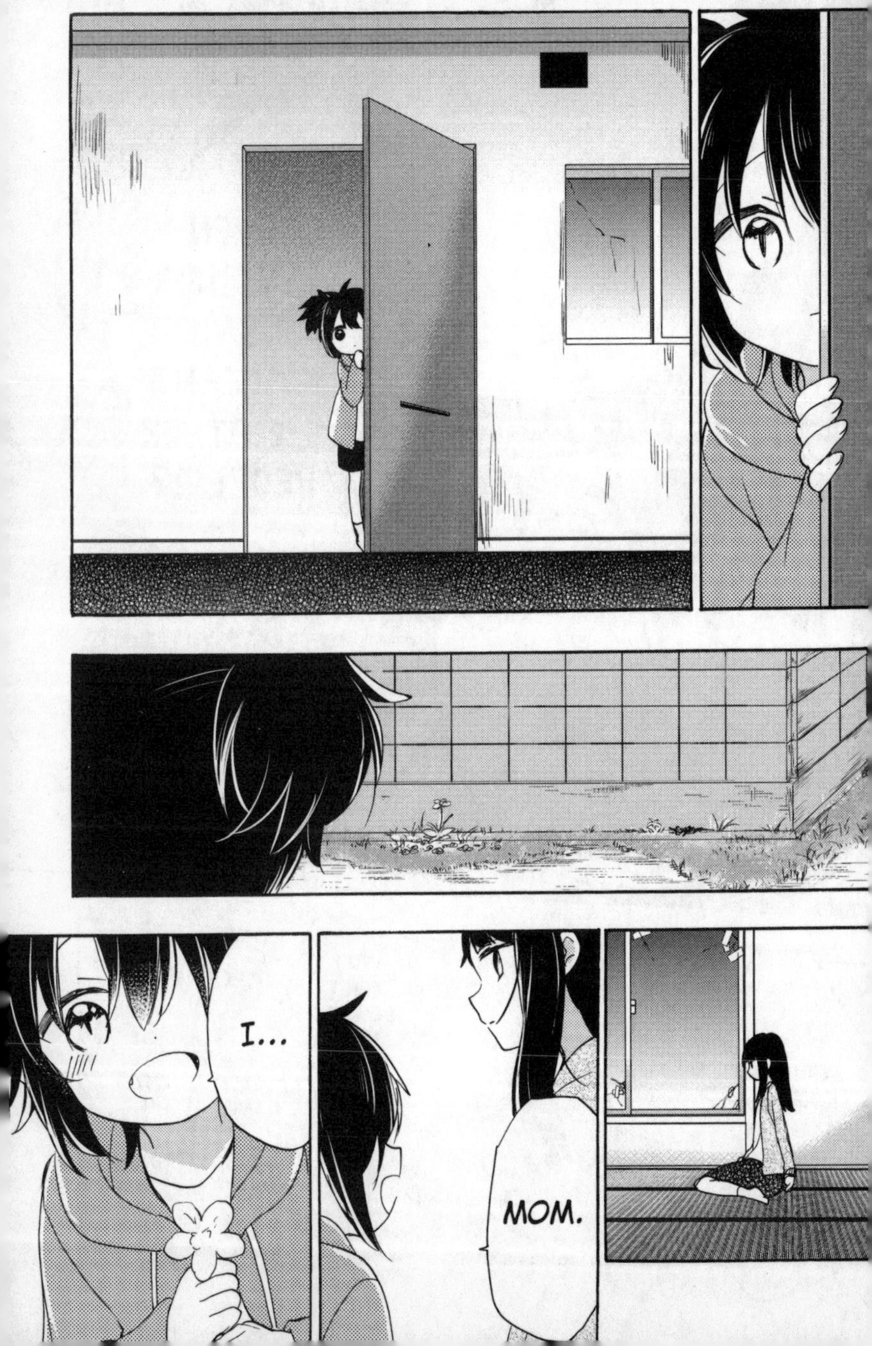
MOM.
I...

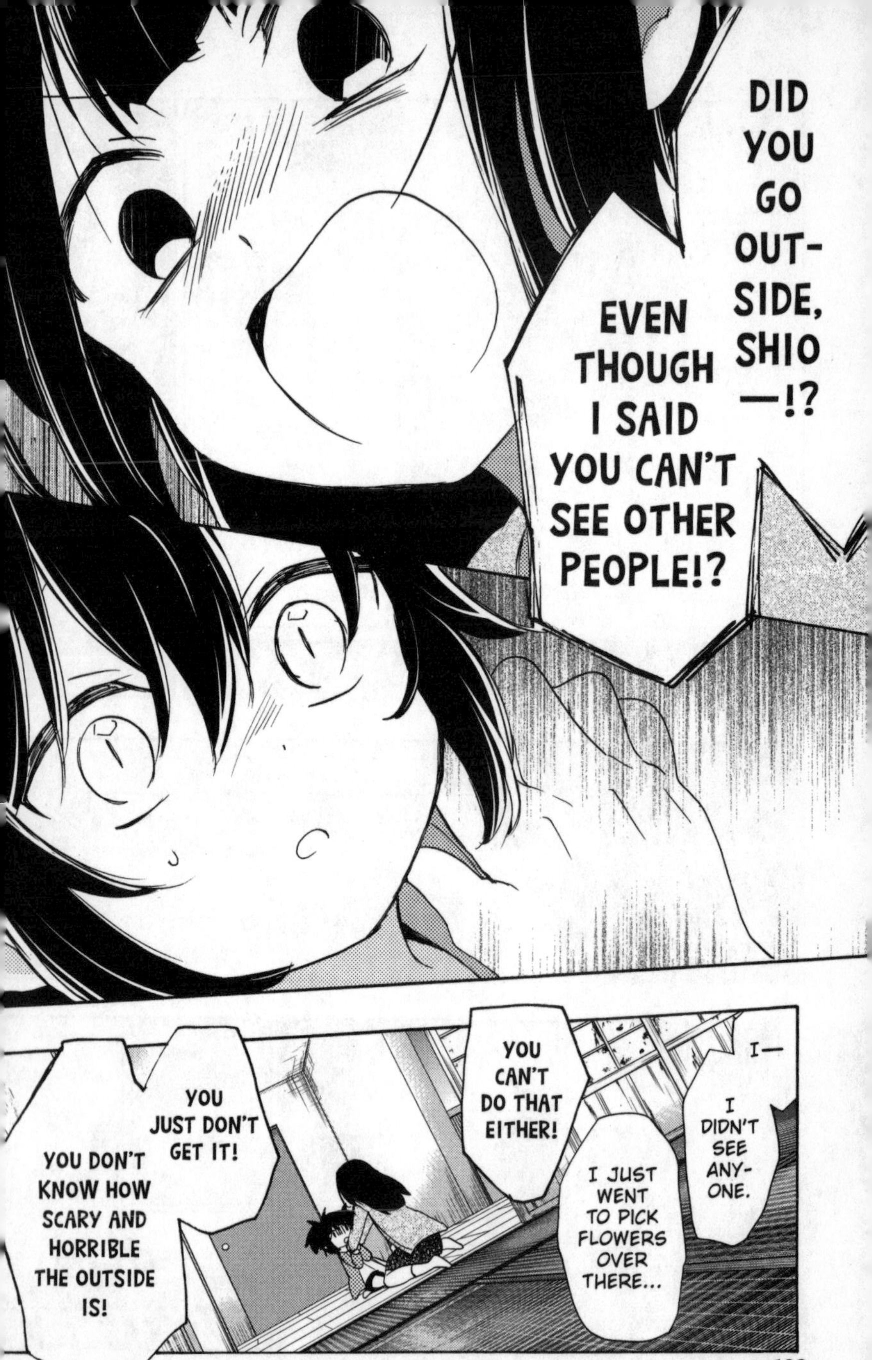
DID YOU GO OUTSIDE, SHIO—!?
EVEN THOUGH I SAID YOU CAN'T SEE OTHER PEOPLE!?
I—
I DIDN'T SEE ANYONE.
I JUST WENT TO PICK FLOWERS OVER THERE...
YOU CAN'T DO THAT EITHER!
YOU JUST DON'T GET IT!
YOU DON'T KNOW HOW SCARY AND HORRIBLE THE OUTSIDE IS!

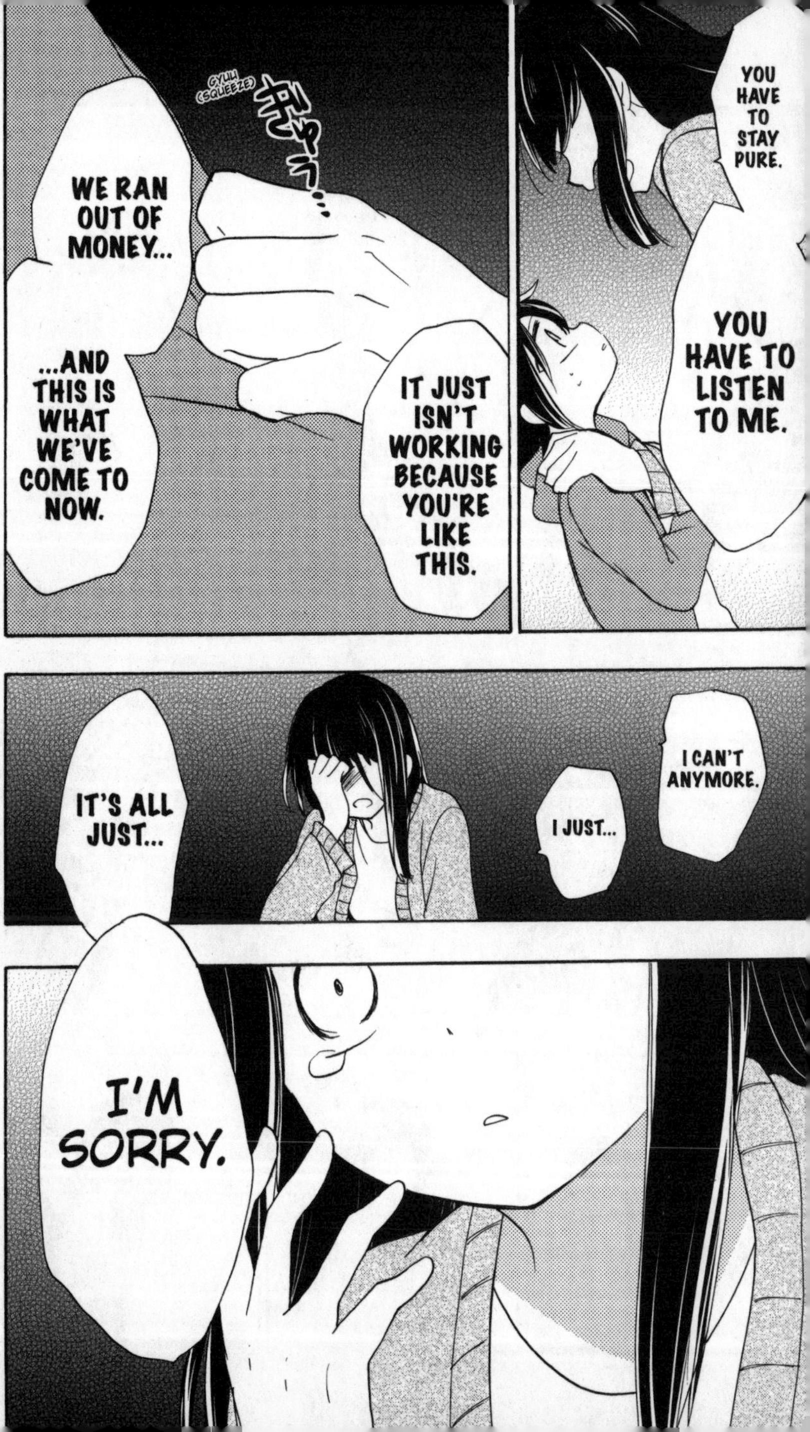
YOU HAVE TO STAY PURE.
YOU HAVE TO LISTEN TO ME.
GYUU (SQUEEZE)
WE RAN OUT OF MONEY...
...AND THIS IS WHAT WE'VE COME TO NOW.
IT JUST ISN'T WORKING BECAUSE YOU'RE LIKE THIS.
I CAN'T ANYMORE.
I JUST...
IT'S ALL JUST...
I'M SORRY.

I'M SORRY, MOM.

......

UGHH.

UGH. ......

IT'S NOT YOU.

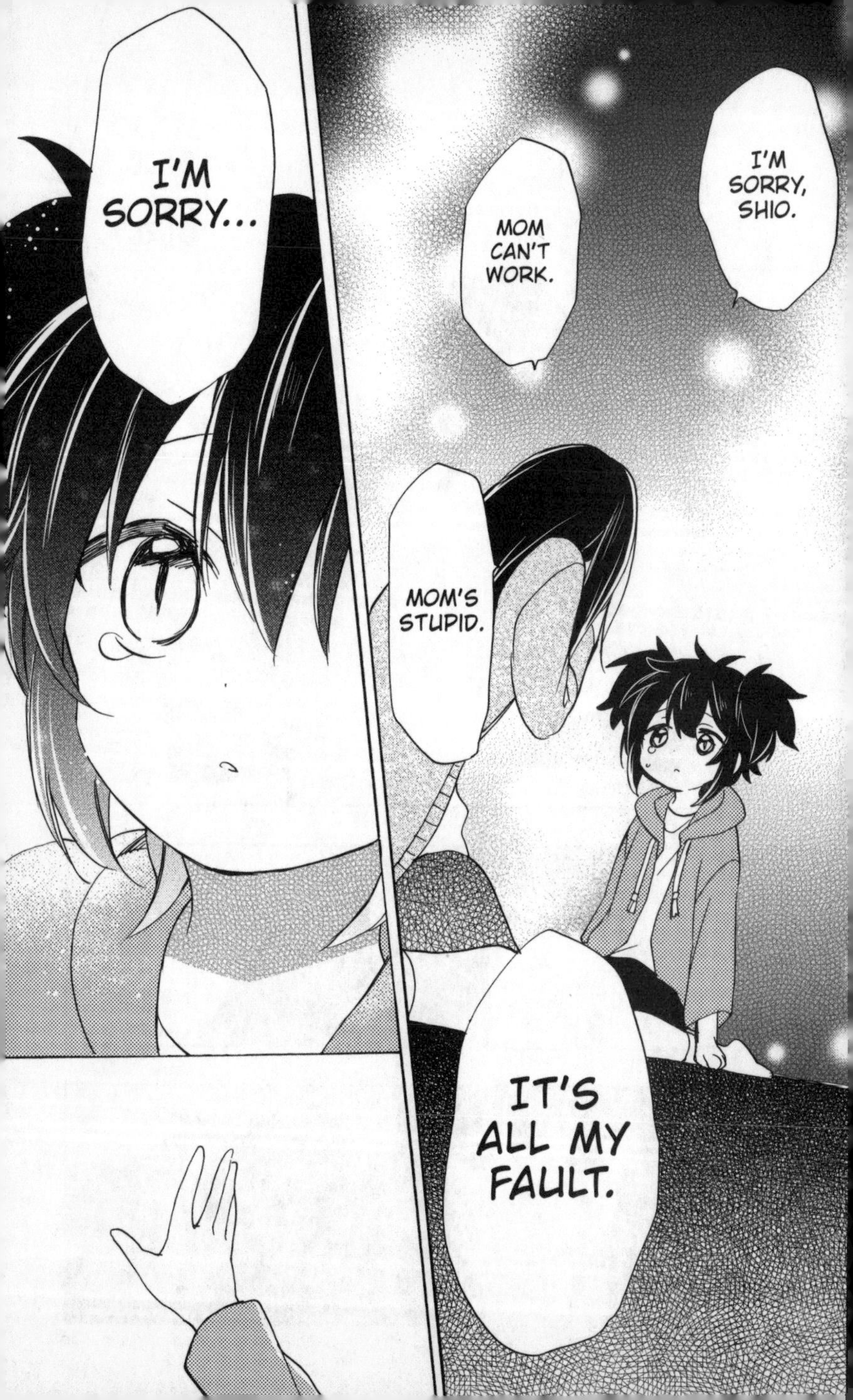
I'M SORRY, SHIO.
MOM CAN'T WORK.
MOM'S STUPID.
IT'S ALL MY FAULT.
I'M SORRY...

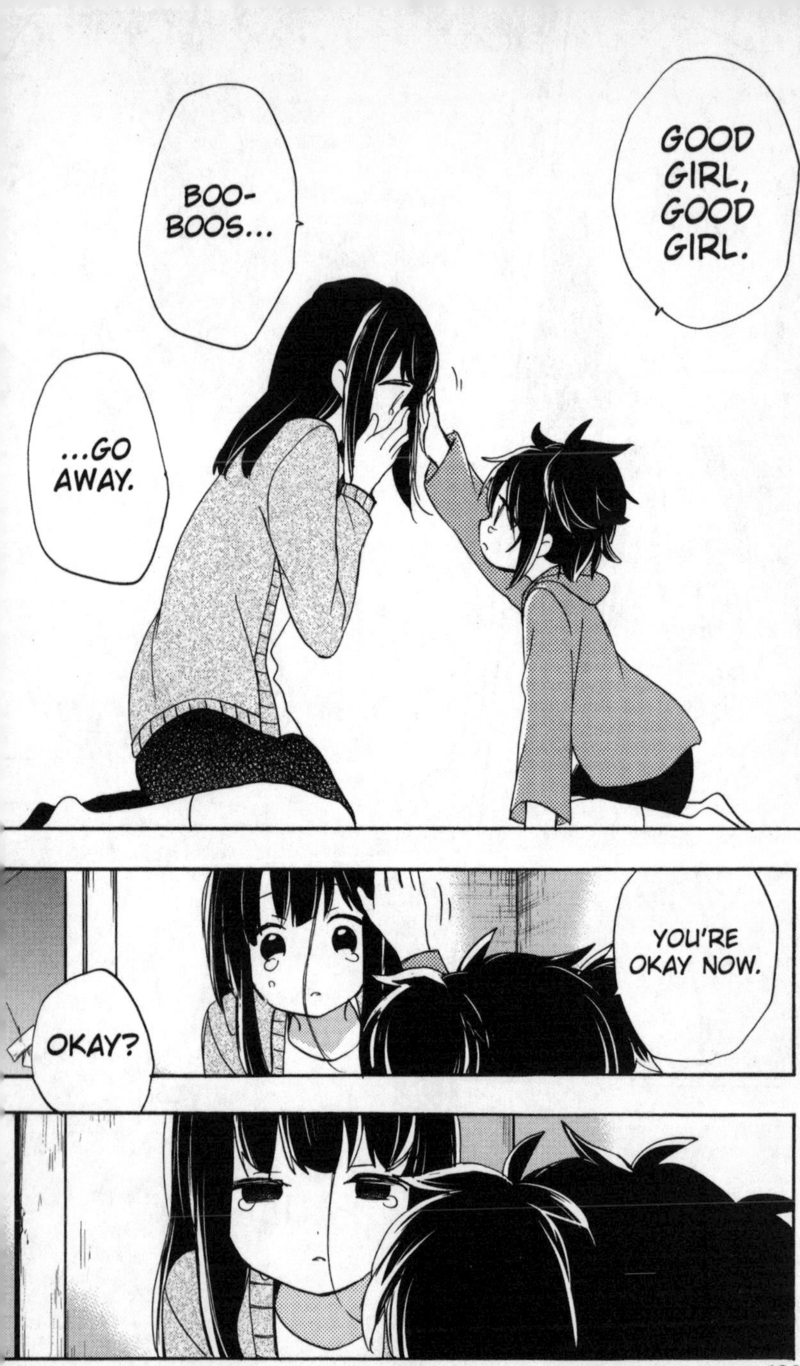
GOOD GIRL, GOOD GIRL.
BOO-BOOS...
...GO AWAY.
YOU'RE OKAY NOW.
OKAY?

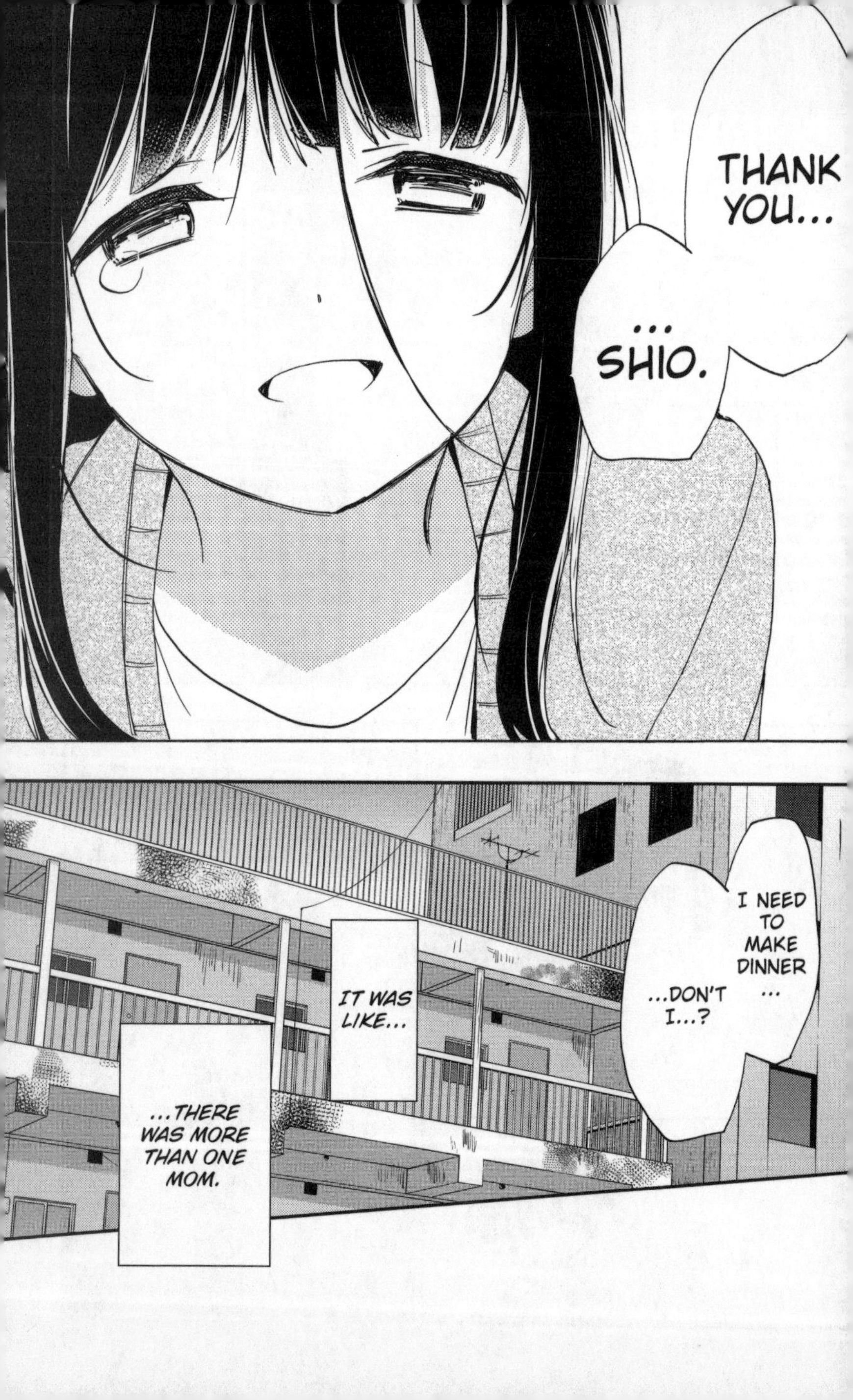
THANK YOU...
... SHIO.
I NEED TO MAKE DINNER ...
...DON'T I...?
IT WAS LIKE...
...THERE WAS MORE THAN ONE MOM.

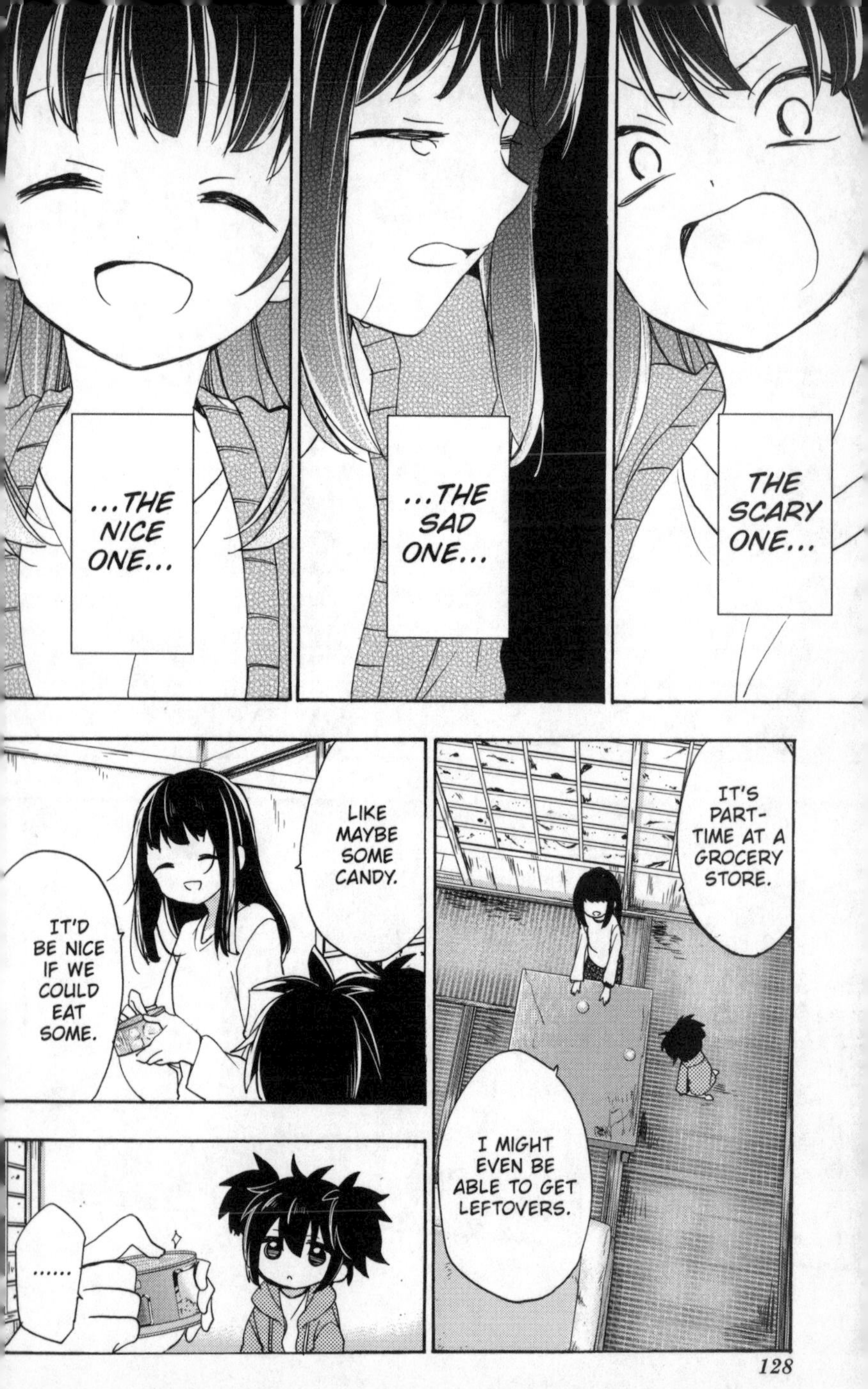
THE SCARY ONE...
...THE SAD ONE...
...THE NICE ONE...
IT'S PART-TIME AT A GROCERY STORE.
I MIGHT EVEN BE ABLE TO GET LEFTOVERS.
LIKE MAYBE SOME CANDY.
IT'D BE NICE IF WE COULD EAT SOME.
......

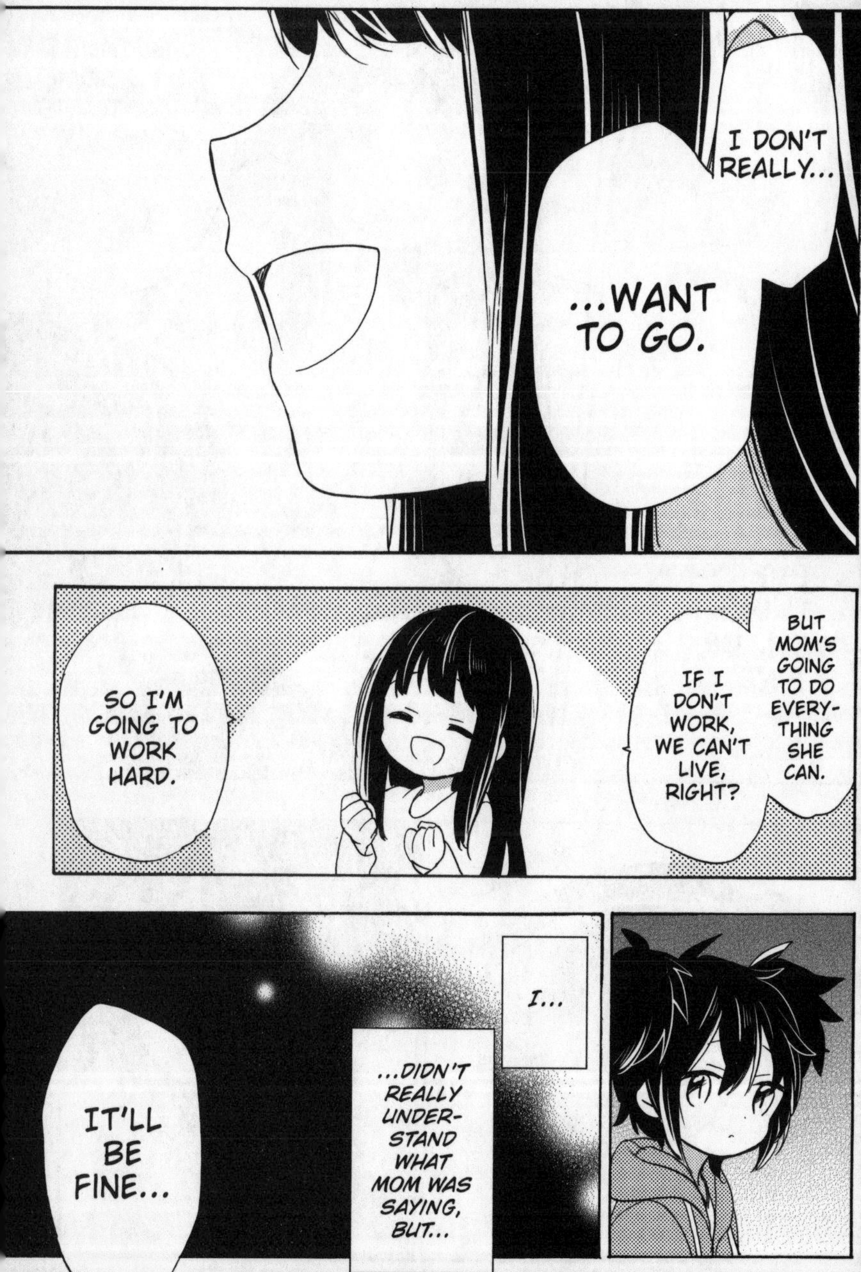
I DON'T REALLY...
...WANT TO GO.
BUT MOM'S GOING TO DO EVERY-THING SHE CAN.
IF I DON'T WORK, WE CAN'T LIVE, RIGHT?
SO I'M GOING TO WORK HARD.
I...
...DIDN'T REALLY UNDER-STAND WHAT MOM WAS SAYING, BUT...
IT'LL BE FINE...

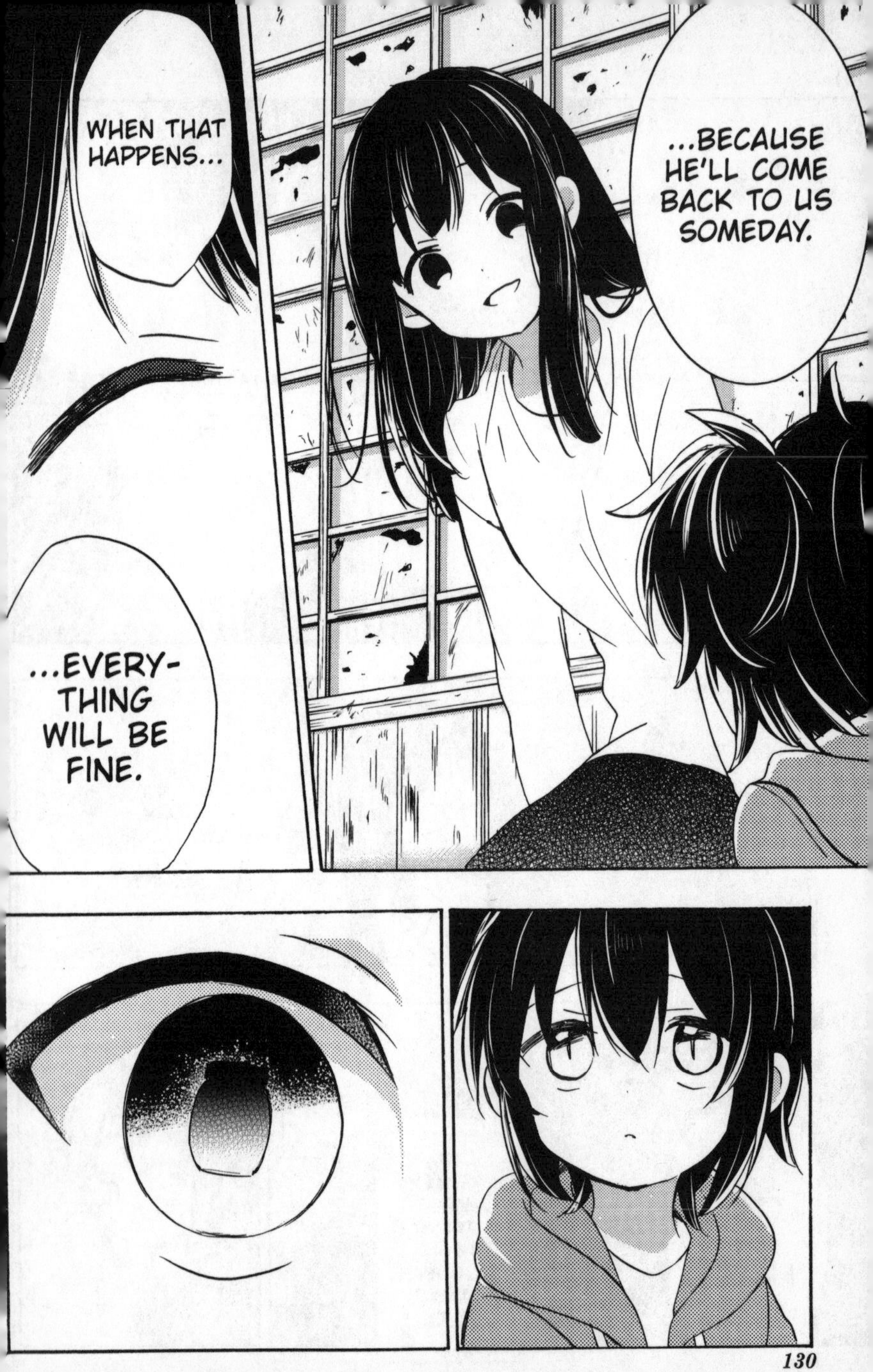
...BECAUSE HE'LL COME BACK TO US SOMEDAY.
WHEN THAT HAPPENS...
...EVERY-THING WILL BE FINE.

YOU CAN'T KEEP GOING LIKE THIS...

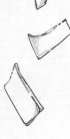

IT'LL BREAK FOR SURE.

WHAT'LL I DO IF IT BREAKS?

WHERE CAN I FIND...

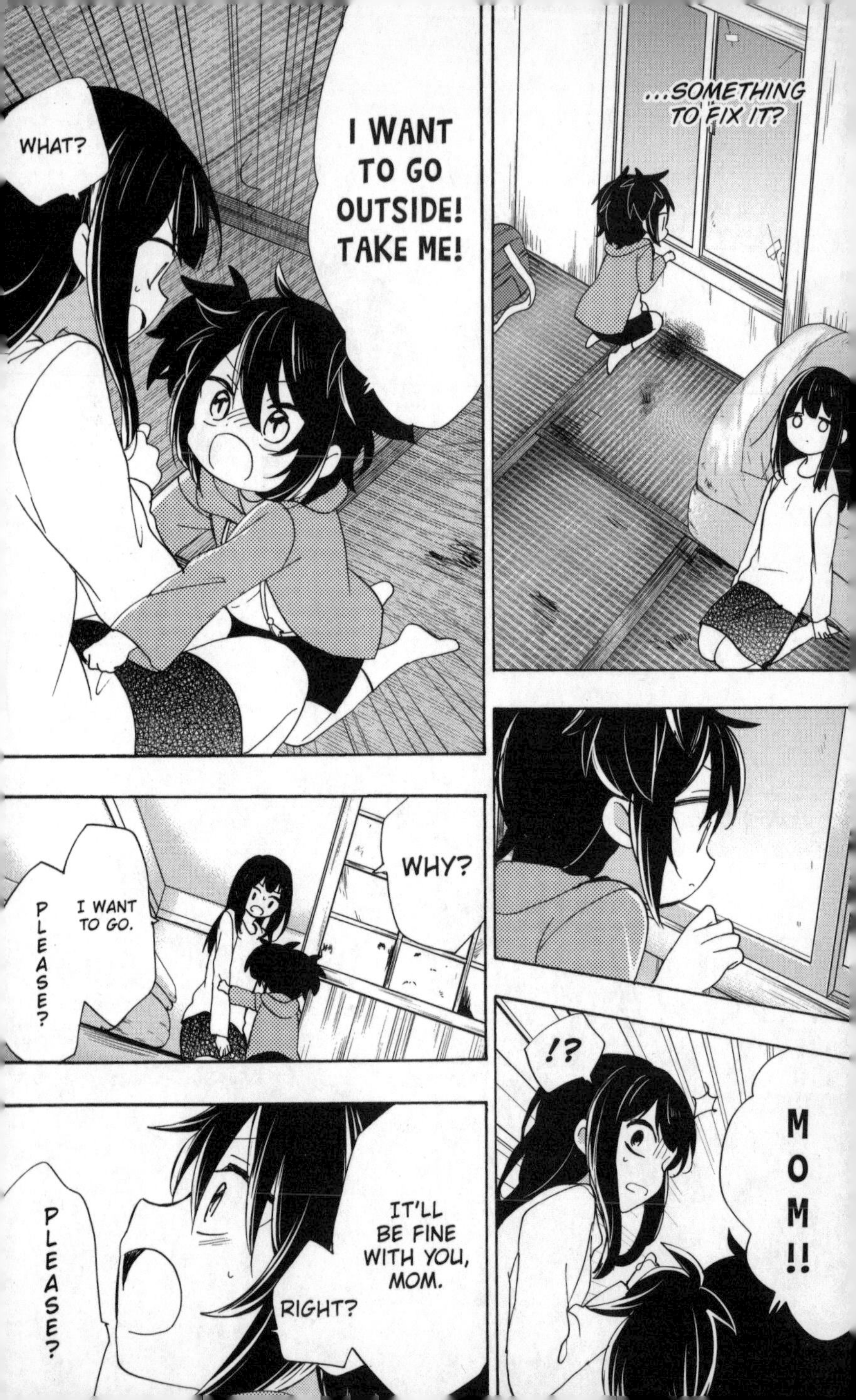
...SOMETHING TO FIX IT?
I WANT TO GO OUTSIDE! TAKE ME!
WHAT?
WHY?
I WANT TO GO.
PLEASE?
MOM!!
!?
IT'LL BE FINE WITH YOU, MOM.
RIGHT?
PLEASE?

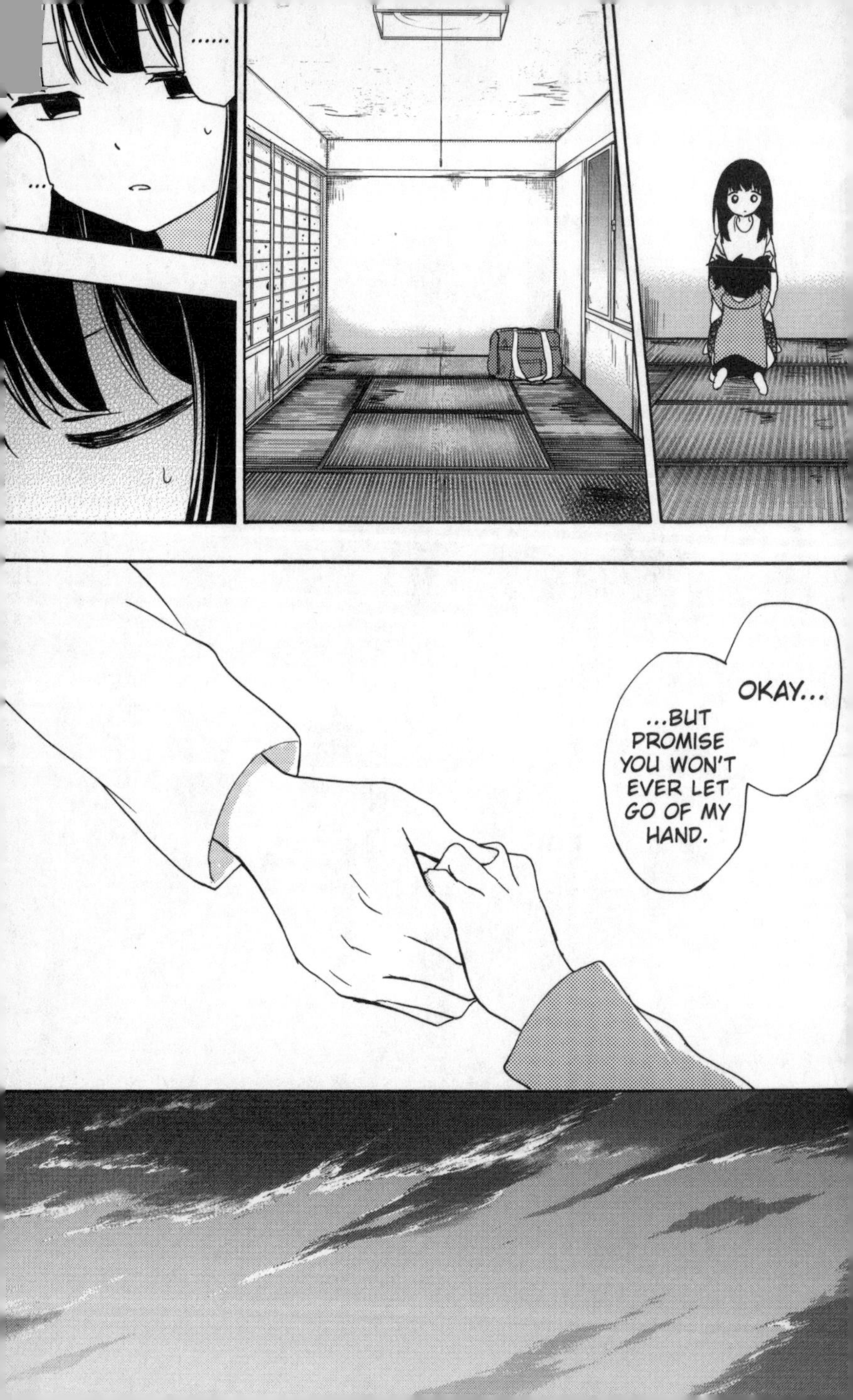
......
...
OKAY...
...BUT PROMISE YOU WON'T EVER LET GO OF MY HAND.

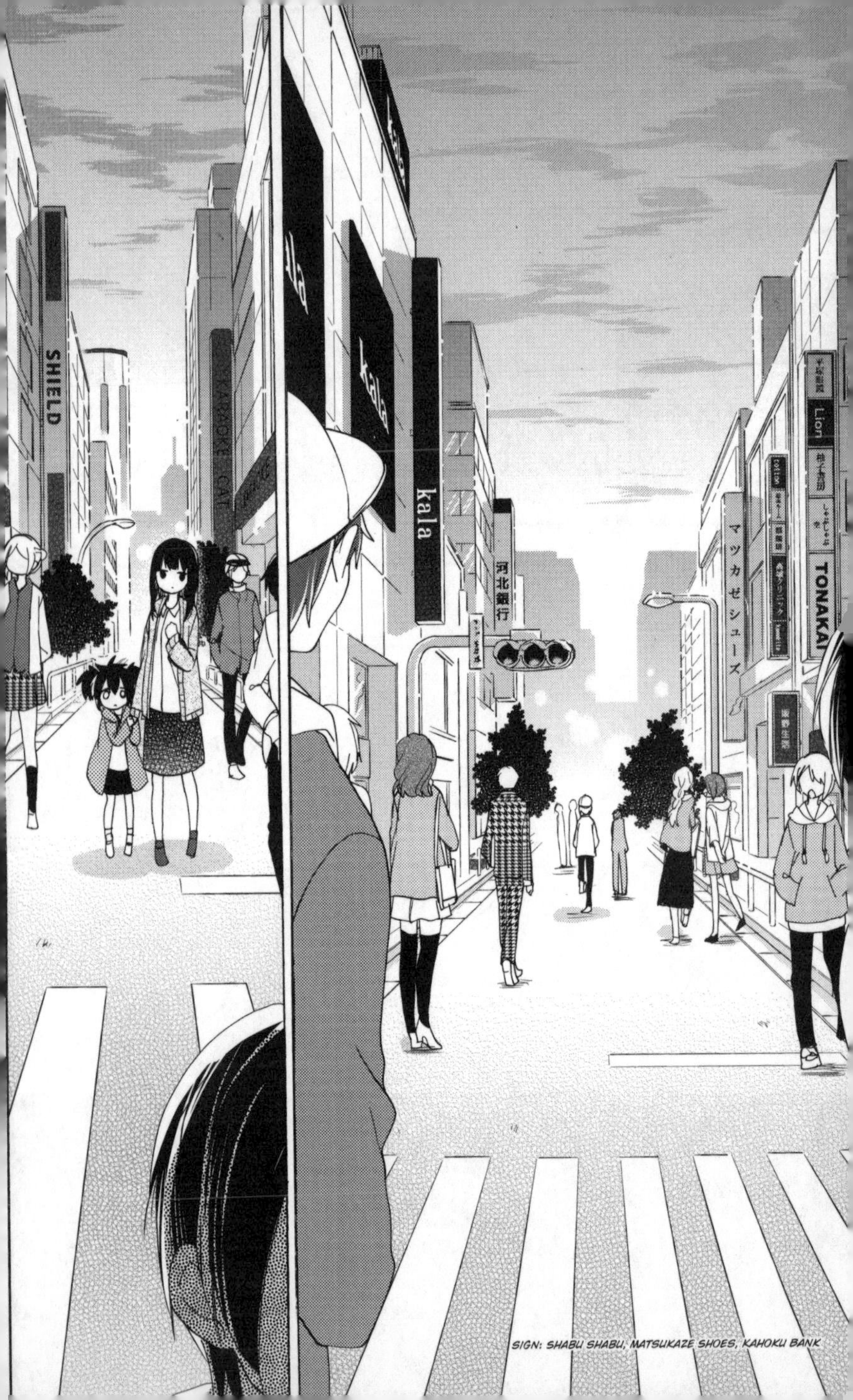
SHIELD
KARAOKE CAT
kala
kala
kala
kala
河北銀行
マツカゼシューズ
Lion
TONAKAI
SIGN: SHABU SHABU, MATSUKAZE SHOES, KAHOKU BANK

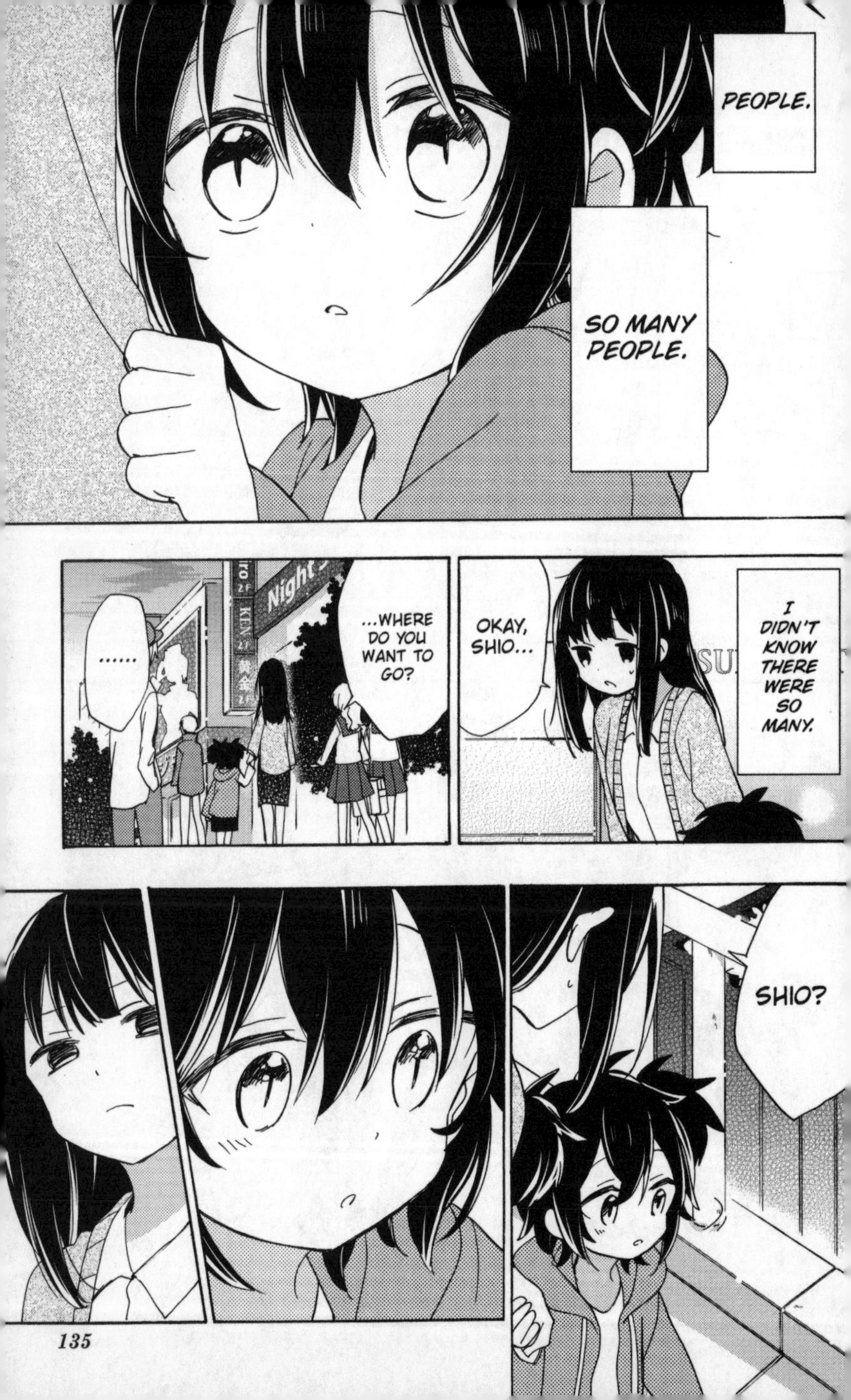
PEOPLE.
SO MANY PEOPLE.
I DIDN'T KNOW THERE WERE SO MANY.
OKAY, SHIO...
...WHERE DO YOU WANT TO GO?
......
SHIO?

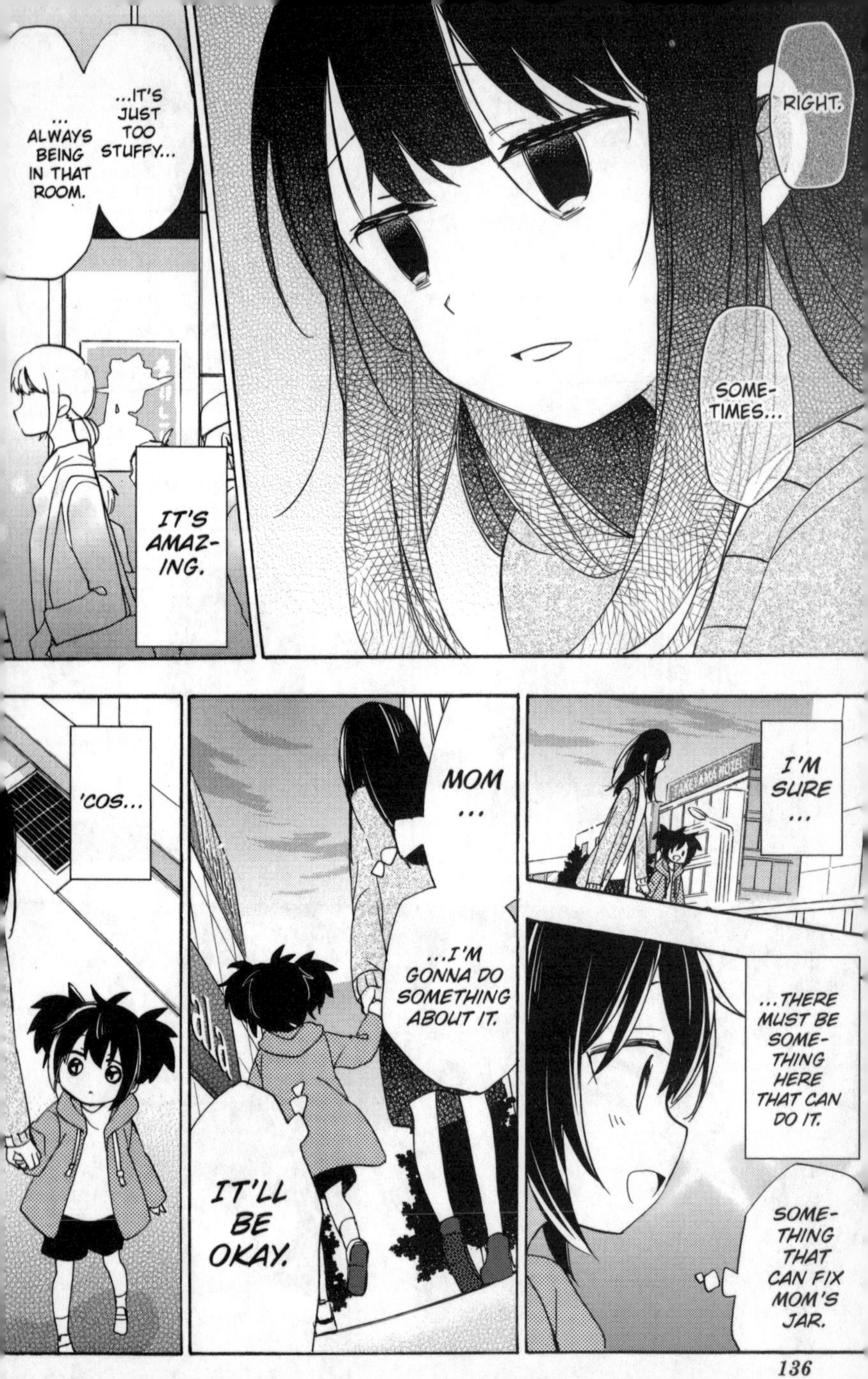
RIGHT.
SOME-TIMES...
...IT'S JUST TOO STUFFY...
...ALWAYS BEING IN THAT ROOM.
IT'S AMAZ-ING.
I'M SURE...
...THERE MUST BE SOME-THING HERE THAT CAN DO IT.
SOME-THING THAT CAN FIX MOM'S JAR.
MOM...
...I'M GONNA DO SOMETHING ABOUT IT.
IT'LL BE OKAY.
'COS...

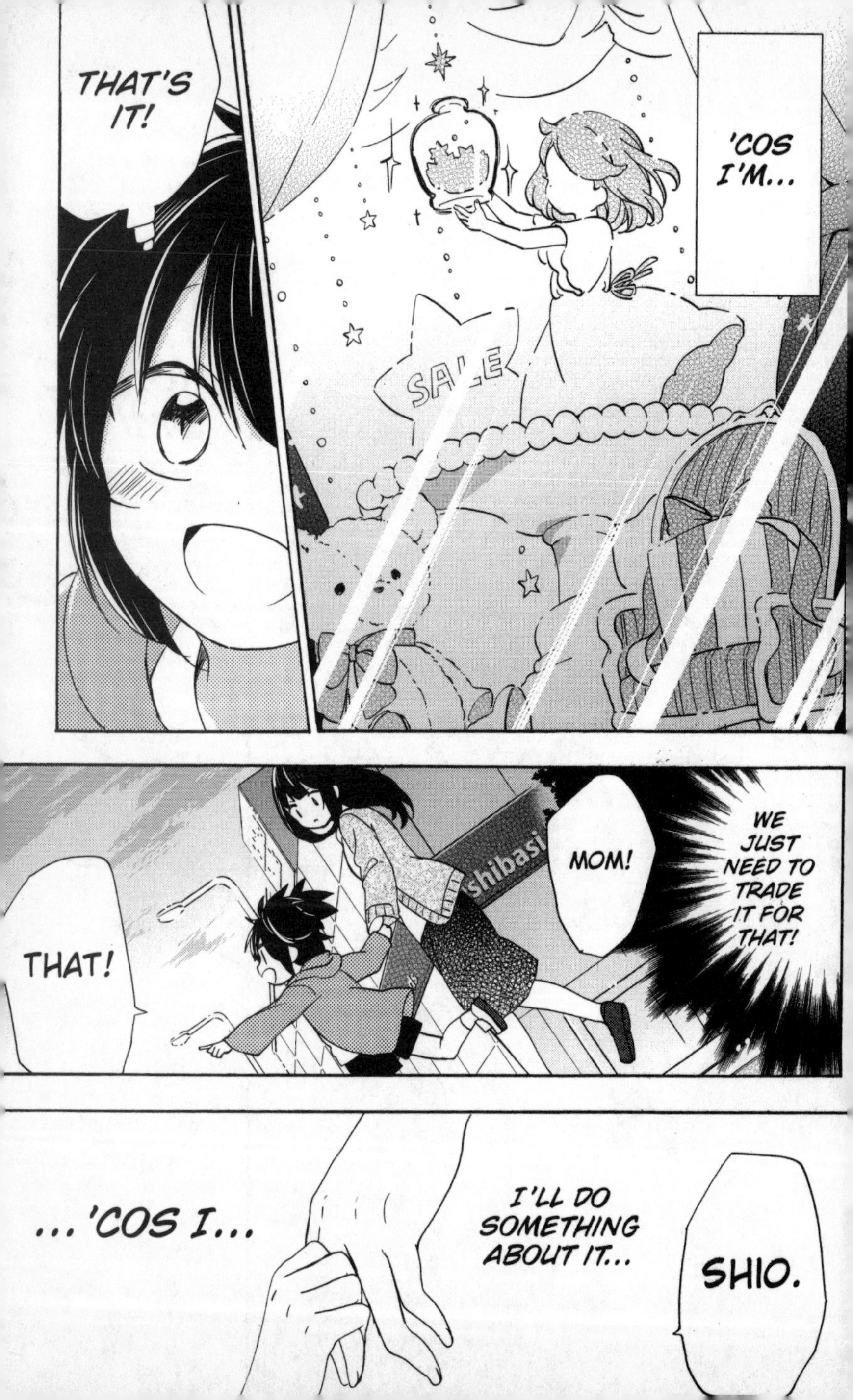
'COS I'M...
SALE
THAT'S IT!
WE JUST NEED TO TRADE IT FOR THAT!
MOM!
shibasi
THAT!
SHIO.
I'LL DO SOMETHING ABOUT IT...
...'COS I...

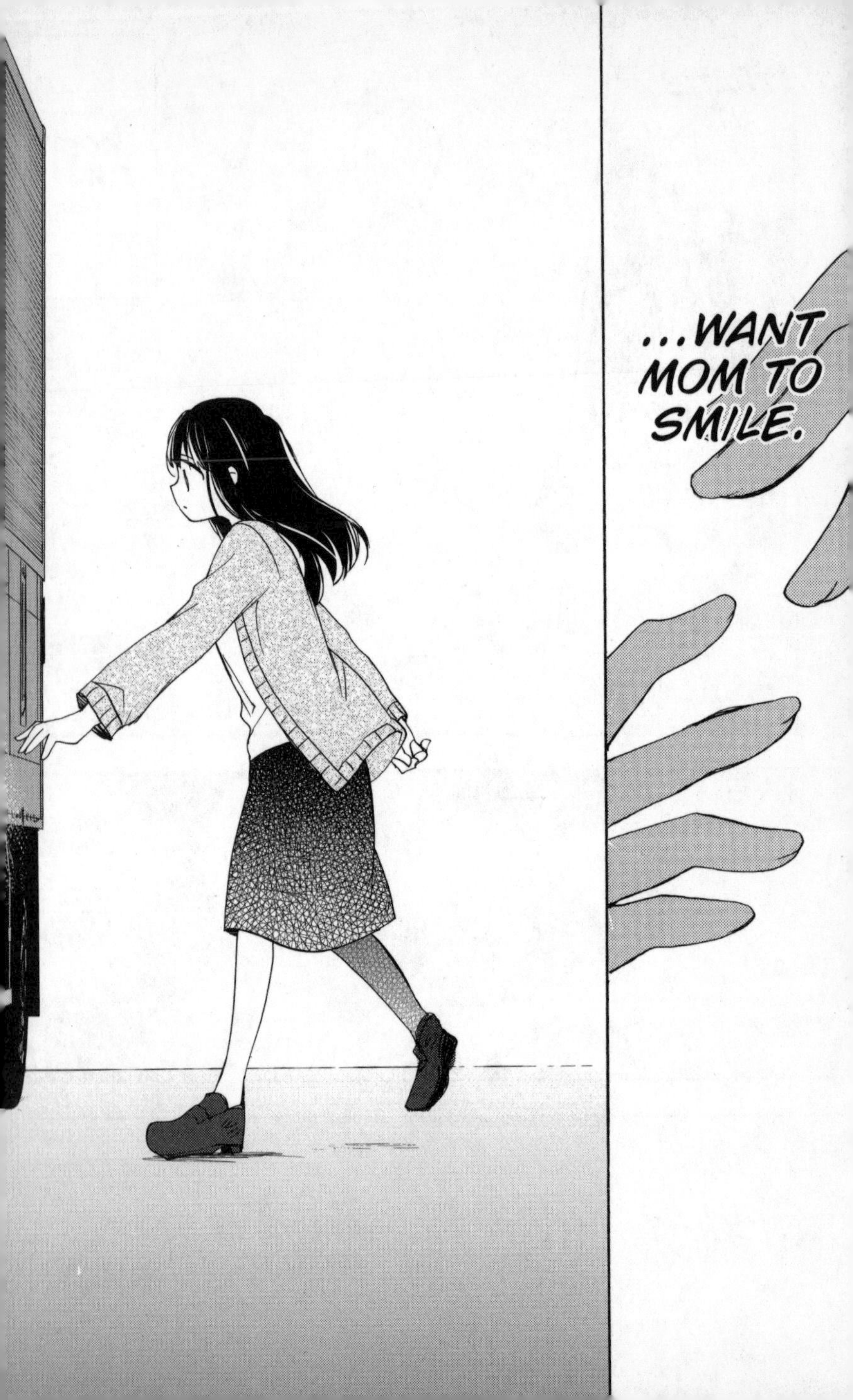
...WANT MOM TO SMILE.

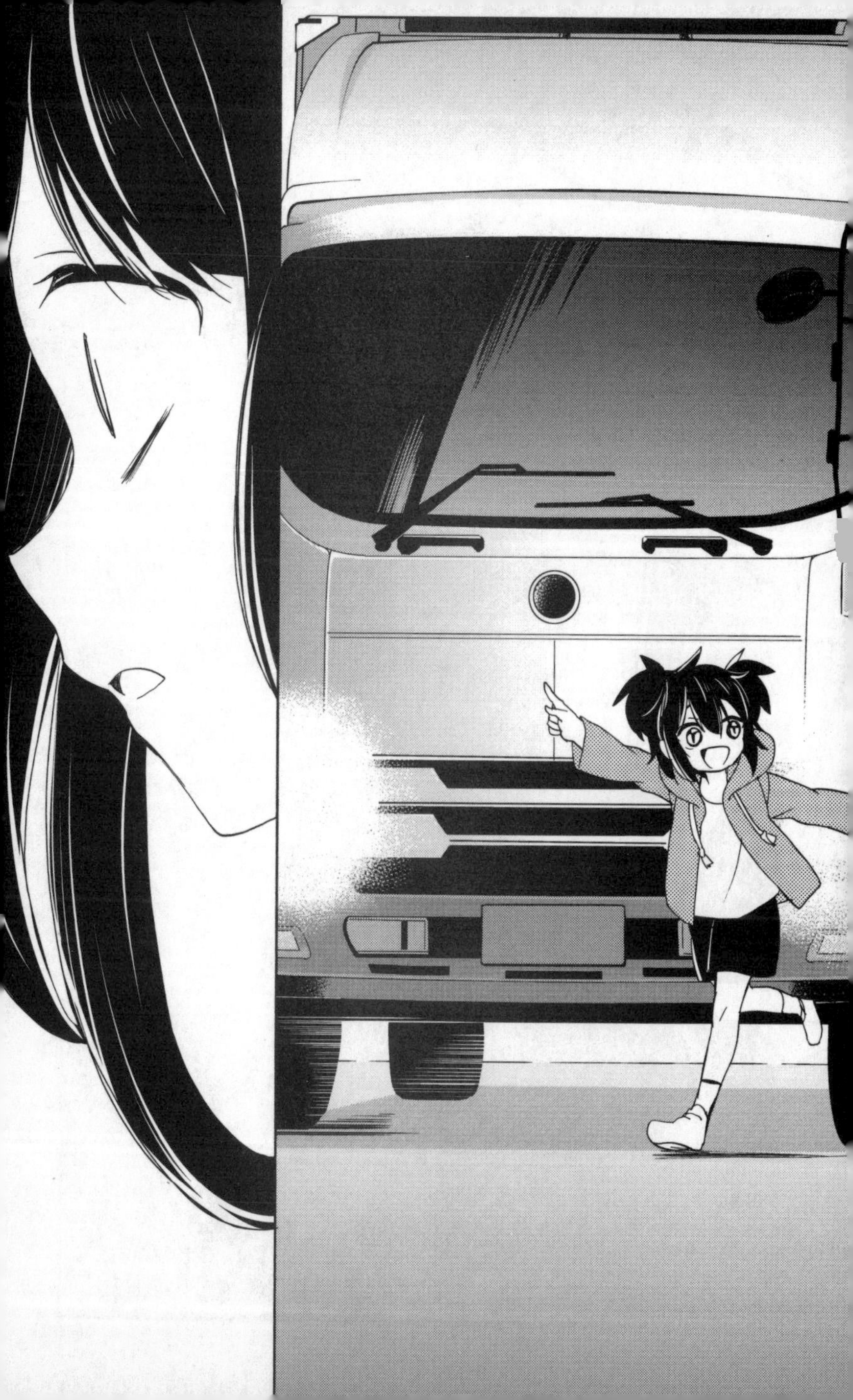

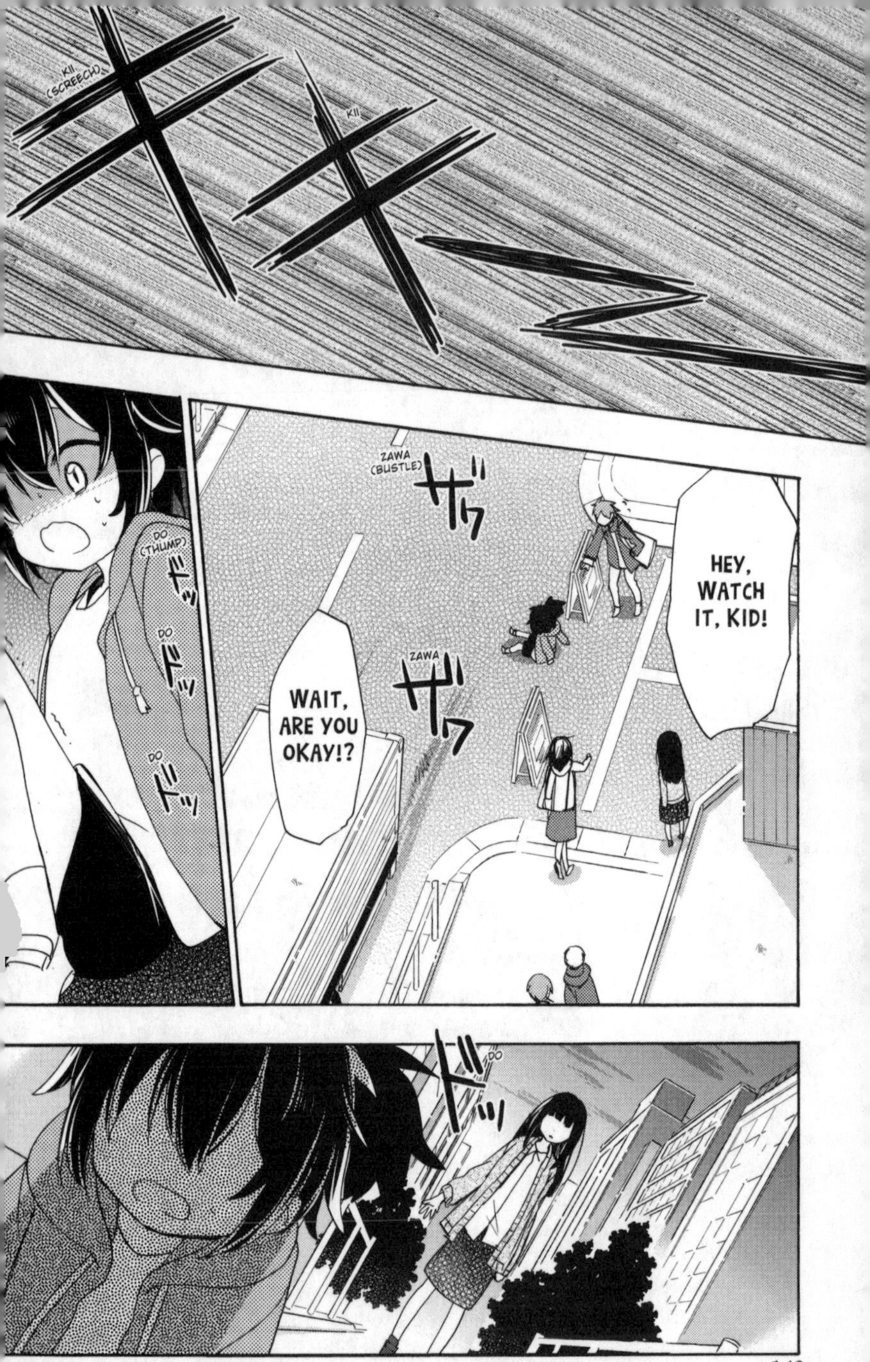
KII (SCREECH)
KII
HEY, WATCH IT, KID!
ZAWA (BUSTLE)
ZAWA
WAIT, ARE YOU OKAY!?
DO (THUMP)
DO
DO
DO

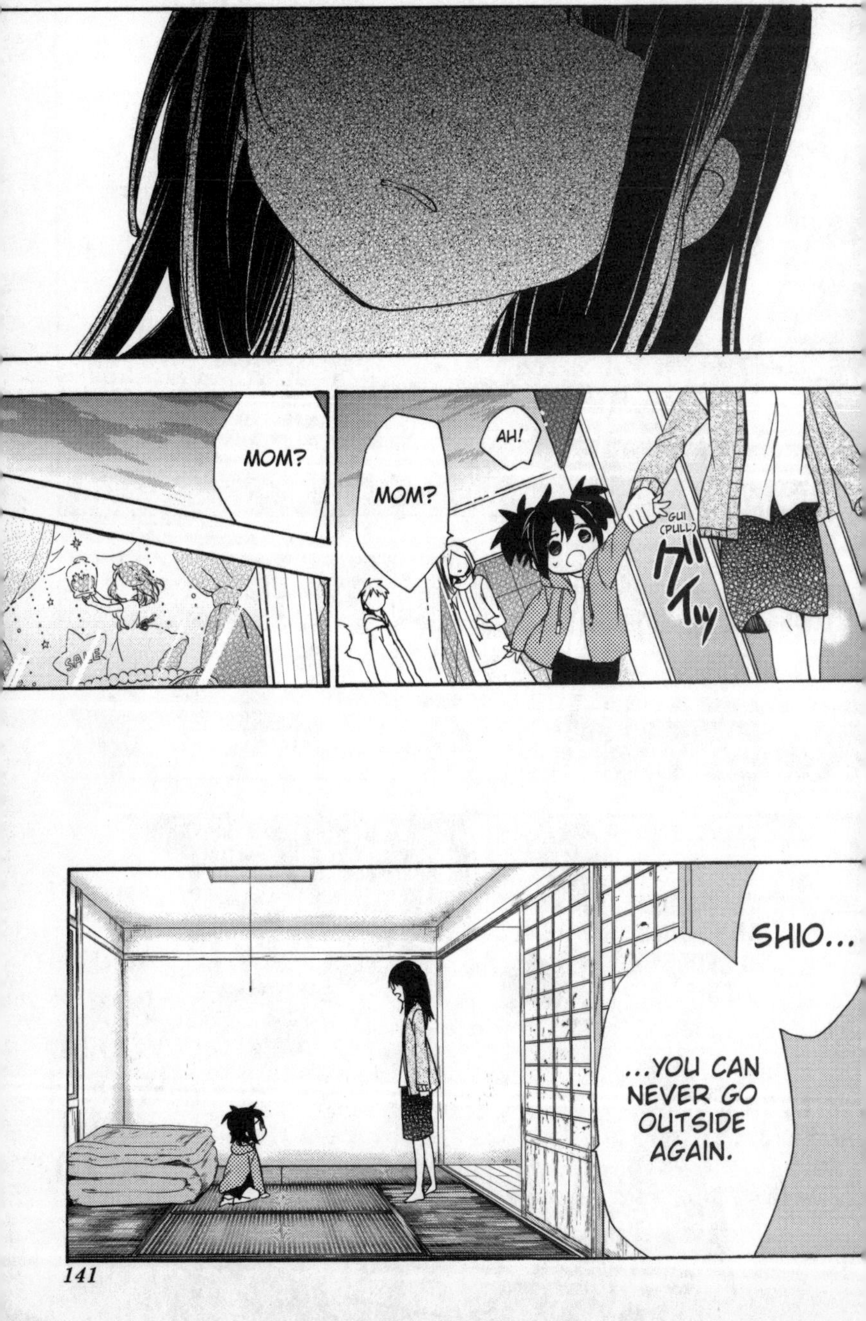
AH!
MOM?
GUI (PULL)
グイッ
MOM?
SHIO...
...YOU CAN NEVER GO OUTSIDE AGAIN.

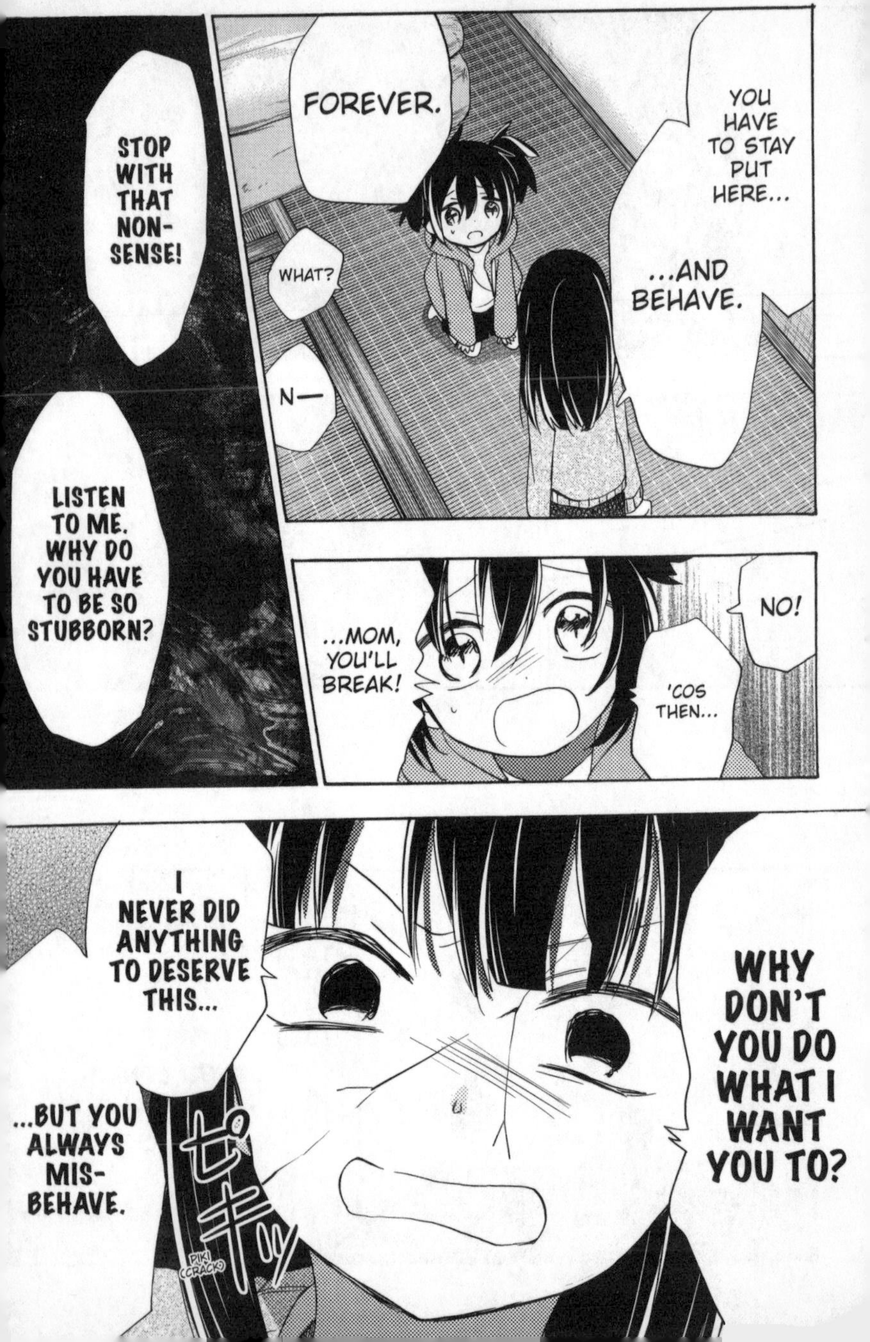
YOU HAVE TO STAY PUT HERE...
FOREVER.
...AND BEHAVE.
WHAT?
N—
NO!
'COS THEN...
...MOM, YOU'LL BREAK!
STOP WITH THAT NON-SENSE!
LISTEN TO ME. WHY DO YOU HAVE TO BE SO STUBBORN?
WHY DON'T YOU DO WHAT I WANT YOU TO?
I NEVER DID ANYTHING TO DESERVE THIS...
...BUT YOU ALWAYS MIS-BEHAVE.
PIKI (CRACK)

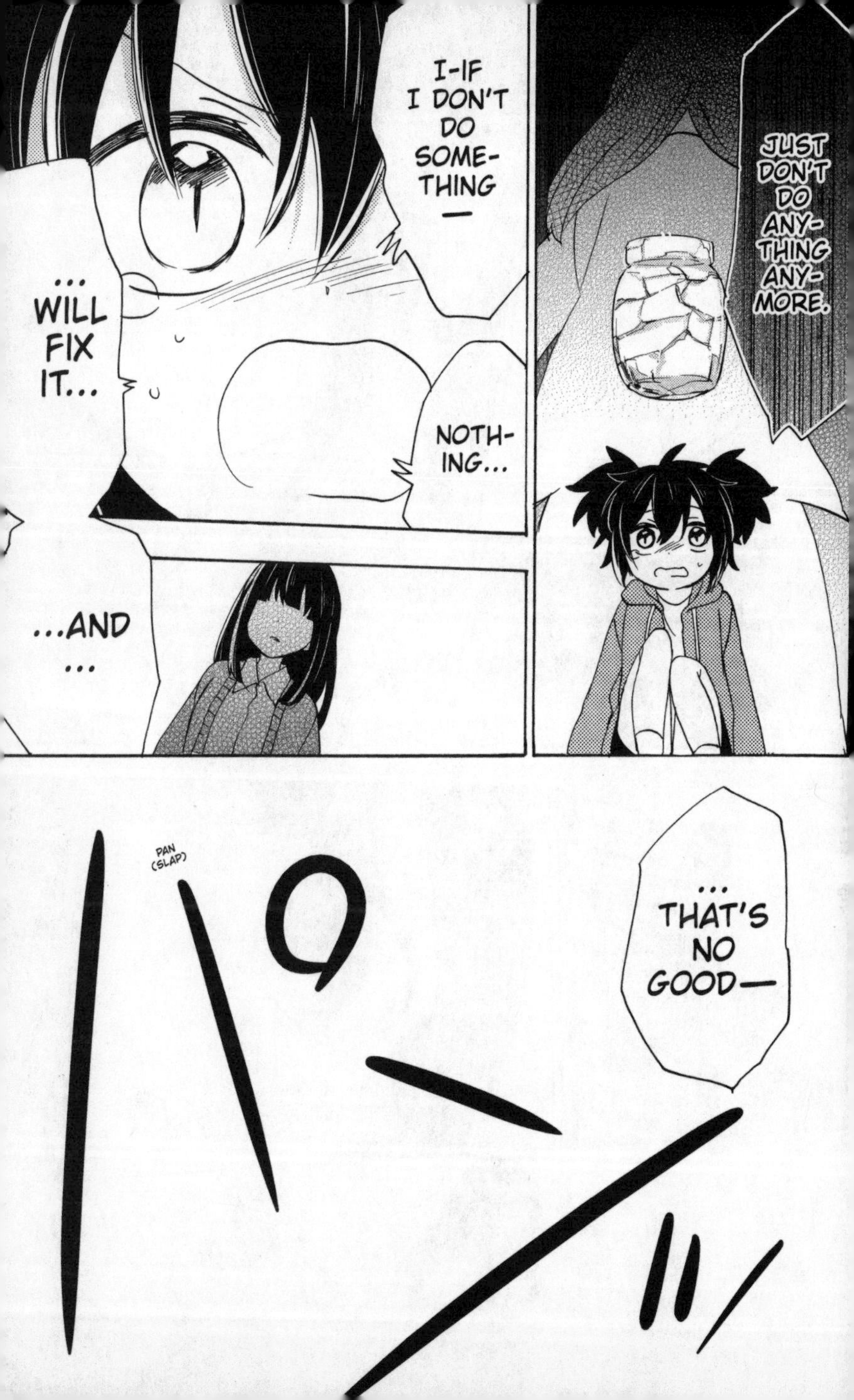
JUST DON'T DO ANYTHING ANYMORE.
I-IF I DON'T DO SOMETHING—
NOTHING...
...WILL FIX IT...
...AND ...
...THAT'S NO GOOD—
PAN (SLAP)

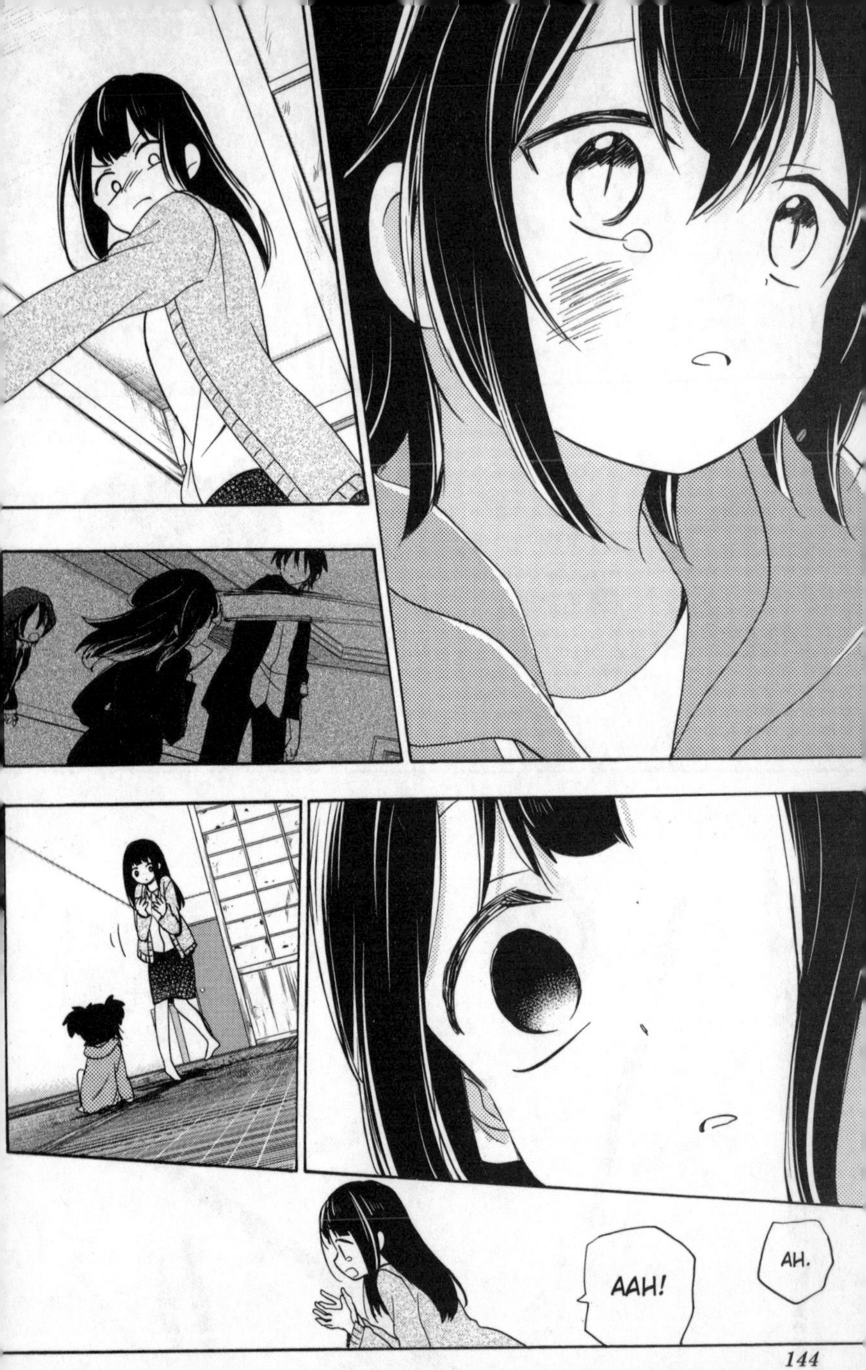
AH.
AAH!

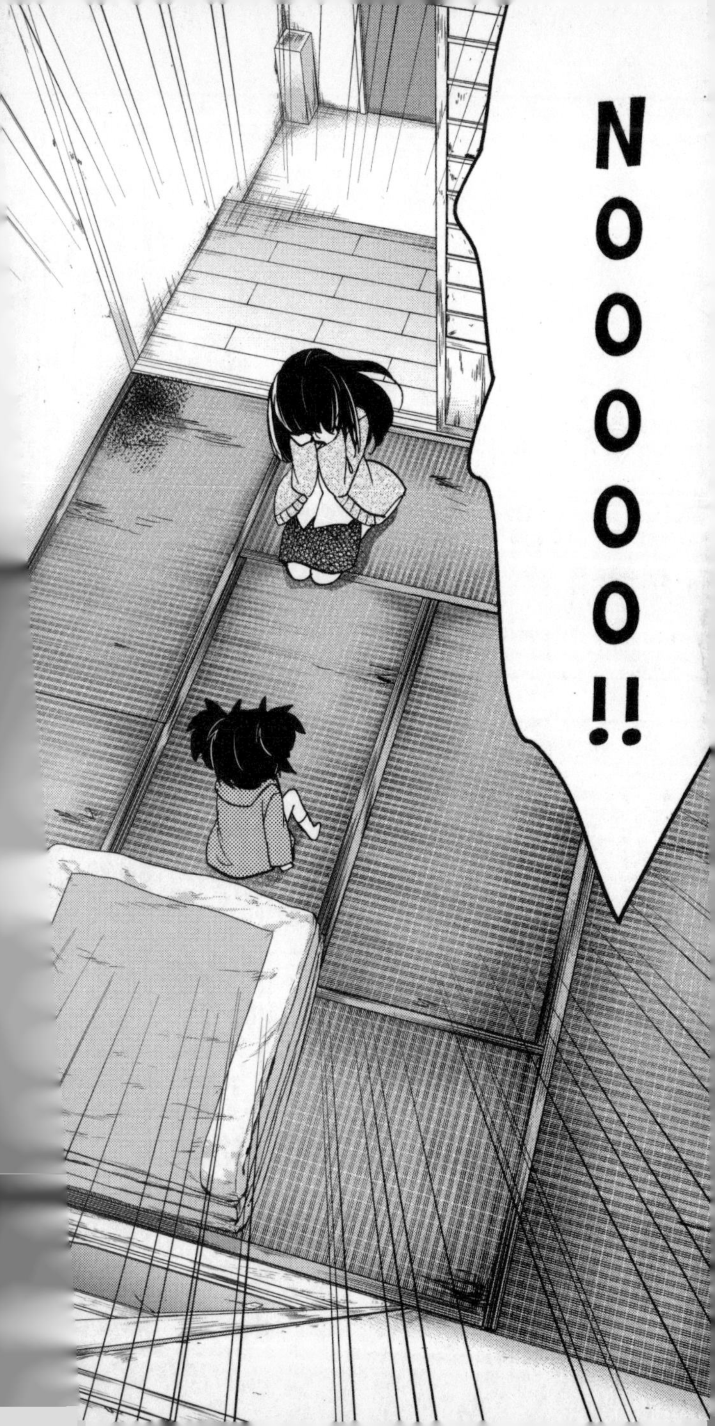
NOOOOO!!

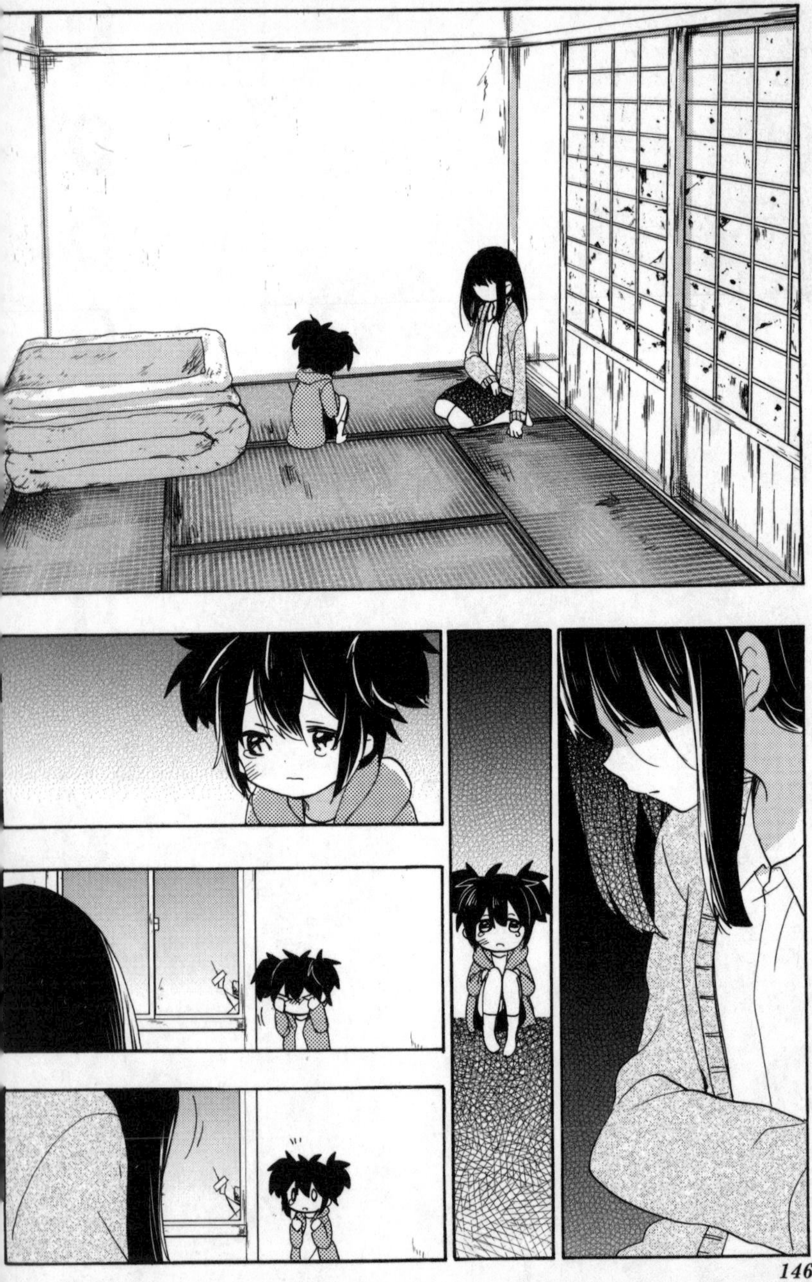

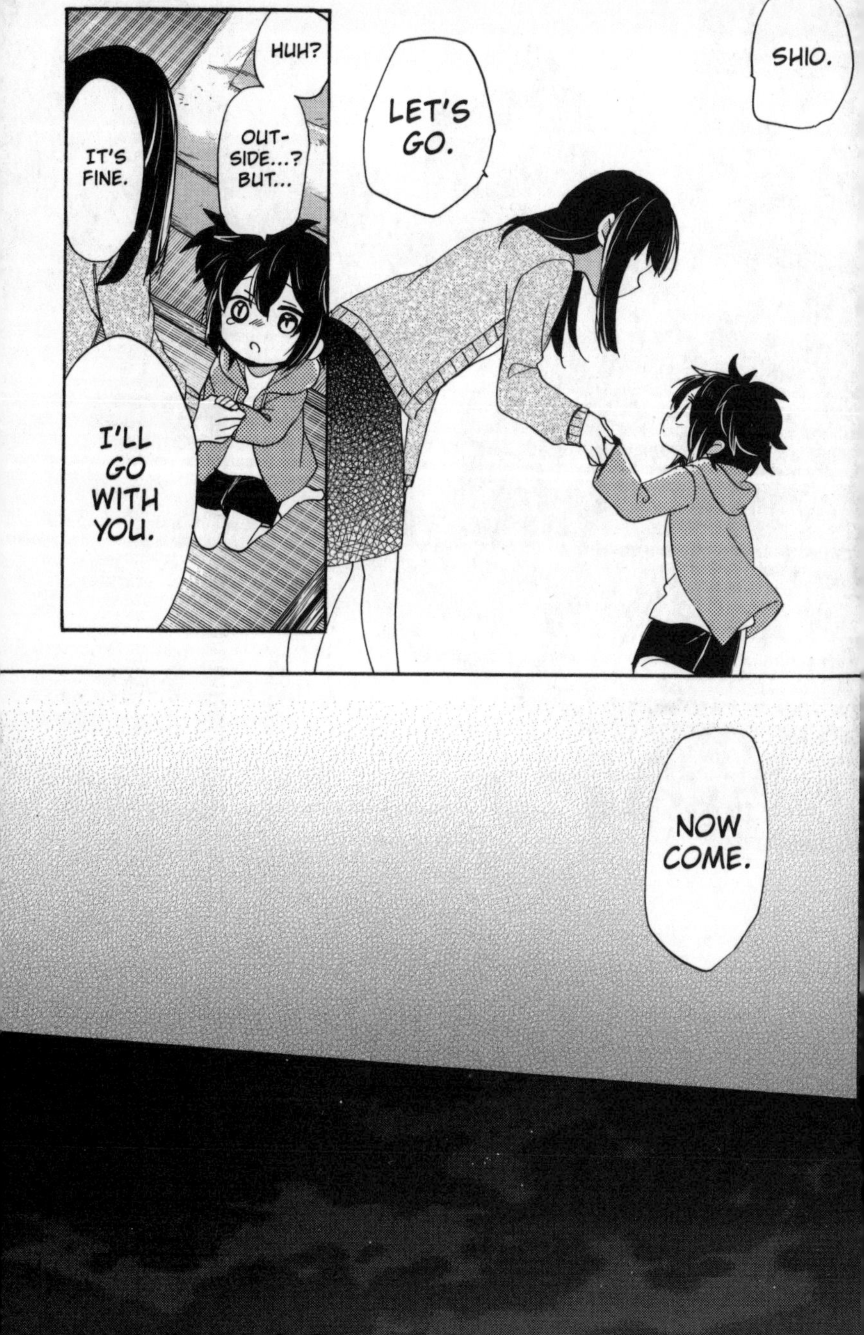
SHIO.
LET'S GO.
HUH?
OUT-SIDE...? BUT...
IT'S FINE.
I'LL GO WITH YOU.
NOW COME.

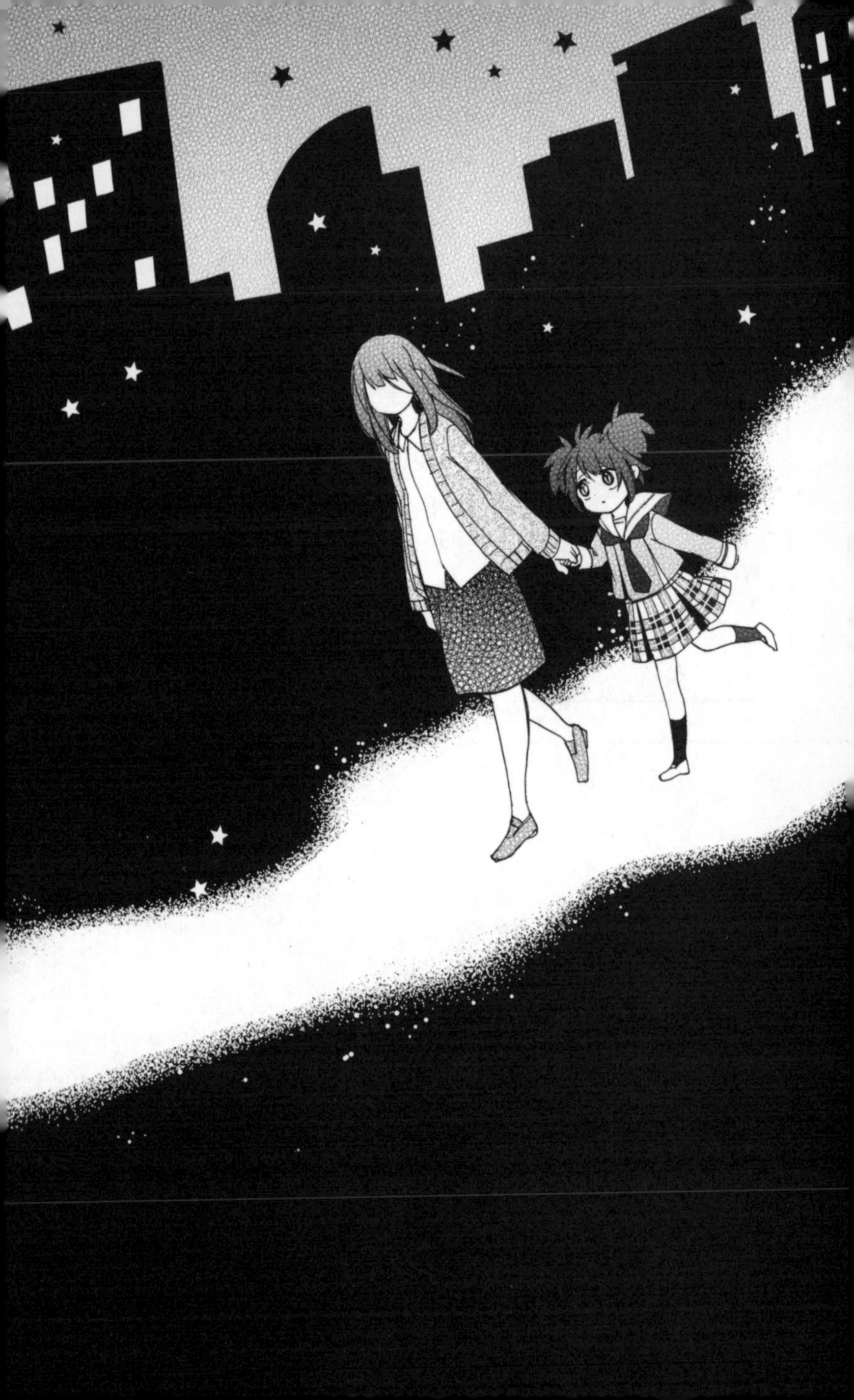

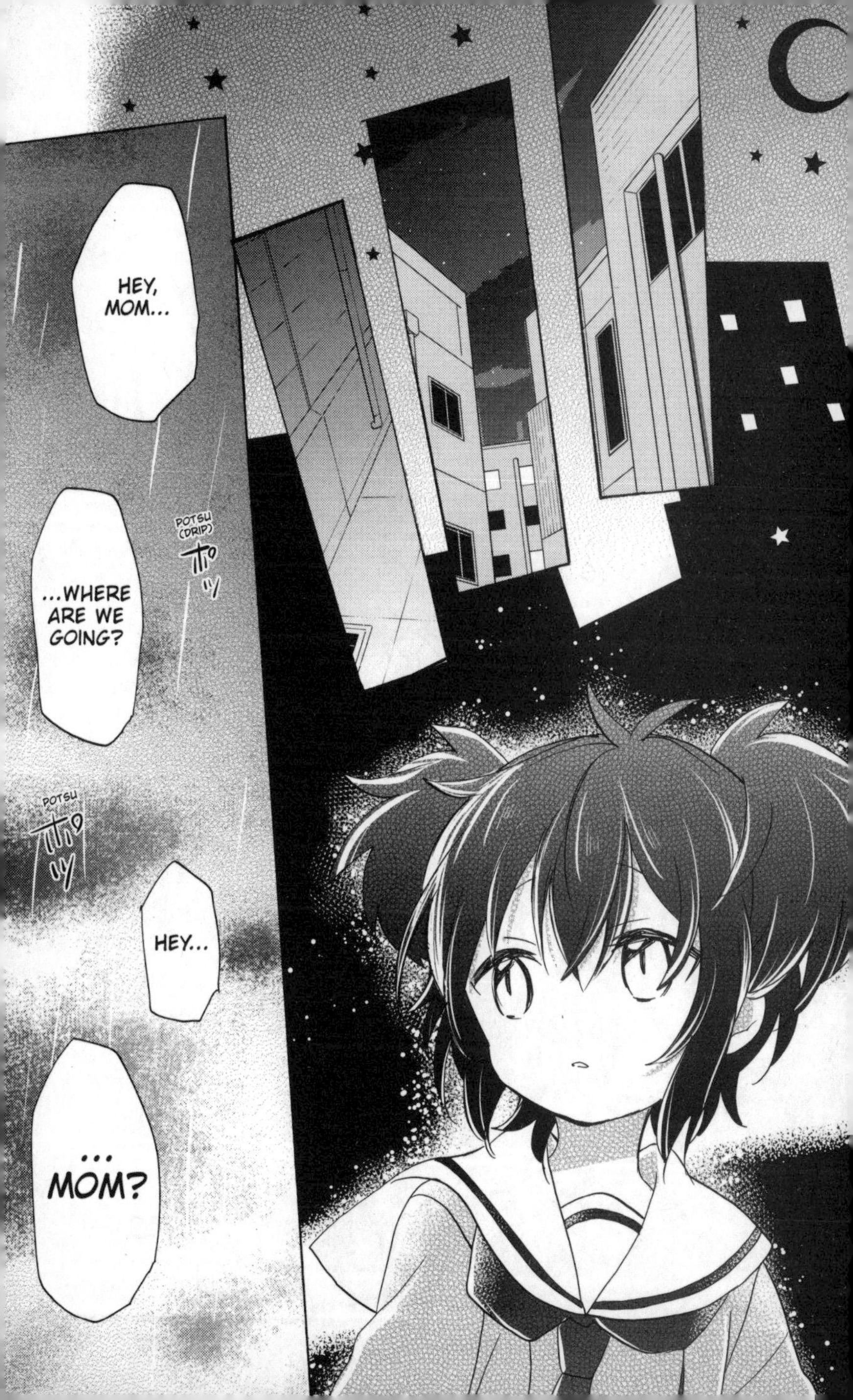
HEY, MOM...
POTSU (DRIP)
ポツ
...WHERE ARE WE GOING?
POTSU
ポツ
HEY...
... MOM?

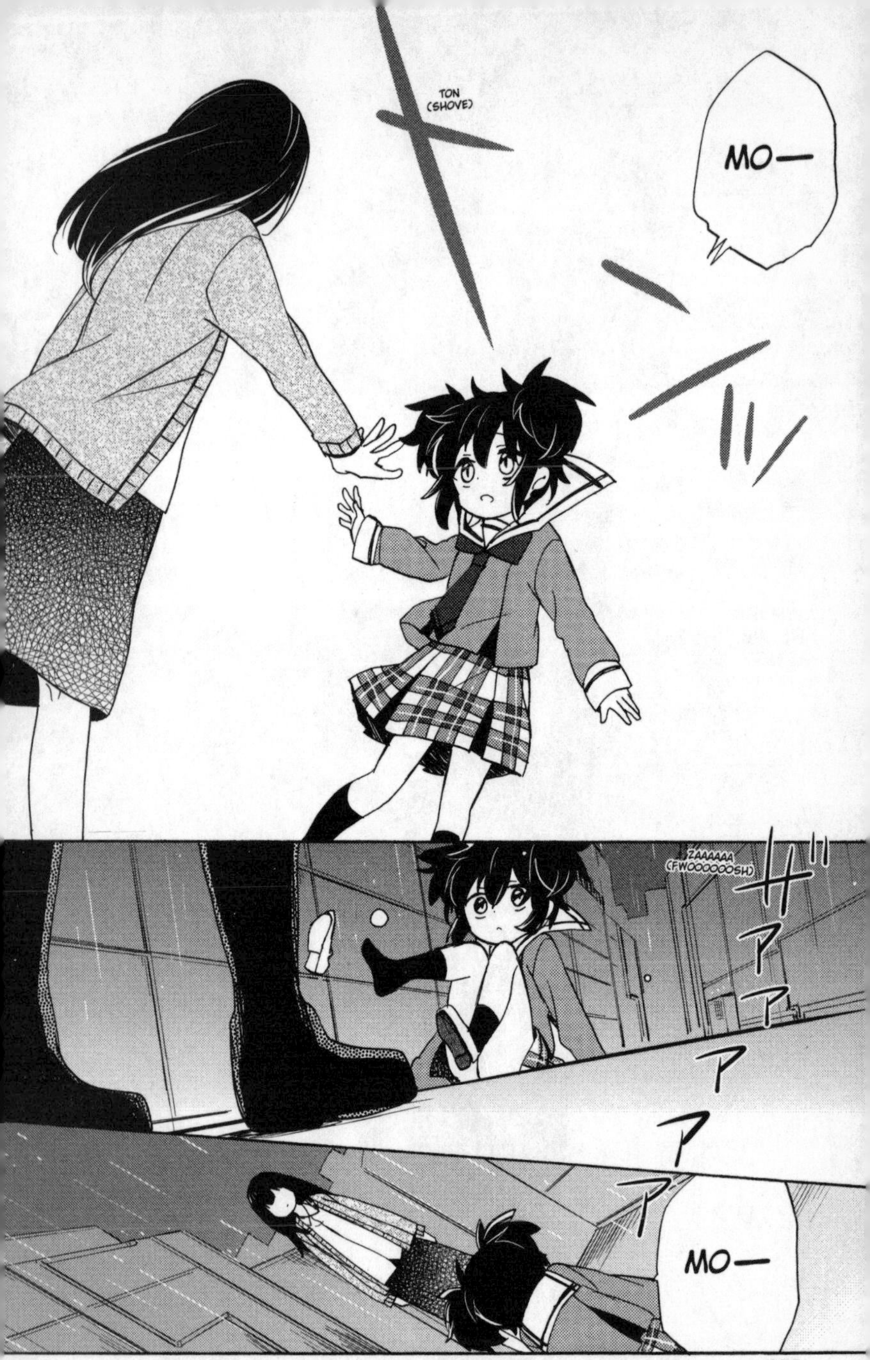
MO—
TON (SHOVE)
ZAAAAAA (FWOOOOOOSH)
ザァァァァ
MO—

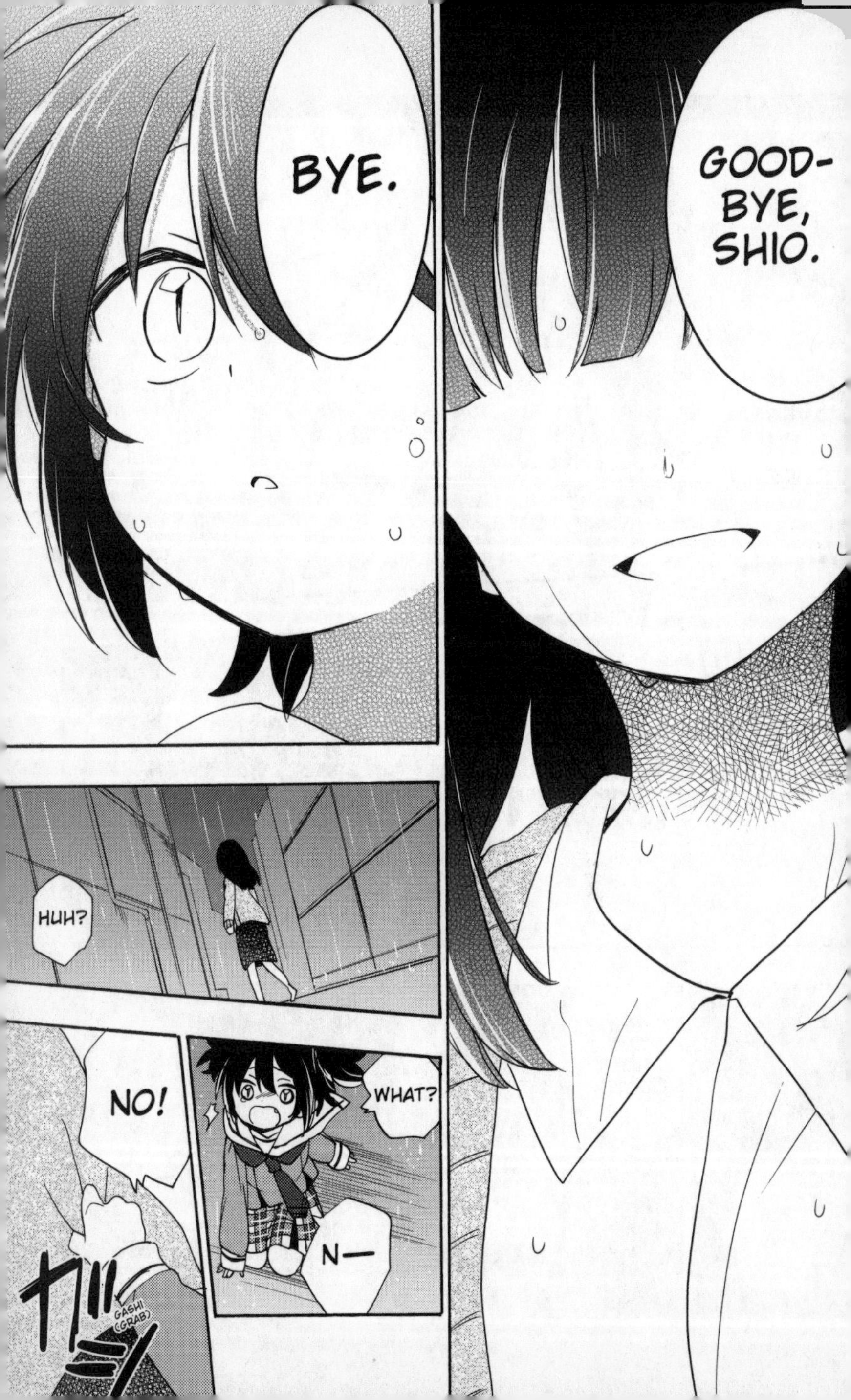
GOOD-BYE, SHIO.
BYE.
HUH?
WHAT?
N—
NO!
GASHI (GRAB)

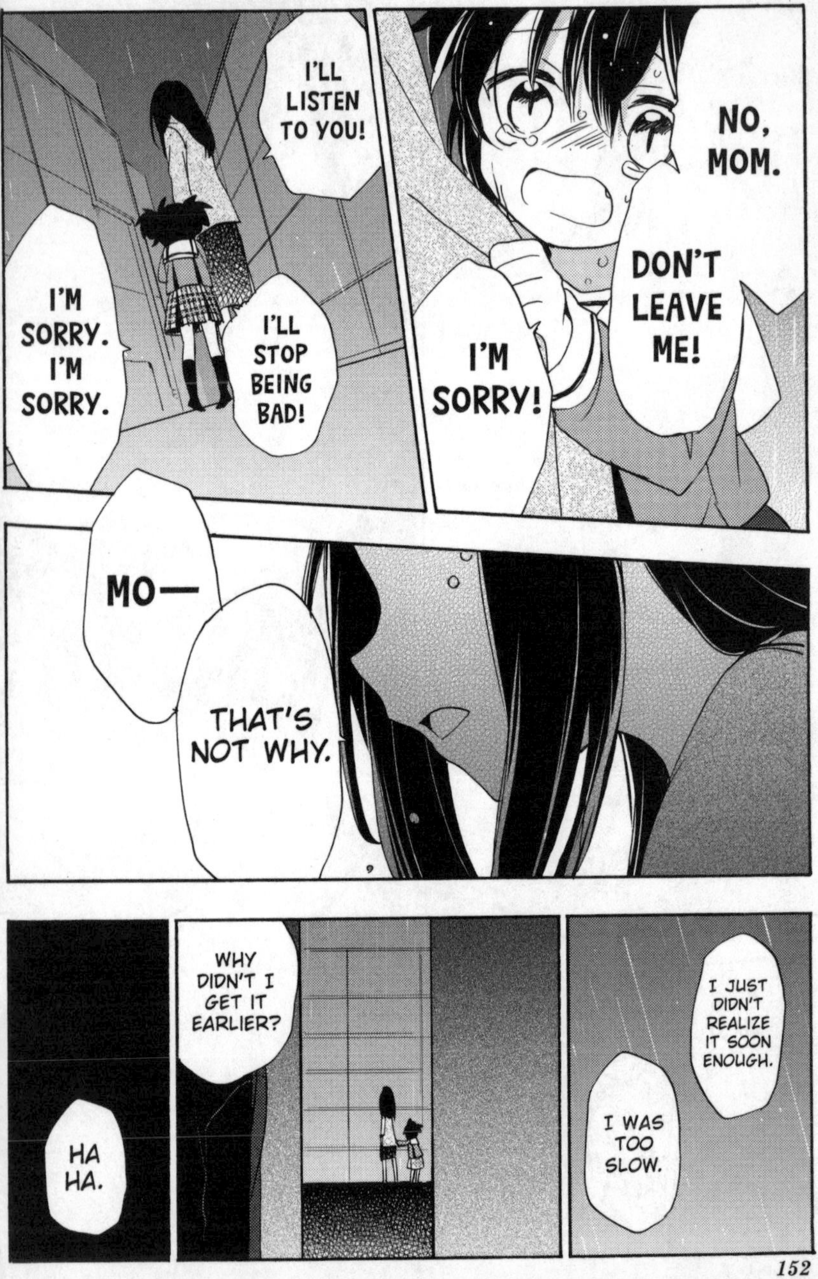
NO, MOM.
DON'T LEAVE ME!
I'M SORRY!
I'LL LISTEN TO YOU!
I'LL STOP BEING BAD!
I'M SORRY. I'M SORRY.
MO—
THAT'S NOT WHY.
I JUST DIDN'T REALIZE IT SOON ENOUGH.
I WAS TOO SLOW.
WHY DIDN'T I GET IT EARLIER?
HA HA.

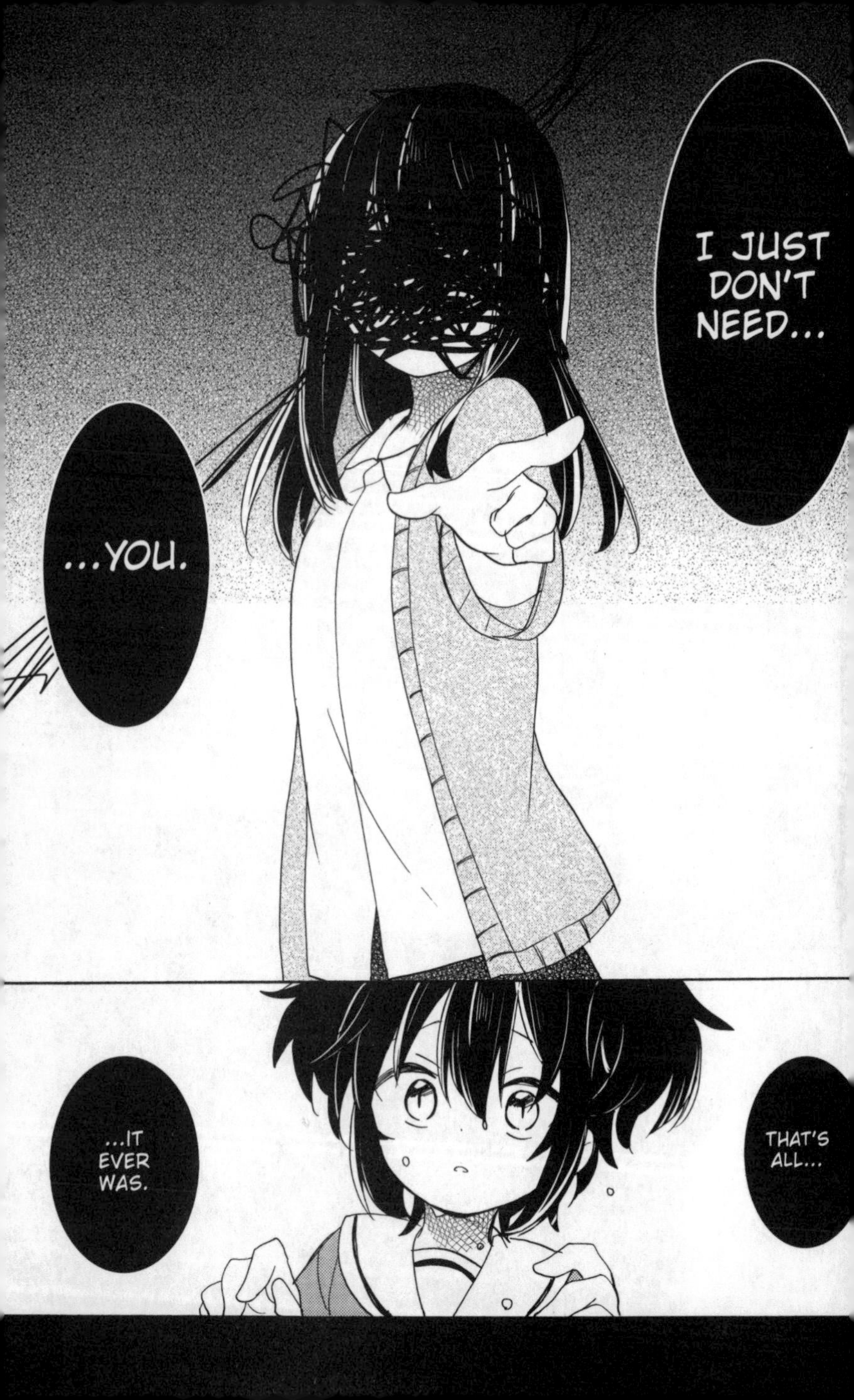
I JUST DON'T NEED...
...YOU.
THAT'S ALL...
...IT EVER WAS.

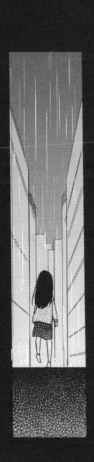

SO...

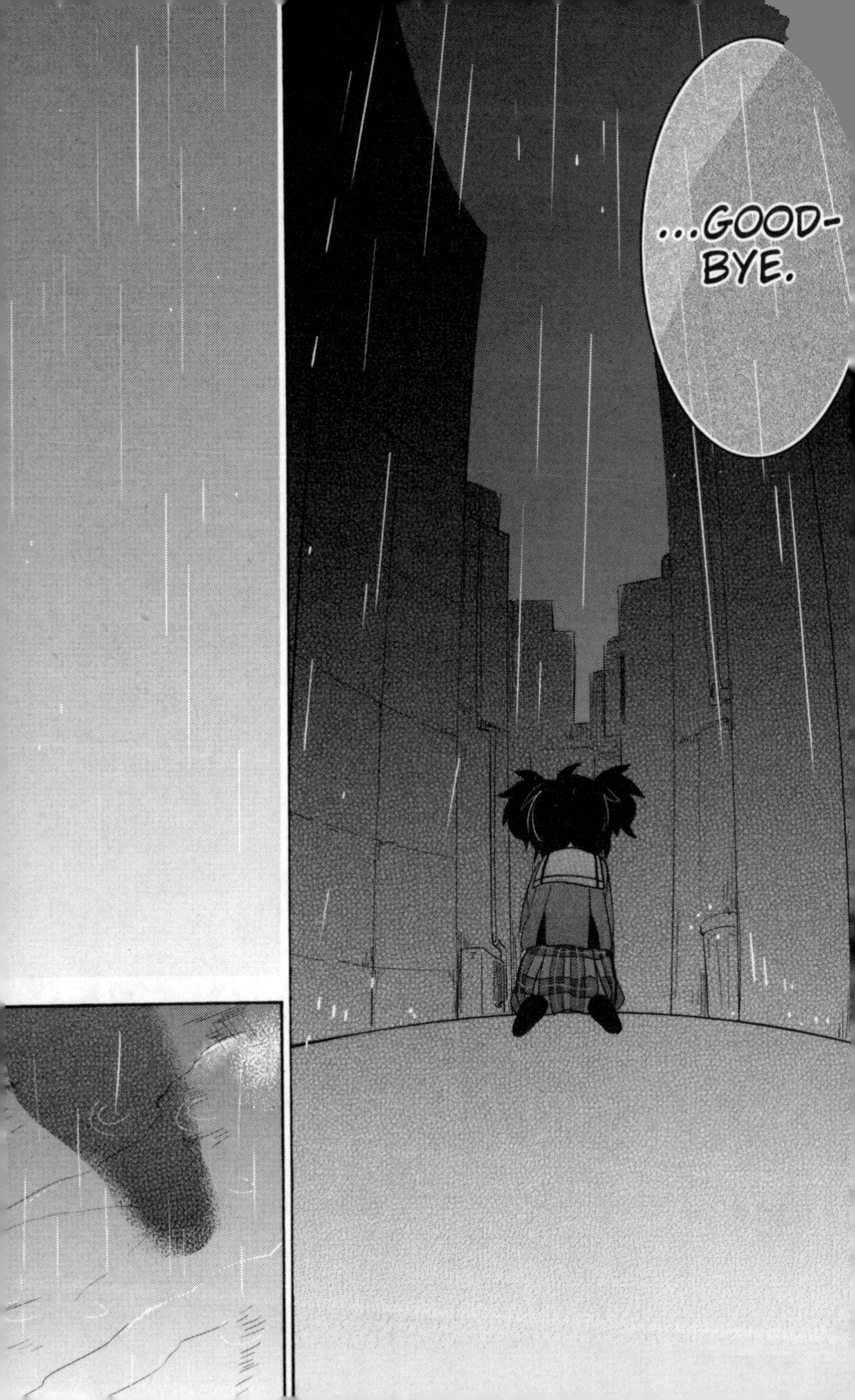
...GOOD-BYE.

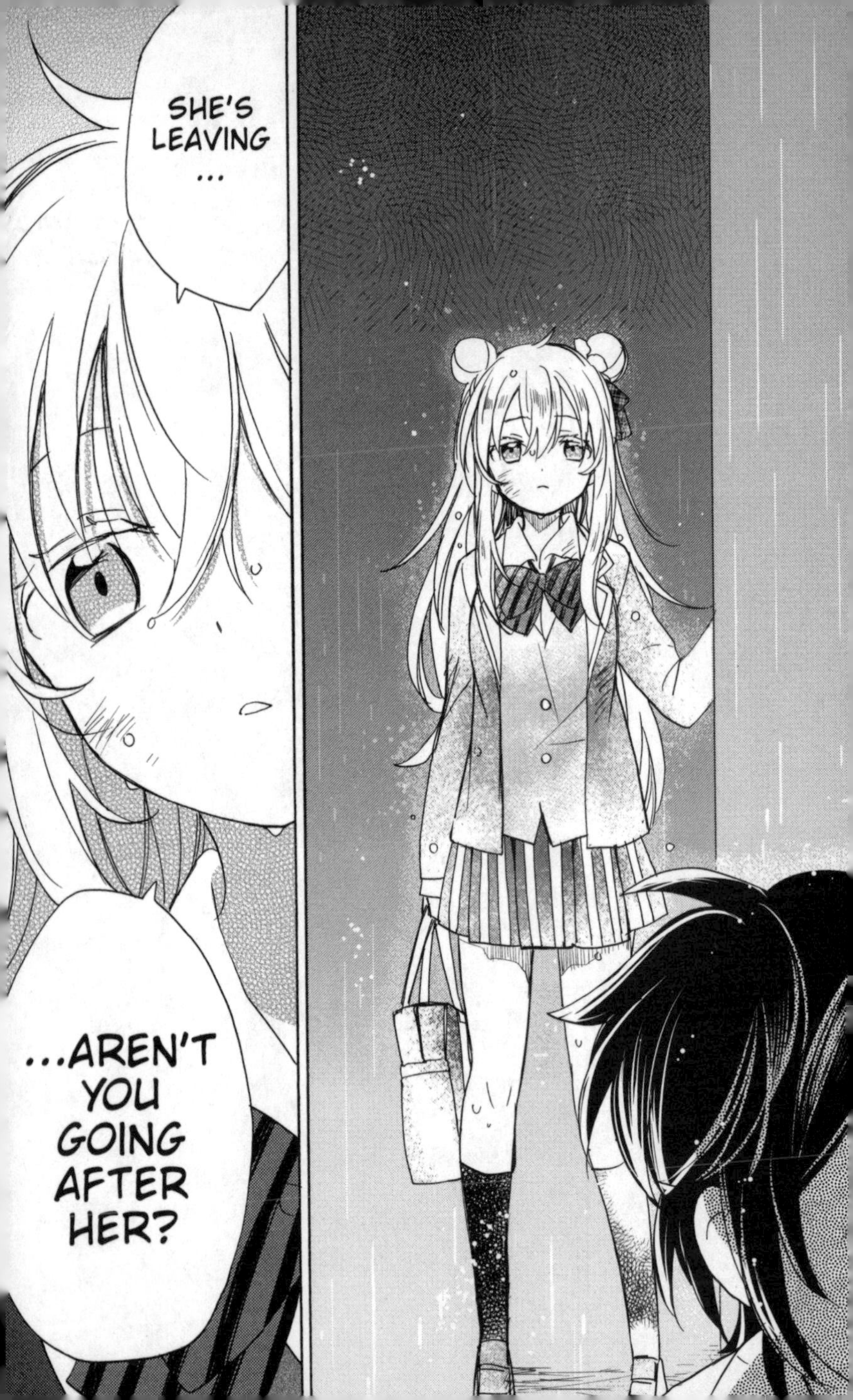
SHE'S LEAVING ...
...AREN'T YOU GOING AFTER HER?

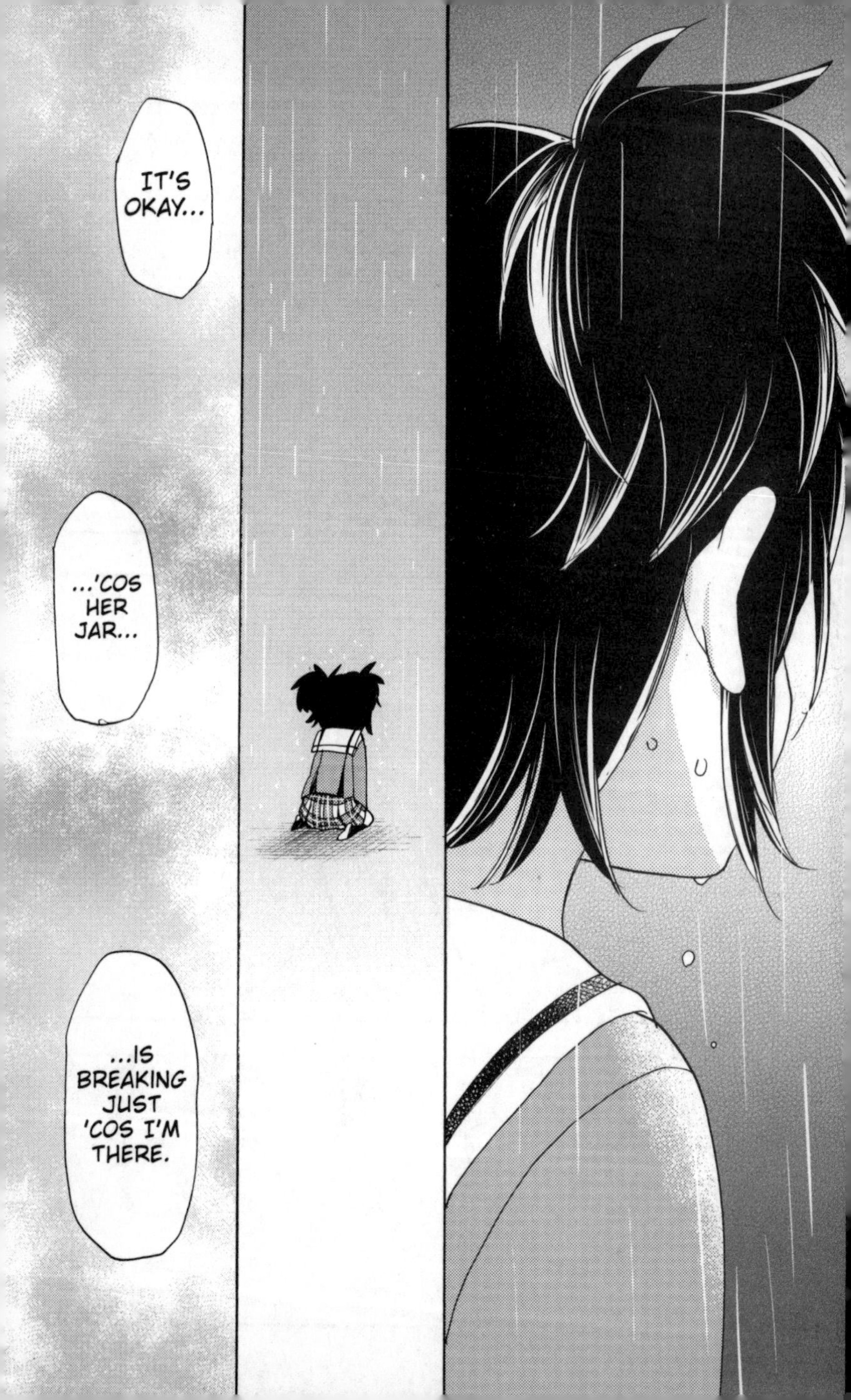
IT'S OKAY...
...'COS HER JAR...
...IS BREAKING JUST 'COS I'M THERE.

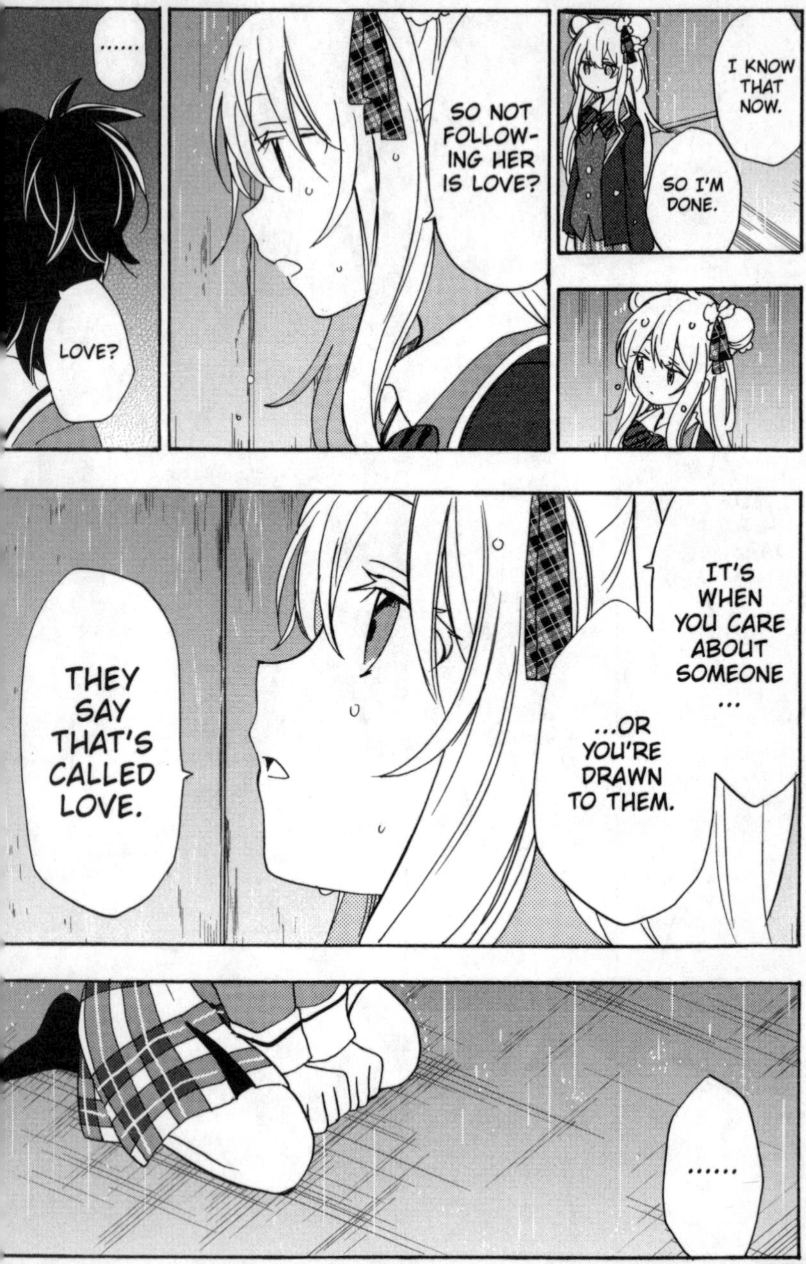
I KNOW THAT NOW.
SO I'M DONE.
SO NOT FOLLOWING HER IS LOVE?
......
LOVE?
IT'S WHEN YOU CARE ABOUT SOMEONE...
...OR YOU'RE DRAWN TO THEM.
THEY SAY THAT'S CALLED LOVE.
......

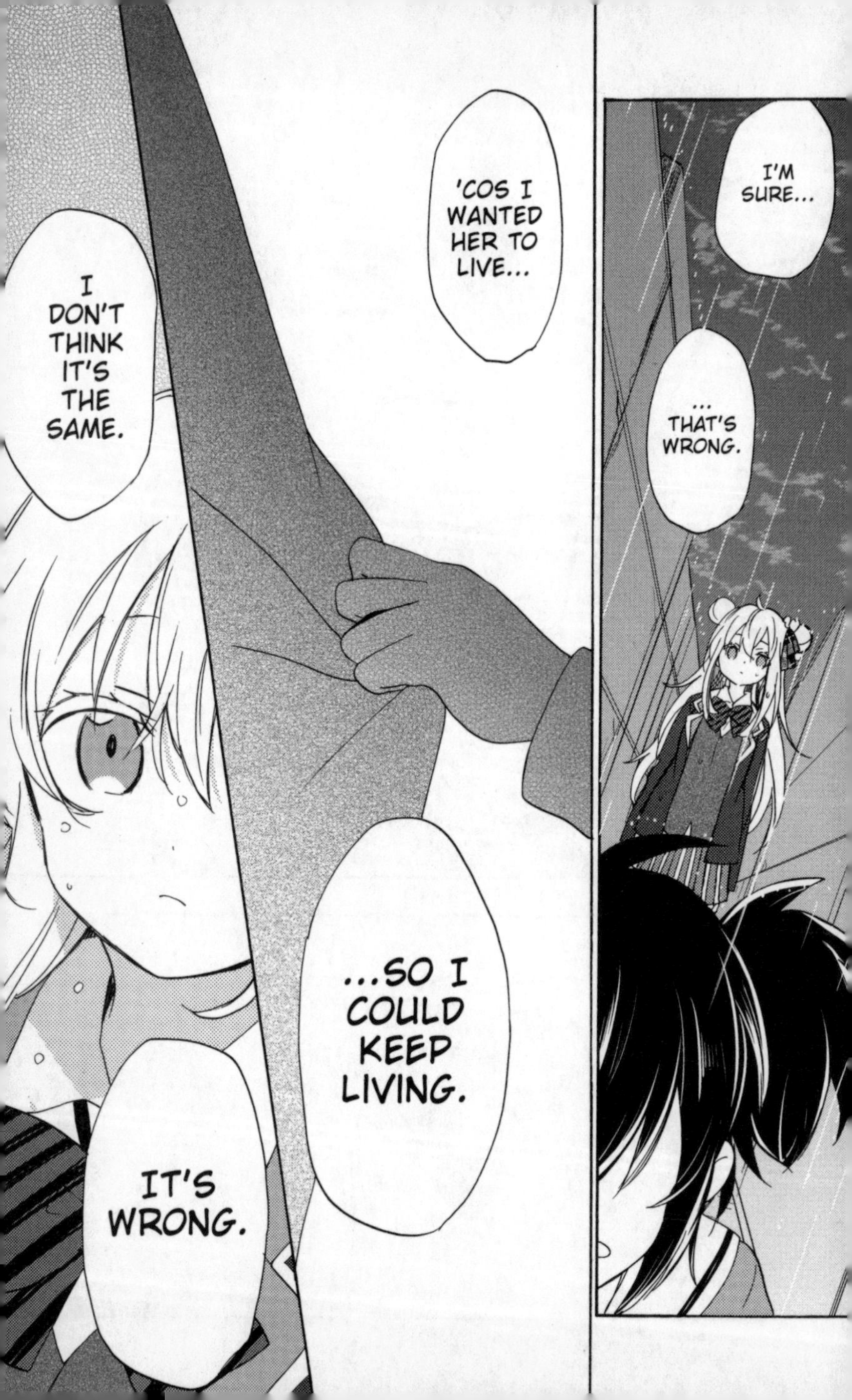
I'M SURE...
...THAT'S WRONG.
'COS I WANTED HER TO LIVE...
I DON'T THINK IT'S THE SAME.
...SO I COULD KEEP LIVING.
IT'S WRONG.

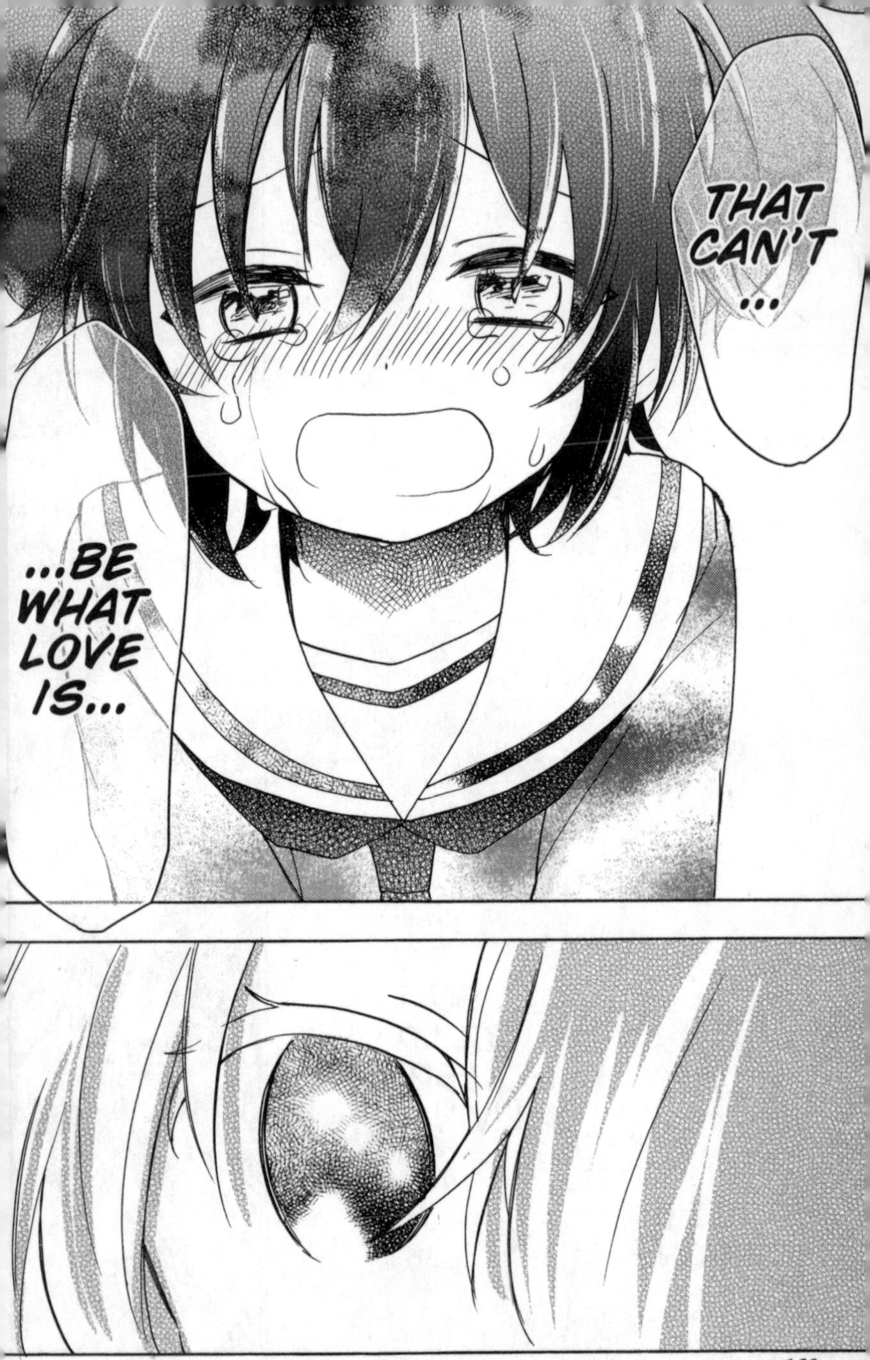
THAT CAN'T ...
...BE WHAT LOVE IS...

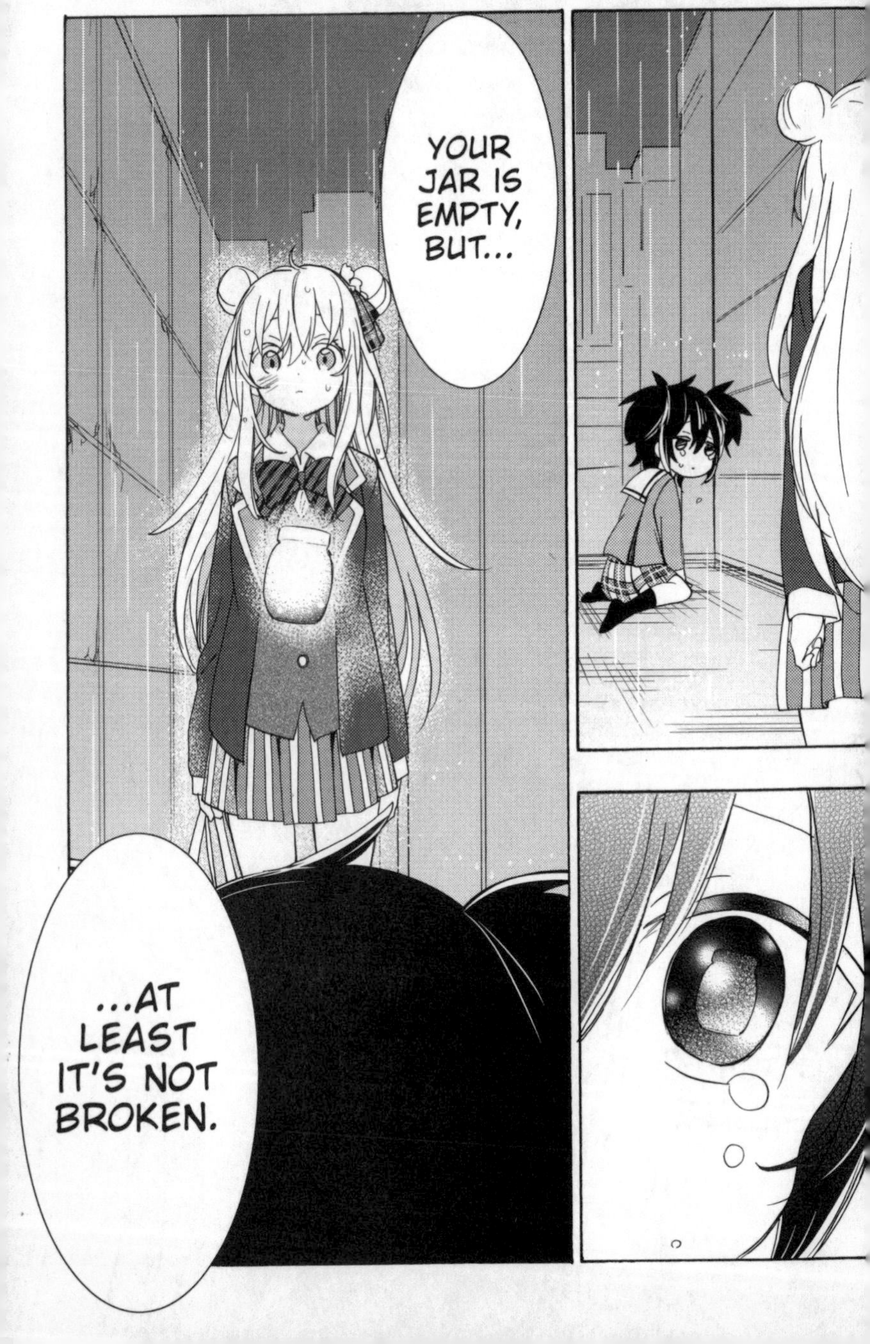
YOUR JAR IS EMPTY, BUT...
...AT LEAST IT'S NOT BROKEN.

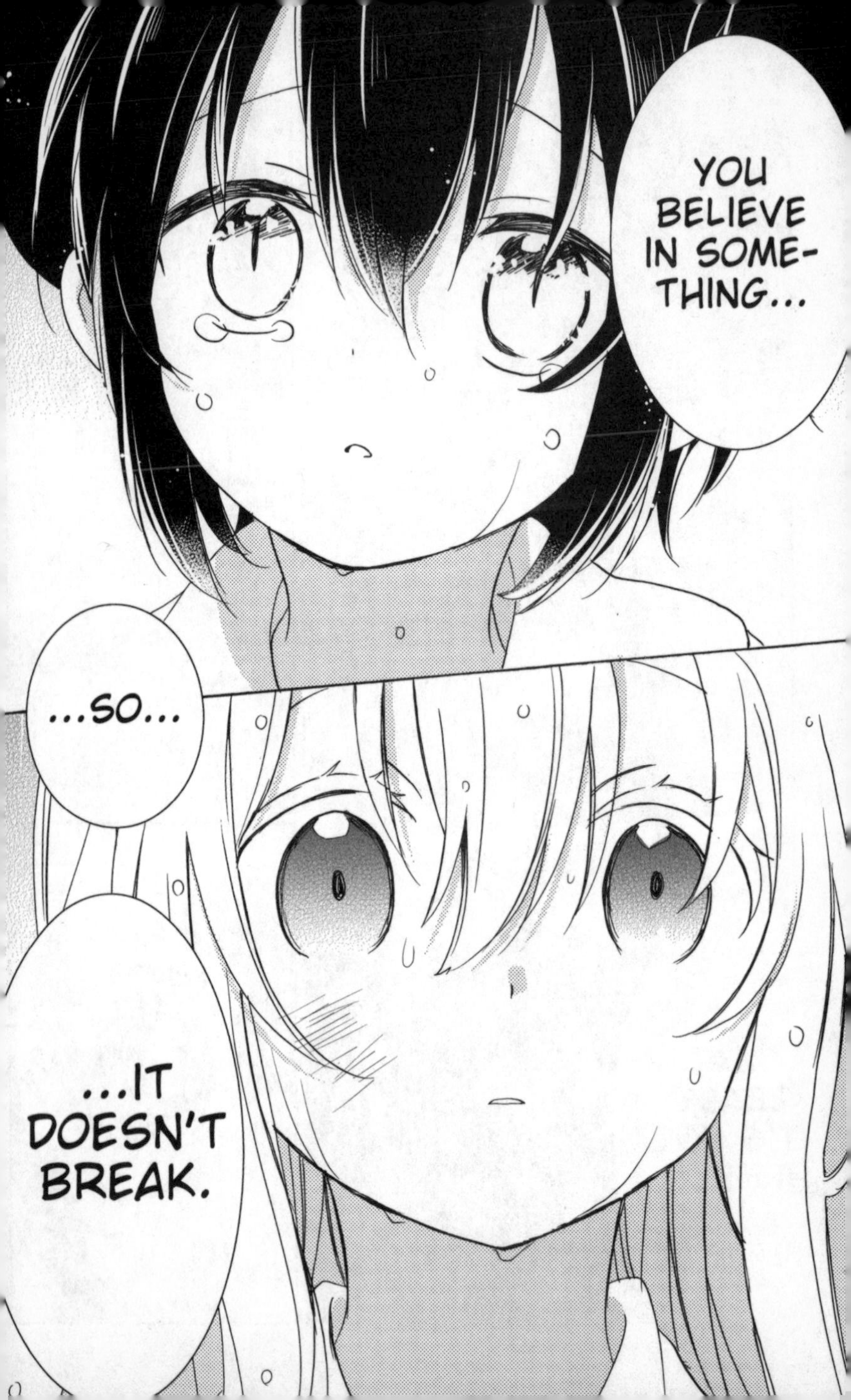
YOU BELIEVE IN SOME-THING...
...SO...
...IT DOESN'T BREAK.

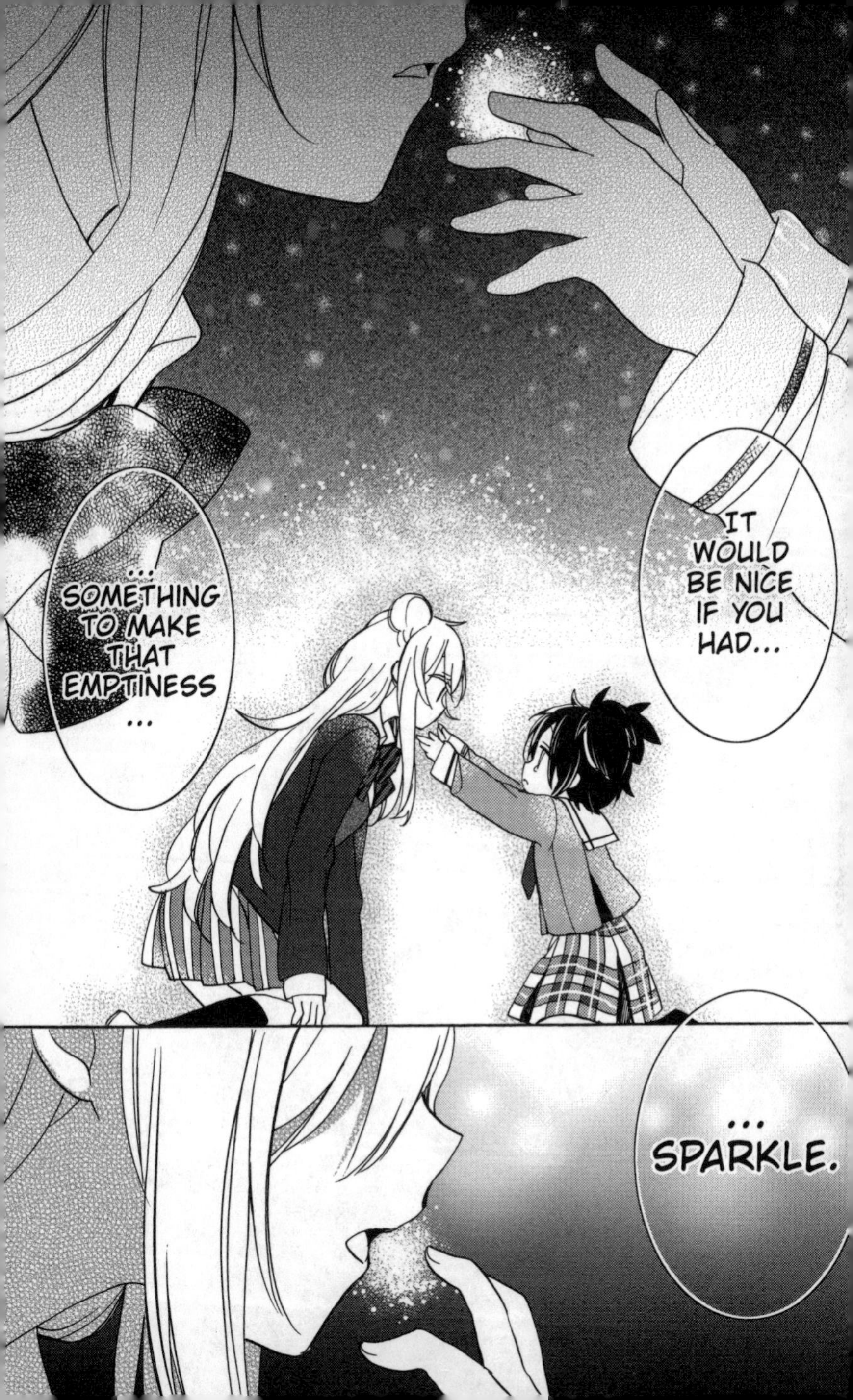
IT WOULD BE NICE IF YOU HAD...
...SOMETHING TO MAKE THAT EMPTINESS...
...SPARKLE.

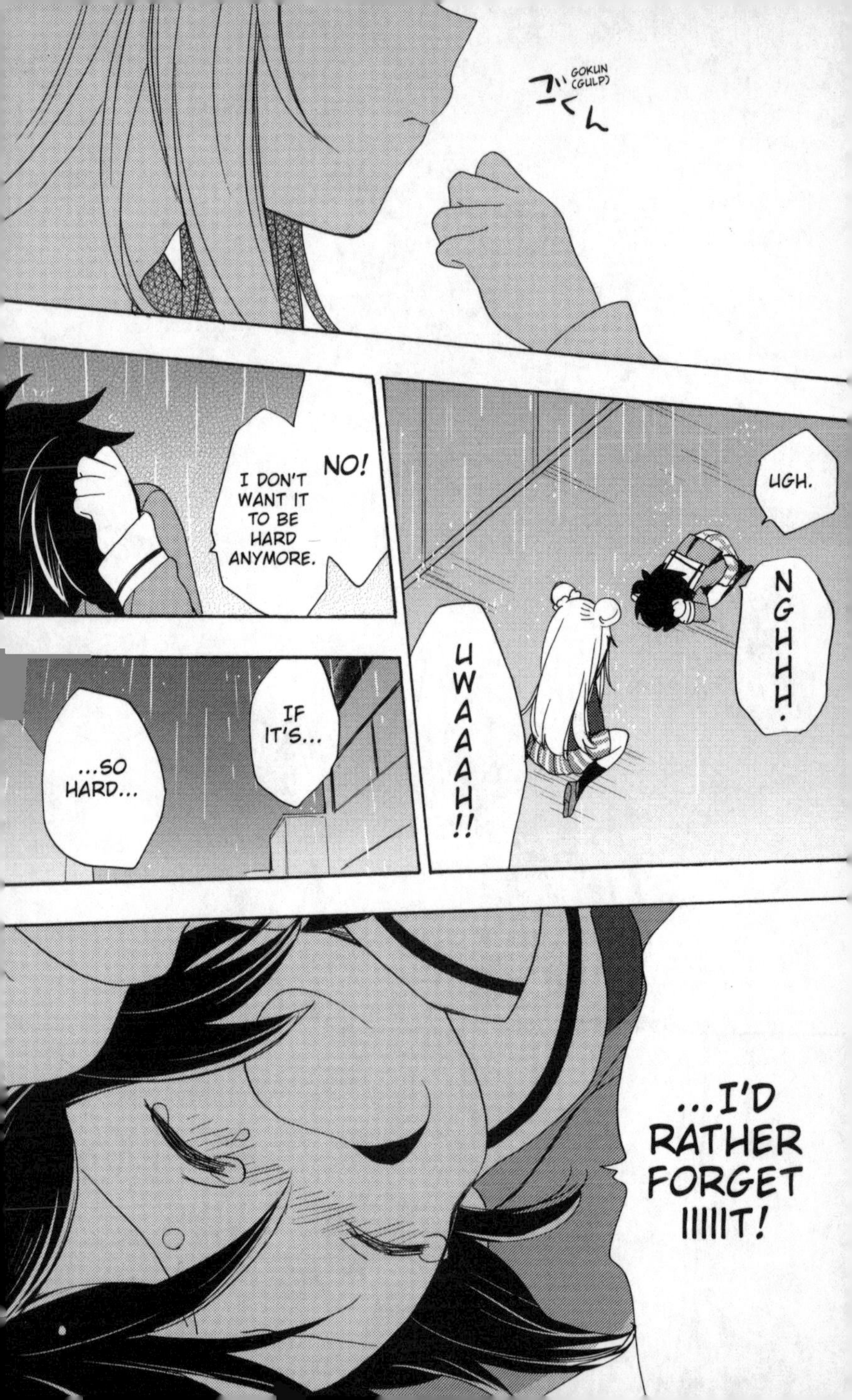
GOKUN (GULP)
ごくん
UGH.
NGHHH.
UWAAAAH!!
NO!
I DON'T WANT IT TO BE HARD ANYMORE.
IF IT'S...
...SO HARD...
...I'D RATHER FORGET IIIIIIT!

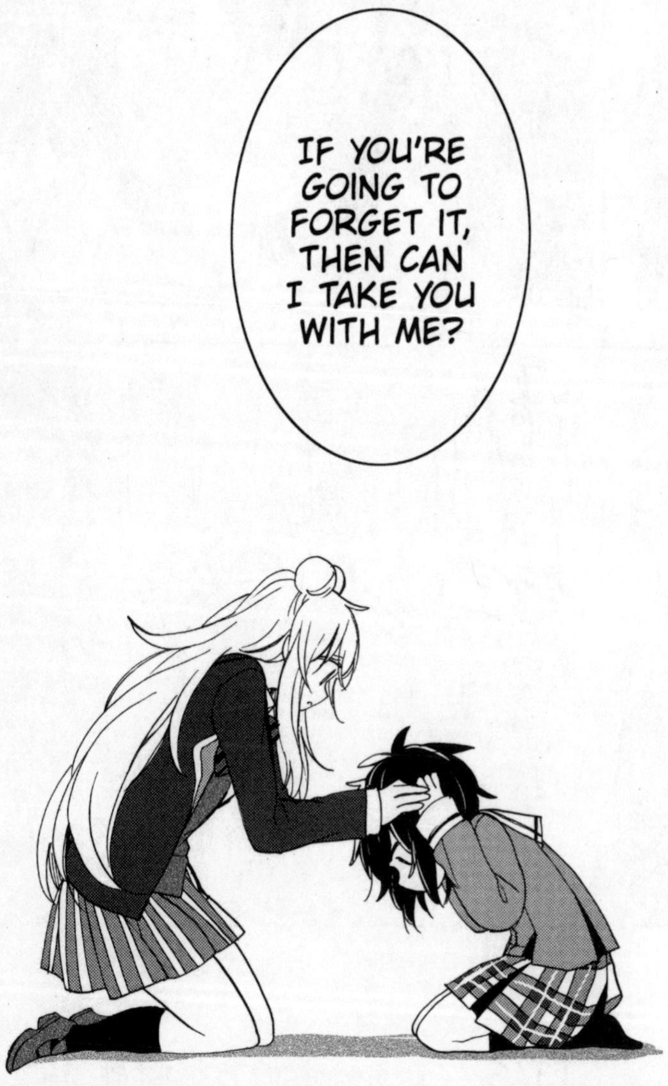
IF YOU'RE GOING TO FORGET IT, THEN CAN I TAKE YOU WITH ME?

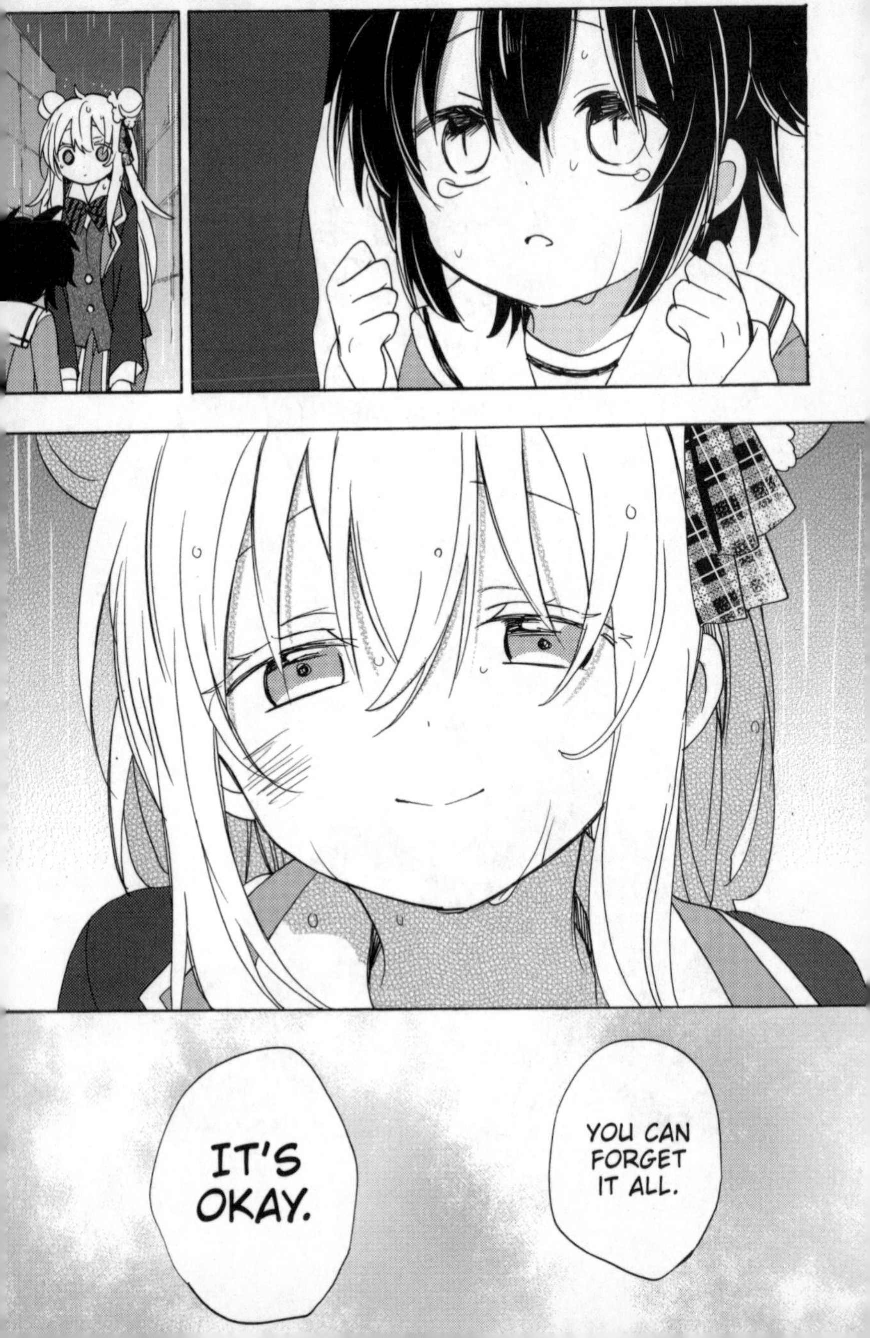
YOU CAN FORGET IT ALL.
IT'S OKAY.

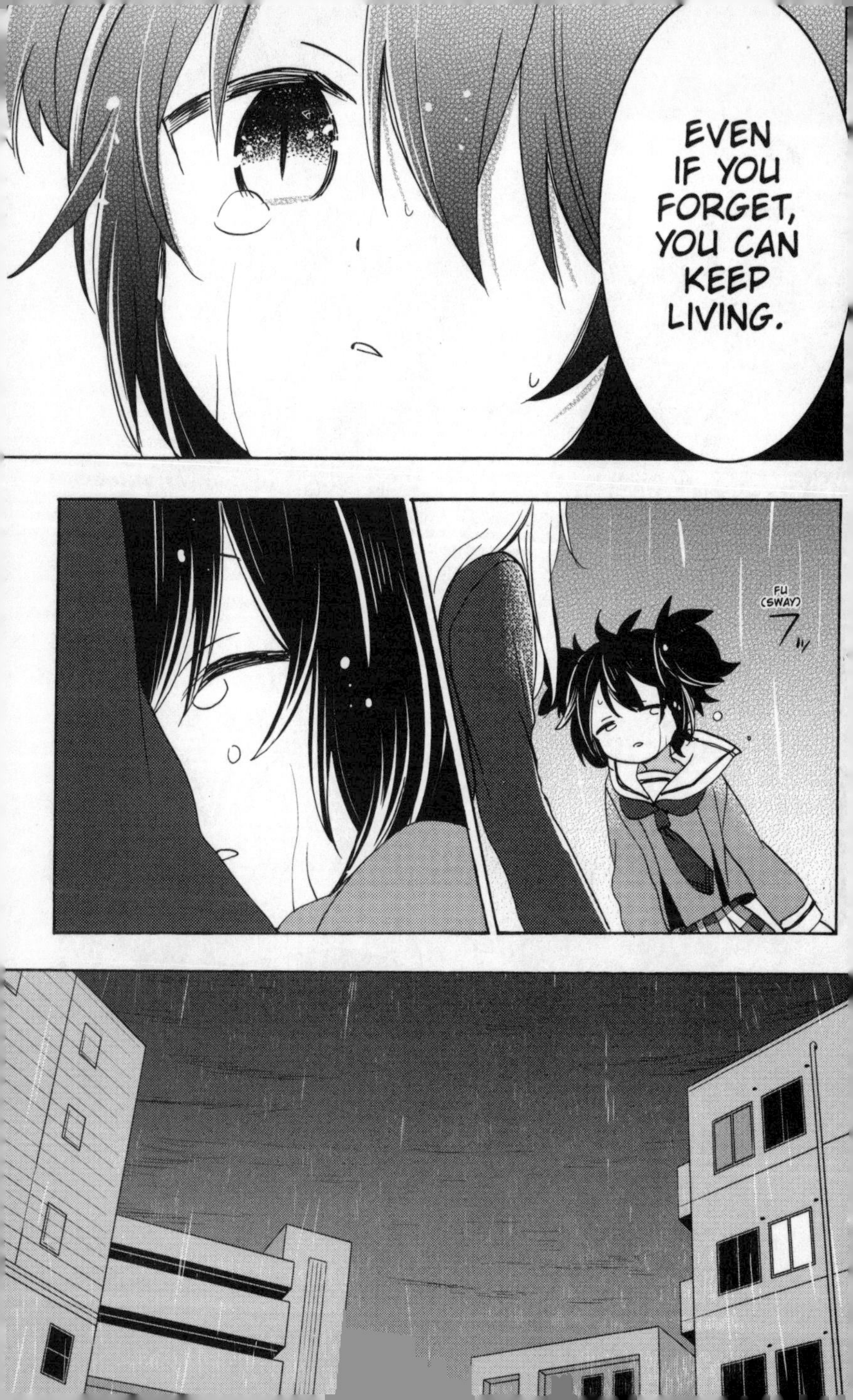
EVEN IF YOU FORGET, YOU CAN KEEP LIVING.
FU (SWAY)

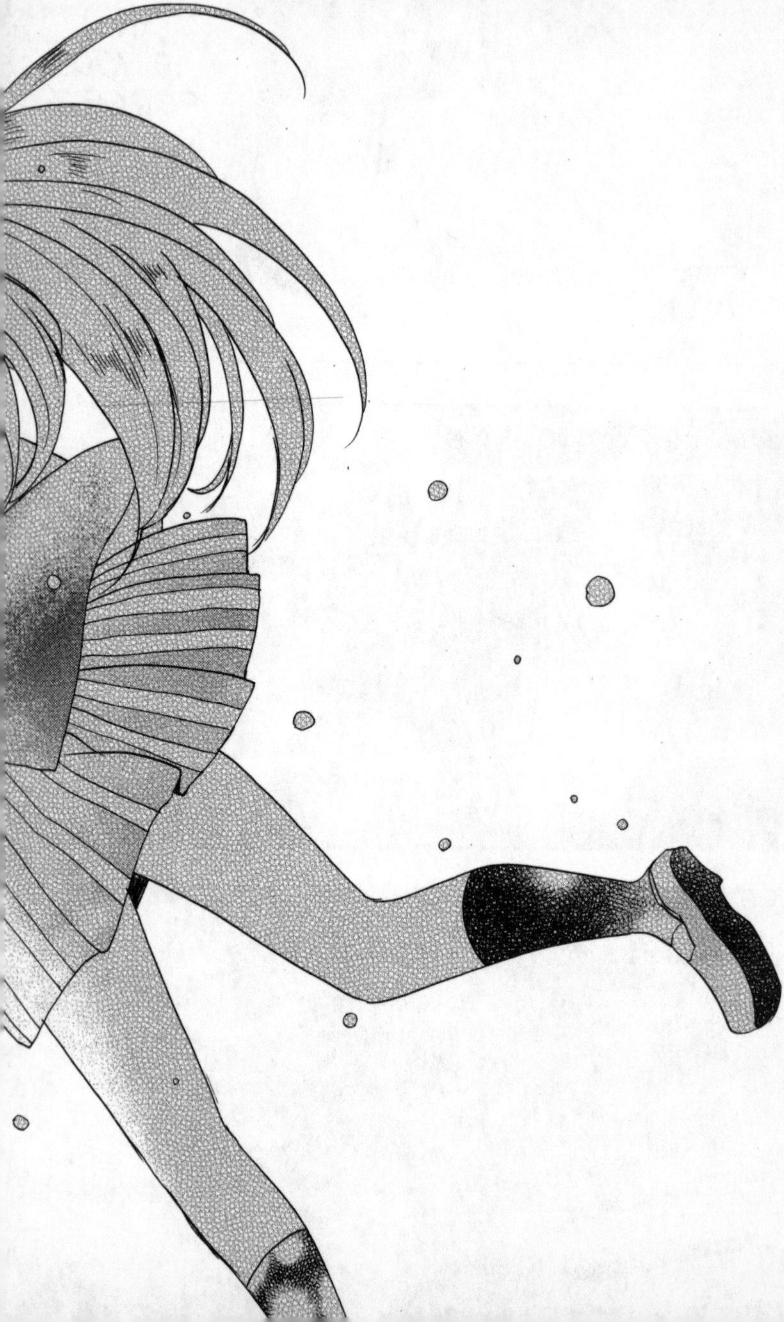

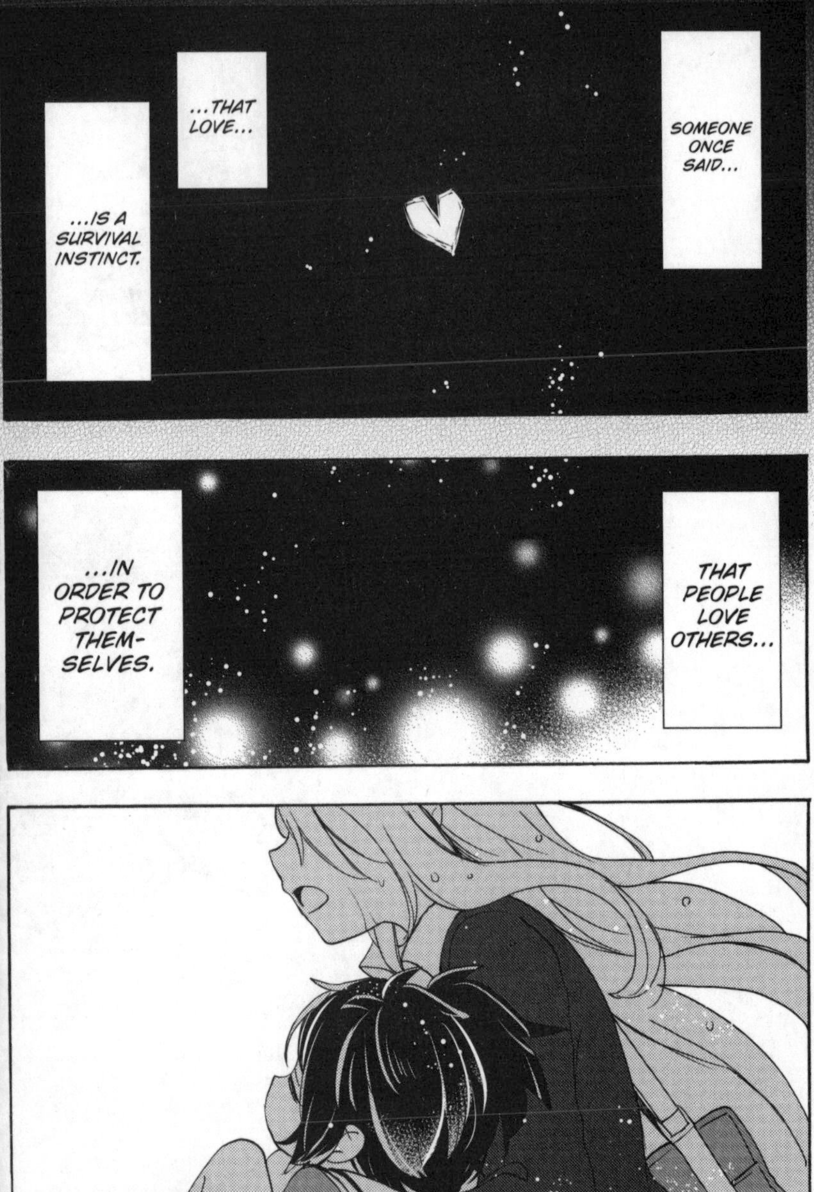
SOMEONE ONCE SAID...
...THAT LOVE...
...IS A SURVIVAL INSTINCT.
THAT PEOPLE LOVE OTHERS...
...IN ORDER TO PROTECT THEM-SELVES.

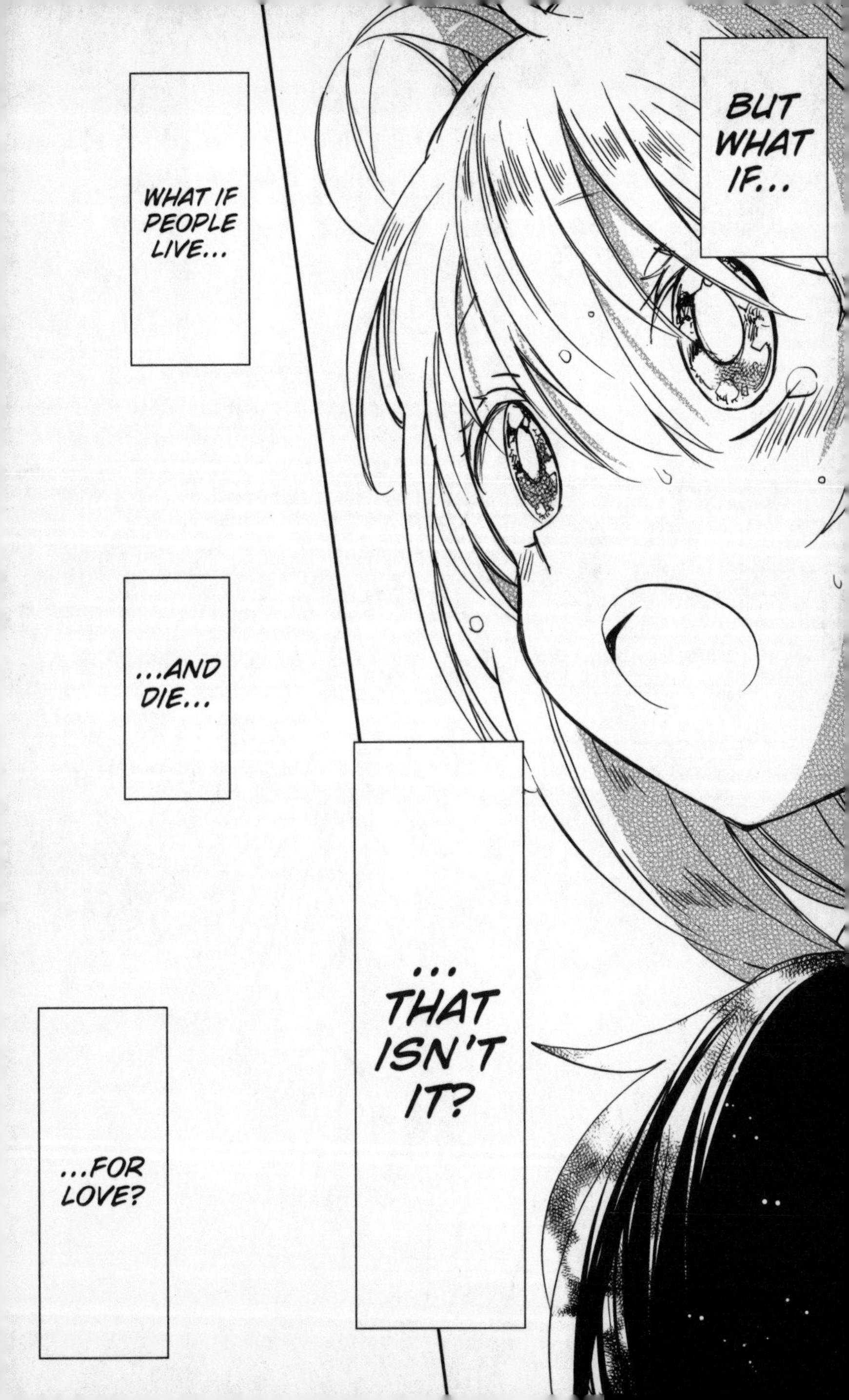
BUT WHAT IF...
...THAT ISN'T IT?
WHAT IF PEOPLE LIVE...
...AND DIE...
...FOR LOVE?

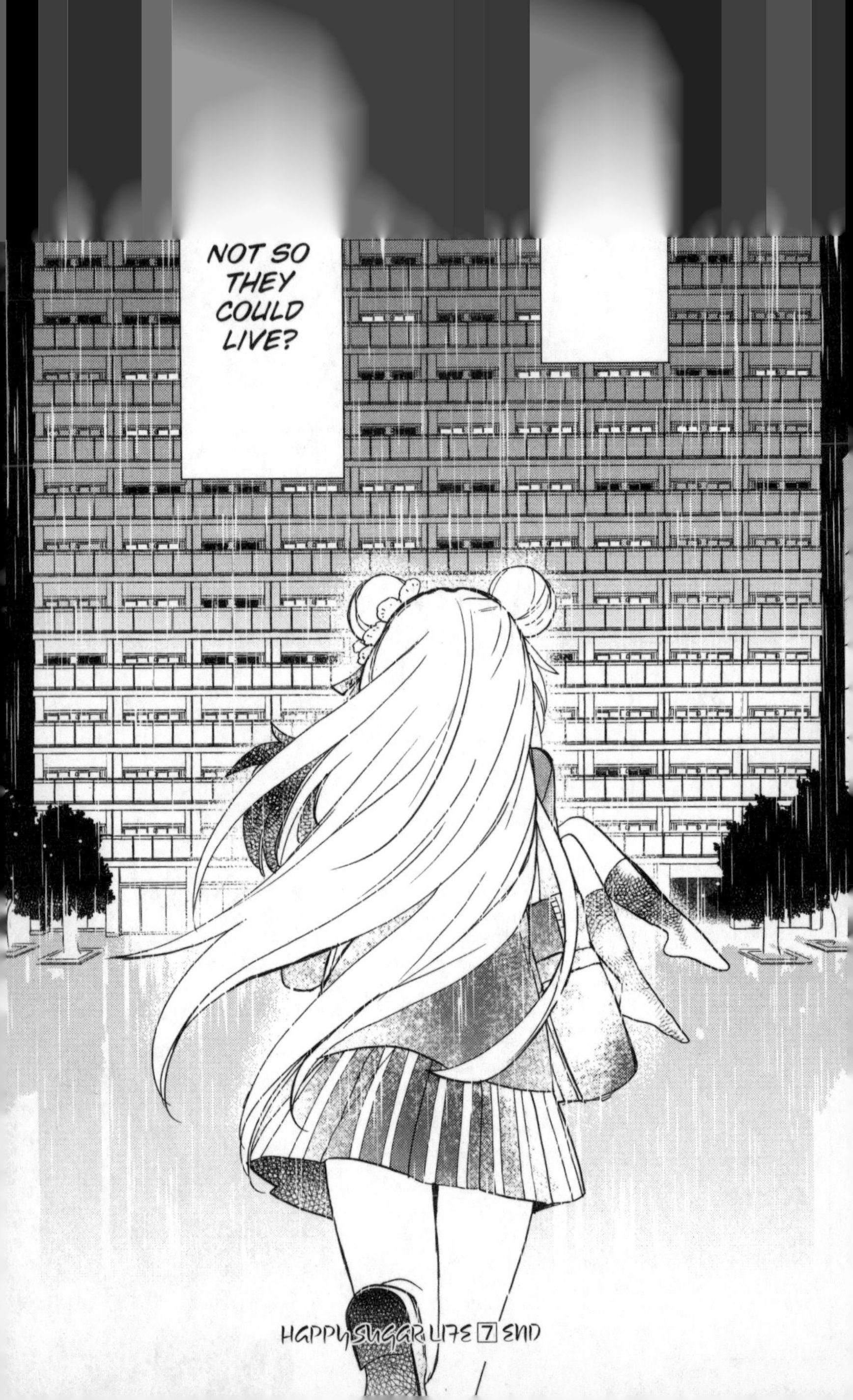
NOT SO THEY COULD LIVE?
HAPPY SUGAR LIFE 7 END

Happy
Sugar
Life

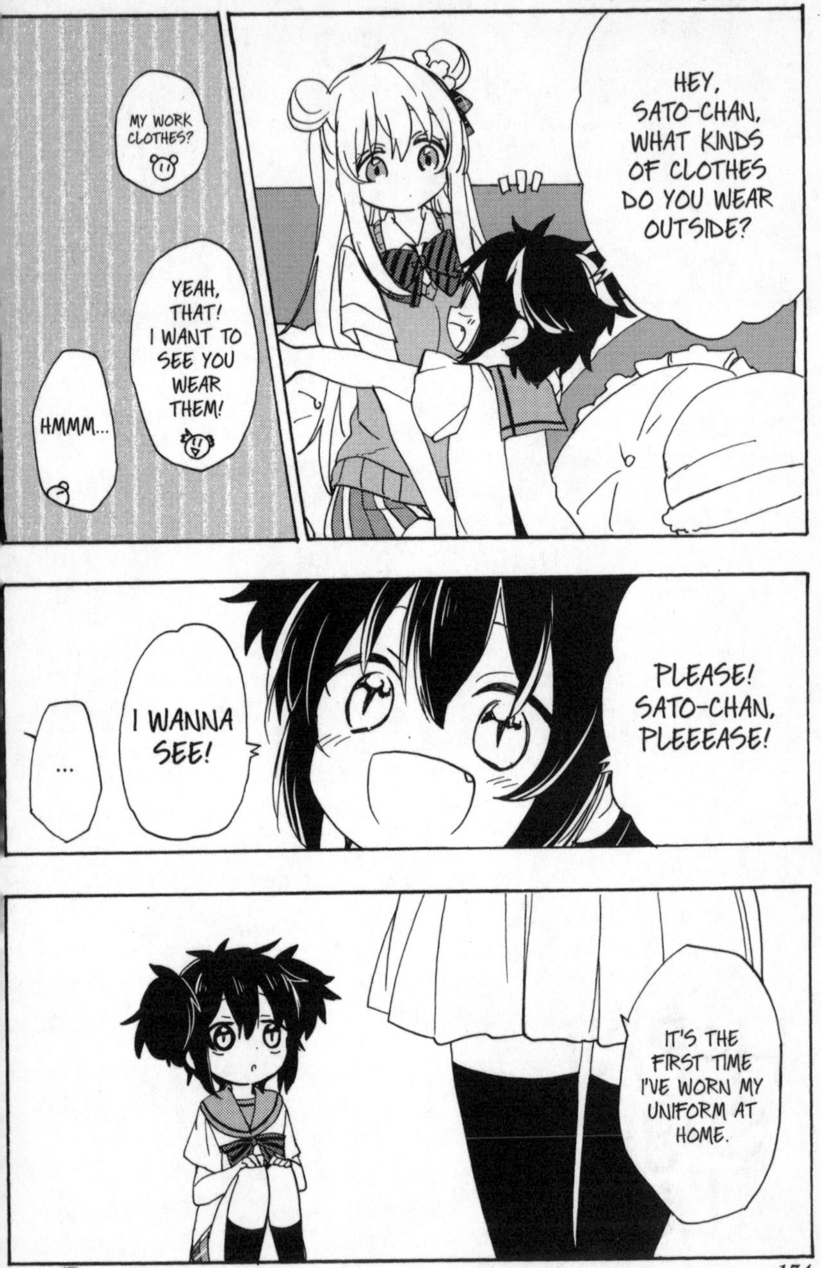
HEY, SATO-CHAN, WHAT KINDS OF CLOTHES DO YOU WEAR OUTSIDE?
MY WORK CLOTHES?
YEAH, THAT! I WANT TO SEE YOU WEAR THEM!
HMMM...
PLEASE! SATO-CHAN, PLEEEASE!
I WANNA SEE!
...
IT'S THE FIRST TIME I'VE WORN MY UNIFORM AT HOME.

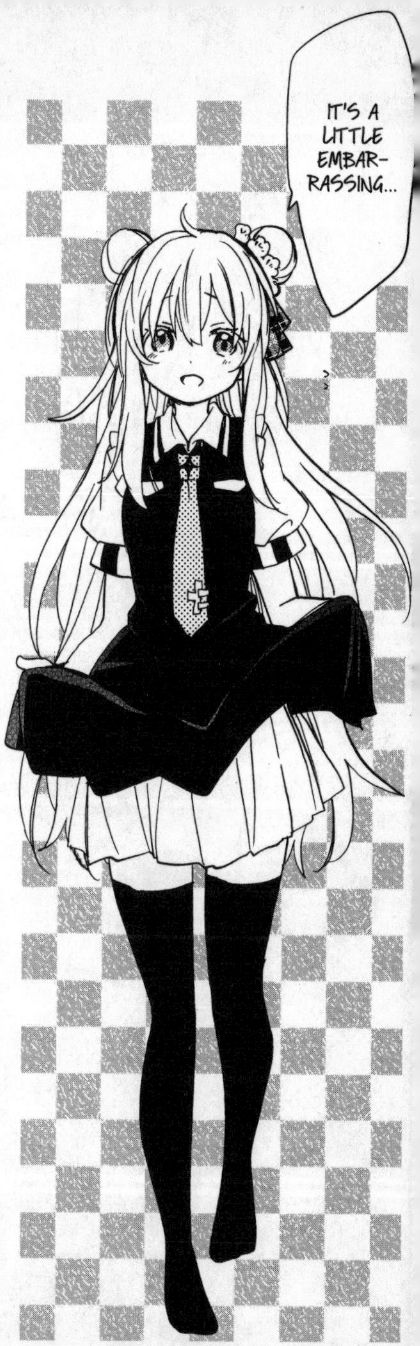
IT'S A LITTLE EMBAR-RASSING...

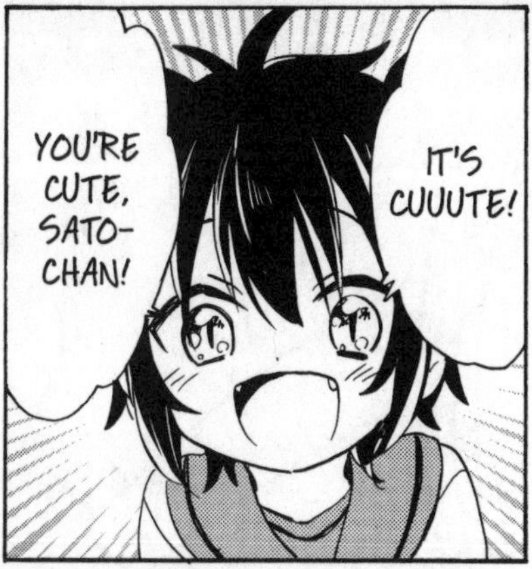
IT'S CUUUTE!
YOU'RE CUTE, SATO-CHAN!

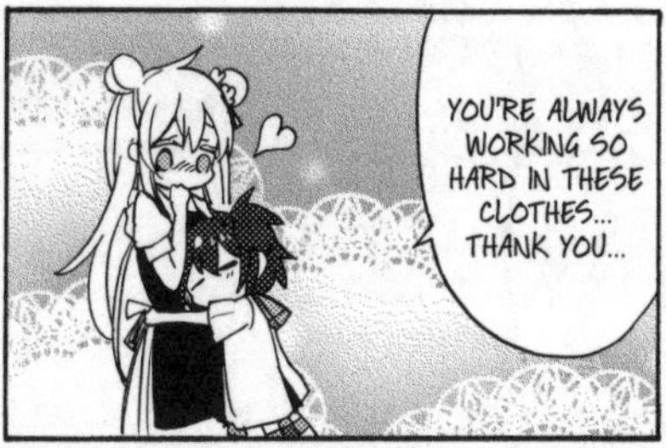
YOU'RE ALWAYS WORKING SO HARD IN THESE CLOTHES... THANK YOU...

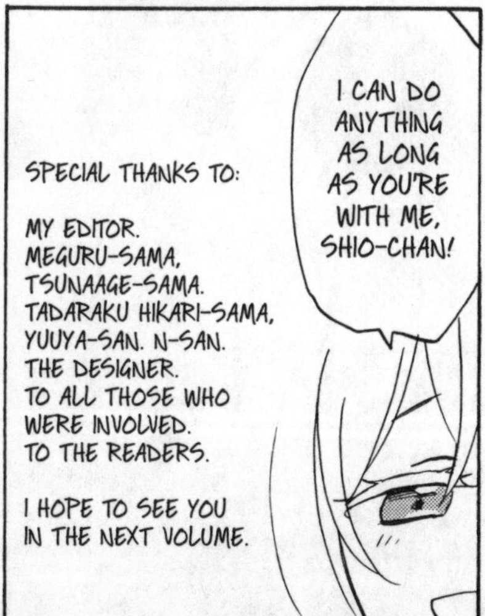
I CAN DO ANYTHING AS LONG AS YOU'RE WITH ME, SHIO-CHAN!
SPECIAL THANKS TO:
MY EDITOR.
MEGURU-SAMA,
TSUNAAGE-SAMA.
TADARAKU HIKARI-SAMA,
YUUYA-SAN. N-SAN.
THE DESIGNER.
TO ALL THOSE WHO WERE INVOLVED.
TO THE READERS.
I HOPE TO SEE YOU IN THE NEXT VOLUME.

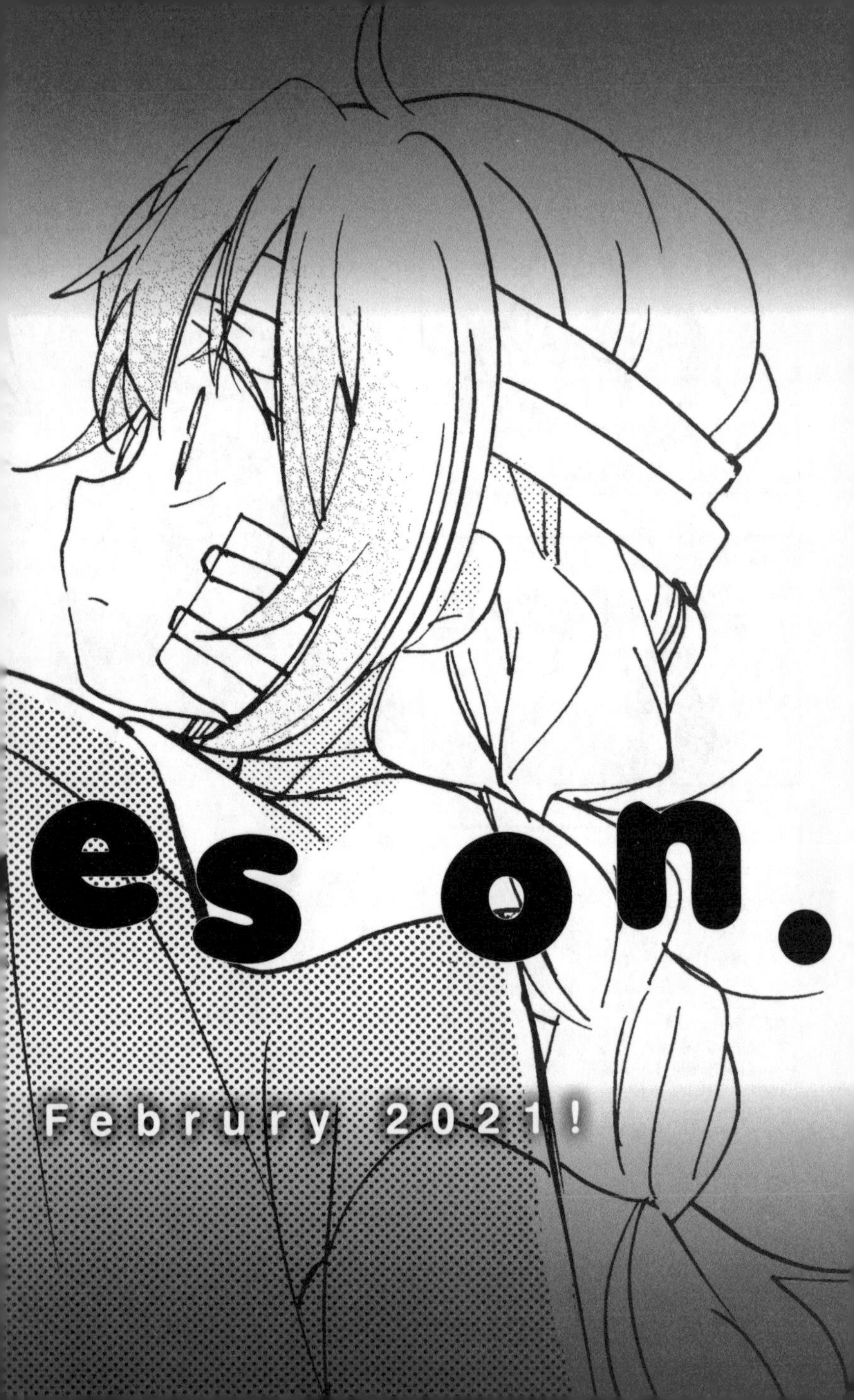
es on.
Februry 2021!

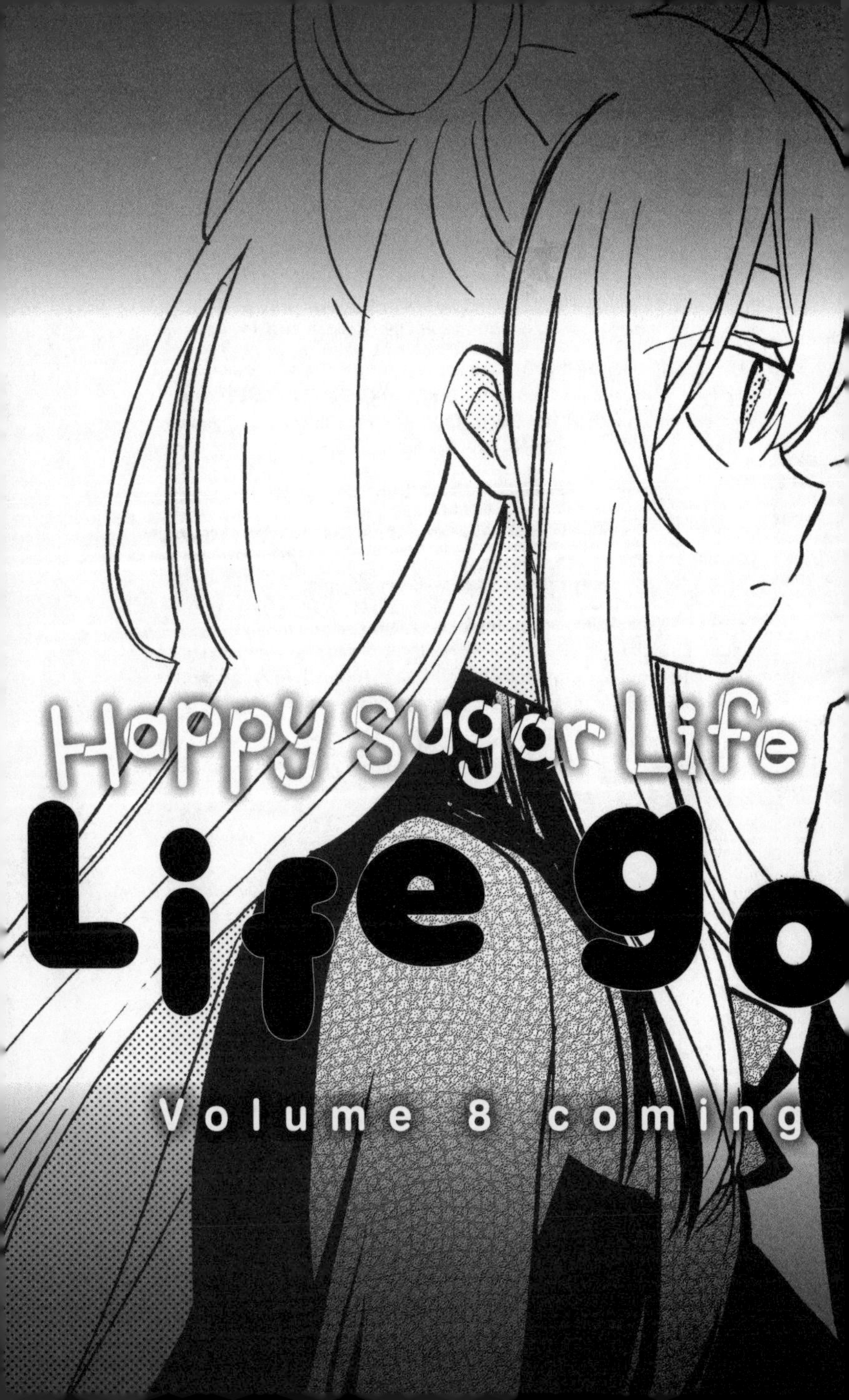
Happy Sugar Life
Life go
Volume 8 coming

Happy Sugar Life 7

Tomiyaki Kagisora

Translation: JAN MITSUKO CASH

Lettering: CHIHO CHRISTIE

HAPPY SUGAR LIFE vol. 7 ©2018 Tomiyaki Kagisora / SQUARE ENIX CO., LTD.
First published in Japan in 2018 by SQUARE ENIX CO., LTD. English translation rights arranged with SQUARE ENIX CO., LTD. and Yen Press, LLC through Tuttle-Mori Agency, Inc.

English translation ©2020 by SQUARE ENIX CO., LTD.

Yen Press
150 West 30th Street, 19th Floor
New York, NY 10001

Visit us at yenpress.com
facebook.com/yenpress
twitter.com/yenpress
yenpress.tumblr.com
instagram.com/yenpress

First Yen Press Edition: November 2020

Yen Press is an imprint of Yen Press, LLC.
The Yen Press name and logo are trademarks of Yen Press, LLC.

The publisher is not responsible for websites (or their content) that are not owned by the publisher.

Library of Congress Control Number: 2019932474

ISBNs: 978-1-9753-0336-5 (paperback)
978-1-9753-8718-1 (ebook)

10 9 8 7 6 5 4 3 2 1

BVG

Printed in the United States of America